MACHINE CONTROL SYSTEMS

- SYSTEMS -

Proceedings of the 2nd International Conference

12·14 May 1987
Birmingham, UK

MACON·2

IFS (Publications) Ltd, Bedford, UK

Springer-Verlag Berlin · Heidelberg · New York · London · Paris · Tokyo

MACHINE CONTROL SYSTEMS
Proceedings of the
2nd International Conference

The MACON-2 Conference is an international event organised and sponsored by:
IFS (Conferences) Ltd, 35-39 High Street, Kempston, Bedford MK42 7BT, UK

It is one of the five international events which form the ADVANCED MANUFACTURING SUMMIT '87

SPONSORS
The principal sponsor is the British Robot Association, and other sponsoring bodies are:

Association de Robotique Industrielle Athena (Belgium)
Asociacion Española de Robotica (AER)
Association Française de Robotique Industrielle (AFRI)
Australian Robot Association Incorp
Belgian Institute for Regulation and Automation (BIRA)
CIRP (International Institution for Production Engineering Research)
Dansk Robot Forening (DIRA)
Dutch Robotic Association (CIR — Contactgroep Industrielle Robots)
Finnish Association of Materials Management
Flemish Organisation for Robotics and Automation (FLORA)
Fraunhofer Institute for Production Automation (IPA), Stuttgart, West Germany

Institut Belge de Regulation et d'Automatisme (IBRA)
International Federation of Robotics
Japan Industrial Robot Association (JIRA)
Japan Society for Laser Technology (JSLT)
Laser Institute of America (LIA)
Ontario Robotics Center
Pulsar SA
Robot Industries Association, USA
The Robotics Society in Finland
Robotics Society of Japan
Societá Italiana di Robotica Industrial
Society for Machine Intelligence, USA
Swedish Industrial Robot Association
Warwick Manufacturing Roundtable

MACON-2 Programme Committee
Professor D S Ross, (Chairman), University of Strathclyde
D G S Avrell, Fanuc Europe SA
Dr D Bell, National Engineering Laboratory
P M Cooper, IBM United Kingdom Ltd
M E Grange, Allen-Bradley Industrial Automation Products
M Henderson, Siemens Ltd
R A C Jennings, IFS (Conferences) Ltd
M R Jones, Gould Electronics Ltd
A Kochan, IFS (Publications) Ltd
J P Leighfield, Istel Ltd
A Lodge, Cincinnati Milacron Ltd
D Mather, GEC Electrical Projects Ltd
F Popplewell, Deckel Ltd
P Shaw, Texas Instruments
Dr M Thorneycroft, TI Machine Tools Ltd

British Library Cataloguing in Publication Data

International Conference on Machine Control Systems *(2nd: 1987: Birmingham)*
Proceedings of the 2nd International Conference on Machine Control Systems, 12-14 May 1987, Birmingham, UK: an international event organised and sponsored by IFS (Conferences) Ltd.
1. Control theory — Data processing
I. Title II. IFS (Conferences) III. Ross, D. S. (Donald S.)
629.8'312   QA402.3

ISBN 0-948507-52-7   IFS (Publications) Ltd, 35-39 High Street, Kempston, Bedford MK42 7BT, UK
ISBN 3-540-17852-X   Springer-Verlag Berlin Heidelberg New York London Paris Tokyo
ISBN 0-387-17852-X   Springer-Verlag New York Heidelberg Berlin London Paris Tokyo

Printed by: Cotswold Press Ltd, Oxford, UK

This book is to be returned on or before
the last date stamped below.

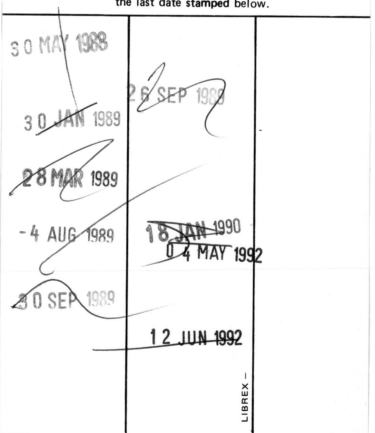

CONTENTS

Official Opening and Plenary Session

Communications I

Communications II

Control Systems

Applications

The Future

Late Papers

AUTHOR INDEX

CORPORATE
INDEX

Late Papers

FOREWORD

Professor Donald S. Ross
University of Strathclyde

MANUFACTURING industry has passed through the phase of envisaging 'the Factory of the Future' and needs to know what is possible and achievable in the factory of today. The integration of the systems essential for the achievement of economic manufacturing is heavily dependent on communications, communications standards and machine control systems.

The contributors to this conference present the results of their practical experience in these important areas of manufacturing system development, highlighting what has been done successfully so far, and indicating areas where further work needs to be done.

The subject areas of manufacturing communications, control systems and networking provide lively topics for discussion on the present state-of-the-art, and the lessons to be learned from the experience of the contributors should prove invaluable.

OFFICIAL OPENING AND PLENARY SESSION

Proc. 2nd Int. Conf. Machine Control Systems, 1-8
May 1987, © IFS (Conferences) Ltd and authors, ISBN 0-948507-52-7

The role of technology in regenerating UK manufacturing industry

A Barr
Austin Rover Group Ltd, UK

Four key requirements for a successful manufacturing activity are
discussed: high productivity, the application of technology, the
importance of quality and meeting the needs of the customer. The
essential partnership between technology and people is highlighted.

There are few locations in Britain that could be more appropriate than the West Midlands at which to hold a conference, where amongst other subjects, the regeneration of manufacturing industry is to be discussed.

It is probably of no surprise to you to hear this from a representative of the motor industry.

To emphasise this parochial point I should say that each year the Rover Group spends £2,300 millions with 2000 UK companies and much of this activity with all its economic implications takes place within a radius of 50 miles or so from where we are today.

The economic point is underlined by the fact that the Group produces close to half the total UK manufactured - as opposed to UK assembled vehicles and in the West Midlands alone accounts for some 134,000 jobs, directly and indirectly, in the region.

My specific task this morning is to discuss the essential part that technology must play in bringing about a sustained revival in this country's manufacturing sector.

Because, mark my words, if, as a nation we are to get anywhere in the race for industrial survival we must keep in the forefront of our minds four essential ingredients for any successful manufacturing activity.

They are:

.   the need to strive constantly for the highest levels of
         productivity.

.   the intelligent application of technology.

.   making QUALITY the point of focus for the entire
         manufacturing activity

         and

.   meeting the needs of the customer.

I will return to these points in a moment but first I want to say that the competition we face as a country does not just come from mature nations like Japan and the United States, but from emergent ones such as Korea and Taiwan as well.

I think the situation is well described by saying that the race for international competitiveness knows no finishing line. As we get better so too do our competitors.

To illustrate what I have to say, I shall from time to time refer to the experience of the particular part of the Rover Group from which I come, because I believe that we have made considerable progress in improving our productivity, in raising the technological base of the company, in improving quality and in paying a great deal of attention to giving our customers what they want at a price they can afford to pay, rather than what we think they should have.

Better man management was at the heart of our initial advance, but we quickly recognised that this had a finite life, and that further improvement would be dependent on the development of an integrated technical strategy embracing all areas of the business and the complete product cycle.

It is a fact, of course, that our competitive position is affected by some areas of cost such as ever rising rates, the cost of energy and exchange rates fluctuations, over which we have little or no control but which influence our manufacturing expense and the price of our products

PRODUCTIVITY

Returning to my earlier point - the need for constantly rising levels of productivity, nationally there has been a considerable labour shakeout, and this is one of the factors that has contributed to the level of UK unemployment, but at the same time it has had a beneficial effect on our competitive position.

Taking the example of Austin Rover there has been a 150% increase in our productivity between the 1980 level and the position we have reached today.

But in terms of improving the competitive edge of a business the extent of change achievable through labour shakeout and the elimination of lines of demarcation, is limited once the initial thrust has been made.

So it is to technology that we must turn if we are to have a thriving manufacturing sector with its wealth creating capability ensuring constantly rising living standards right across the nation.

The potential effects of advanced manufacturing technology are enormous and are surely the gateway to a "new industrial age".

As a country we have a record of success in original research and technological innovation, but we have often failed to manufacture financially successful products.

There is no doubt in my mind that the technology of manufacturing and of its management will change dramatically in the years ahead.

The spur for this will be the need to drive constantly for greater productivity, reduction in product lead times and rising quality and reliability standards.

APPLYING TECHNOLOGY

At the heart of applying advanced technology on the factory floor is the flexible manufacturing system, which will lead to factories that receive information and raw materials from the outside world, perform relatively complex manufacturing tasks, with the end result of a discrete "product". This type of factory will operate around the clock and be unmanned.

At our Longbridge plant we have a flexible manufacturing installation which machines the Rover 800 16-valve cylinder heads and cam carriers. It is a flexible machining and assembly installation with single-spindle and multi-turret type machine tools linked by robots and automatic guided vehicles, all under the direction of a supervisory host computer.

Individual machines and cells monitor their own performance by the use of probe and vision systems, to ensure consistently high quality levels.

The facility is not restricted to any one product - it is also being used for production of cylinder heads for diesel engines.

The system I have just described is one example of applying technology for economical quality manufacture.

Another example, again at the Longbridge site is the low pressure sand casting technique used for the production of Rover 800 cylinder heads.

Molten metal is pumped rather than poured into a precision formed sand mould and it has made casting a much more precise art.

Reduced porosity has enabled wall sections to be thinner, while the greater precision of the casting means there is less subsequent machining to be done, and less material to be removed.

It is a technique that lends itself to the casting of cylinder heads which is one of the most complex casting shapes of any car component.

What I have just described relates to the production of prismatic parts. We have a similar approach to the production of gears and shafts whereby it is no longer necessary to install dedicated and expensive machining facilities.

Here the majority of forming operations to produce the finished component have been achieved, in the shaping of the blank with consequential capital savings.

QUALITY - THE POINT OF FOCUS

At this point I would like to link the process of applying new technology to manufacturing to the third point I mentioned earlier, making quality the point of focus for the entire manufacturing activity.

This brings us to the power and influence of the computer and the application of computer aided quality control and inspection.

We have to be wary of inspection which to me means the examination of parts or assemblies <u>after</u> manufacture. More often than not inspection relies on human operation and is, therefore, a fallable process.

By contrast, quality control is essential. Properly planned it will produce consistency, reduce costs and shorten lead times.

In Austin Rover it is an element of our computer based integrated technology strategy.

4

At the heart of the strategy is a powerful single source computer aided design system embracing over 330 workstations. These are networked between sites and departments, starting in the styling studio and extending through product engineering, manufacturing, quality and service.

There is one single database which links the system, which is capable of transmitting information in both directions.

The single source origin of the system is vital and ensures total compatibiliy throughout the business, thereby eliminating communication problems.

The system provides the means of achieving a significantly improved level of design and engineering resolution because it gives us the ability to simulate performance not only of the product, but also of the process before metal is cut. Prediction of success in the much reduced prototype programme is vastly improved.

As we introduce automation into any part of the manufacturing process we make it a condition of implementation that the system is integrated into the database, and so we have the means of transmitting control parameters from the original data set up by the product engineer.

STATISTICAL PROCESS CONTROL

As part of our quality control technique we make extensive use of statistical process control (SPC) which is one way of predicting the final quality level of the part being produced. Properly automated it can be totally effective and reliable.

The value of statistical process control lies in its systematic way of scrutinising closely every section of the manufacturing process, to introduce controls to optimise quality and control outputs at every stage.

Among the data gathered on our Rover 800 line, for example, is:

.   body dimensional checks from a laser inspection cell.

.   accuracy of fit data from the robot glazing cell, and

.   electrical results from the vehicle Electrical Test System which we call VETS.

TECHNOLOGY AND PEOPLE - A PARTNERSHIP

Much of what I have said has related to the importance of technology. But technology alone is not enough.

There must be a partnership between technology and people and it is to the effect on people, brought about by the revolution in manufacturing technology that I now want to turn.

One major consequence of the changes that are occurring is the need to re-evaluate the work roles of people in the future as many traditional manufacturing tasks are disappearing.

One of the most obvious consequences of the rapid advance of technology is that the concept of "a job for life" has disappeared. The people starting work now will need to be retrained several times during their working lives to cope with technical change.

There is an imperative to raise progressively the level of intelligence of the total workforce and this has many implications for the education and training systems in this country.

In the future there will be a need for a level of technological literacy equating to the present necessity for reading ability.

To provide the abilities required there must continue to be changes in the education system so that the curricula in schools and colleges prepare young people for coping with the array of technology they will face when they start work.

As to training (as opposed to education) this is becoming a permanent feature of working life and must be regarded as an industry based activity.

In Austin Rover we have recognised the need to raise the intellectual base of the company from the boardroom to the shop floor.

We need a constant supply of young computer literate graduates with the ability to exploit and to manage - let me emphasise manage - the new technologies.

There has to be a new type of Manager. He must have an academic background and be tolerant of th ose less intellectually able with whom he will work.

Universities have a key role in this and our links with the manufacturing systems department of Warwick University provide us with a source of outstanding talent to meet our needs.

In co-operation with Warwick we set up one of the first Teaching Companies in the UK, where highly qualified post experience Associates are contracted for two years to work on Project Based Programmes.

In conjunction with Warwick we operate an Integrated Graduate Development Scheme where through a system of residential modules, selected graduates spend 8 weeks a year in residence at Warwick over a 3 year period.

The University also provides a specially designed Senior Management Training course for Austin Rover, so that all Directors and Senior Managers, over 200 people, become technologically literate.

Through these schemes existing managers become familiar with the new technologies and we have a productive association between established executives and the new talent from the Universities.

Without doubt the new technocrats which are the product of industrial and academic association will play an ever-increasing role in industry. They will work alongside traditional managers and to be effective there must be a band of tolerance between the two.

The importance we attach to intellectual excellence can be judged by the fact that currently we employ some 750 graduates in all areas of the business, with the largest group, some 450, being in Product and Manufacturing Engineering.

This compares with the position ten years ago when the company had twice as many employees as today, but only 200 graduates.

We operate a programme of undergraduate sponsorship supported by the recruitment of graduate trainees and direct entry graduates with an average yearly intake of 100.

Central to the success of our strategy is a determination to have a uniformity of technical excellence throughout the business, and the measures we have taken, and will continue to take in the areas of education and training, are an essential complement to the company's technological base.

Everyone in the company, from the boardroom to the shopfloor has the opportunity to improve their technical literacy through our system of "Open Learning", which is a computer-based training facility available to all employees, and open virtually all hours across our major sites.

We also recognise that our employees, apart from their technical abilities have a lot to offer the company if they have a proper sense of involvement in the business.

This is being fostered under our "Working with Pride" initiative, which is ushering in a new era in the company's employee relations and includes special 5-day courses for new employees at which they are given a full briefing on the company's plans and objectives. They have the opportunity to bring their families to meet company managers before deciding to join.

At the time of new model introduction the employees working on the model have the opportunity to "ride and drive" the vehicle and report on the way it performs from both the viewpoint of driver and passenger.

Another innovation is the formation of "zone circles".

These are made up of volunteers from a particular production zone, who identify work related problems and suggest solutions.

The kind of measures I have just described are under-pinned by an intensive programme of communications, involving the use of electronic notice boards at our major sites and regular briefings of each production zone by the supervisors.

The ultimate objective of these and other measures is to match the aspirations of our employees with Corporate Objectives.

THE FUTURE

Looking to the future it is self-evident that the regeneration of UK manufacturing industry will require increasing levels of investment to achieve even higher productivity and further advances in product quality.

Clearly this investment needs to be in advanced manufacturing technology, in training people to use it, and in research and development.

It is important that industry and those institutions that provide the funds for investment should take the long term view. It must be accepted that profits will come in the longer time frame rather than in the immediate future.

There must also be recognition of the fact that the future of UK manufacturing industry is closely linked to the world economy. This inter-dependence is a natural development in the light of the growth and speed of communications and international transport, and the spread of multi-national companies.

It is essential that British manufacturing industry accepts that the way to meet international competitive pressures is to ensure good design and efficient production through the intelligent use of technology and people.

One of the sources of competition is the United States of America, where the Administration has an Assistant Secretary for Productivity, Technology and Innovation, Dr Bruce Merrifield.

I think the situation manufacturing industry in this country faces today is dramatically brought into focus by Dr Merrifield when he said:

> "What fuelled the world economy in the past were products or processes, that had a 10 to 20 year life, or more! These are now down to three to five years, or even less, in consumer electronics, and rarely more than five to ten years in other areas."

> "What this means is quite simple: Whoever is generating new technology will conquer the market place. Technology is now the engine driving the world economy."

COMMUNICATIONS I

Proc. 2nd Int. Conf. Machine Control Systems, 9-16
May 1987, © IFS (Conferences) Ltd and authors, ISBN 0-948507-52-7

Manufacturing communications — the route to integration
A Preston
Coopers & Lybrand Associates, UK

An examination of the current state of Computer Integrated Manufacturing
and the position of new developments in manufacturing communications. The
paper will consider the importance of information as a business resource,
the opportunities for improving the quality of information brought about by
integration and the role of standard communications networks in supporting
the development of integrated manufacturing systems. Finally it will offer
some practical advice for evaluating integration projects.

Introduction

The intention of this paper is to explore some of the key issues surrounding the new developments in manufacturing communications, to show how and why these issues are important and to draw out some of the key business advantages that they bring. I shall be looking at the current state of Computer Integrated Manufacturing (CIM), the importance of information as a business resource, the meaning and value of integration, the communications tools available to bring it about and, finally, some pratical guidelines for taking on integration.

Much has been said by the pundits and plaudits of CIM but as yet little has been done in practice. It is probably fair to say that users are disinterested, even sceptical of the technology involved and shy of the price that it appears to require.

What by now is clear is that the motivation for integration is well understood and widely accepted. It is not difficult to be motivated by promises of lower manufacturing costs, shorter lead times and improved product quality.

The missing element is an argument which demonstrates the relationship between business advantage and the exploitation of emerging information and communications technologies.

The Information resource

The fundamental issue in the argument is the idea of information as a business resource, a resource like any other: material, men, machines and money. Let us consider it.

Factory information is the means by which decisions are made; put simply, the better the information the better the decisions can be. Consider for example the decision as to which works orders to release to the shopfloor today. You need to know what orders there are, how urgent they are, what the shop's capacity is today, the disposition of machines, what orders are in progress, what material tools and labour are available.

You need to know about material, men and machines, and what you decide will have an effect on money. Leaving technology to one side for a moment, you could go to the planner's filing cabinet, pick out all those orders due to be started today, check them with sales to determine priority, then tour the shopfloor to find out which machines are available, with men and tools, check with stores to see that material is on hand and then, having sifted through all this information, pick out the most urgent orders that can be started. In a small jobbing shop, this is perhaps exactly what you do.

The possession of technology does not alter fundamentally the nature of the problem it merely premits the decision to be made, more precisely and more easily. It does this not so much by intervening in the decision-making process but by gathering and presenting appropriate information to support the decision. If the information is of low quality, if it is out of ate, inaccurate, incomplete, if it is irrelevant, badly presented or hidden amongst a large volume of other information then it will not support an effective decision; it may even encourage a wrong decision.

The value of information lies therefore not only in its content but in its form. Perhaps another way of looking at it would be that information is only of value when it <u>can</u> and when it <u>is</u> used.

Once we have accepted that information is a resource like any other and that it has to be managed just as other resources are managed, we can begin to look at how it is managed. If it can be well managed, by which I mean it can be presented at the right place at the right time, if it is accurate, complete and up to date, the it will be a great asset. It will help to make better decisions more quickly; in short it will begin to contribute to your manufacturing advantage.

The integration issue

Information in a manufacturing environment is usually held near the place where it is created rather than the place where it is used. This tendency comes about because of the principle that he who creates data owns it and therefore manages it. While this principle helps to ensure that the information is 'looked after' it does not to help to get it to the right place at the right time. Indeed it tends to encourage the opposite.

Information, once it has been entered into a system, is not easy to transport to different places. Because communications between different systems are seen as being difficult to achieve, information has traditionally been difficult to move. As we have already said, unless information does move, and above all, unless it moves to where it is used, then it is of little value.

If it were possible to move information more easily, then its value would be enhanced, and it is here that the rationale for integration rests.

Integration is a term which is frequently abused; there are many different definitions of it and they are often interpreted in different ways. I shall attempt to define it in terms of its results, for these are what count in the end.

An essential characteristic of an integrated system is that information is available when and where it is required. Integration means that information must be able to move from its source to it points of usage, irrespective of geographical and time constraints. Its effect results in the value of the total pool of company information exceeding the sum of its individual parts. Integration has therefore added value to a key company resource.

Let us now consider the components of an integrated system to see how it is constructed. The basic components of any system are data and processing logic; apply the logic to the data and you get applications and information. An integrated system merely adds a further ingredient to the recipe: that of communication, the movement of data. In an integrated system you apply logic and communications to data to obtain information. An example would clarify the definition:

Consider a CAD system. Fundamentally it has data in the form of encoded binary and text files and processing logic in the form of graphics and display routines which, when applied to the data provide functions for creating and maintaining drawings and product definitions. Now, if we wished to integrate the CAD system with, say, the bill of materials processor of an MRP system to enable the sharing of that product definition information then it would be necessary, at the very least, to introduce a communications link between the two computer systems to enable the data to move. I say - at the very least - because, as we shall see, a communications link alone is not enough to create an integrated system, but it is the only new component, and without it, integration is not even possible.

<u>Communications - the tool for integration</u>

The requirement for communications networks is not new, indeed, suppliers of computer and shop floor equipment have been offering communications facilities for some time. These have been widely taken up by users who have needed to use specific proprietary network links to resolve limited, usually local, communications problems. In other words, communications problems which have been capable of solution by the use of single vendor or bespoke networks, often have been.

What is new in communications technology is the development and implementation of standards for networking in manufacturing independent of any vendor.

In parallel with the International Standards Organisation's development of OSI standards, major industrial corporations have been exploiting the emerging OSI standards for manufacturing communications.

OSI standards define the seven-layer reference model for implementing common communications protocols over mixed-vendor equipment. General Motor's MAP and Boeing's TOP specifications are both subsets of the OSI model, each designed to provide specific facilities oriented to the shop-floor and technical office respectively.

A detailed discussion of the MAP and TOP specifications lies outside the scope of this paper. I shall instead focus upon the capabilities and limitations of these tools in order to develop a view of the important opportunities that they open up.

With the present specifications the range of application layer facilities offered by MAP and TOP is restricted. Both offer a common file transfer mechanism, FTAM, and MAP also offers an inter-process command syntax for shopfloor devices, MMFS.

FTAM enables the transparent transfer of data files between two network nodes. Given that the requirement, from the application point of view, for file transfer is very common, then FTAM is likely to be useful. It would, for example, provide a solution to our CAD to MRP problem.

12

MMFS provides a set of command formats for directing shopfloor devices, such as NC machines, robot controllers and PLC's. As the command formats are standardised, MMFS greatly simplifies the task of integrating a manufacturing cell. Because of the vast number of possible commands that MMFS tries to specify however, a subset of the full syntax is normally agreed for a specific implementation.

It is true to say that the current specifications are immature and that new versions of the specifications will bring both enhancements to existing functions and the introduction of new facilities.

The importance of MAP and TOP lies not so much in the technology they exploit, nor even in the technical opportunities that they create for linking mixed vendor equipment. In many ways it may be argued that they are not competitive with existing proprietary networks in terms of facilities, track record and, above all cost. In these terms it may still be more practical to go about the integration of, say, a shopfloor cell by using a proprietary network.

The real significance of these developments lies in the opportunity that they open up for laying the foundations of an integrated information processing system addressing the needs of all engineering and manufacturing operations. In other words, MAP and TOP are important because of their potential for supporting the development of real CIM.

Applications integration - the missing link

What neither MAP or TOP do is to attempt to standardise the data that can be transported over the networks. The content, and hence the meaning of data in files and messages is still, and for the time being will remain, the responsibility of the application. As we have seen, only meaningful data can provide information.

The creation of an integrated manufacturing system will depend therefore not only on the availability of a communications network but also on applications which can use it.

To use the network to provide information to the end user an application must be capable both of sending and receiving data over it and of understanding the meaning of that data.

The application layer standards offered by MAP and TOP make application integration somewhat easier, by providing to application programs a common interface to the facilities offered by the protocols, although even this interface is likely to vary with vendors' implementations of the standards and the constraints of their operating environments.

In the main, application integration issues have not yet been squarely addressed by vendors, with the result that it is in this area that most work will be needed and so most cost incurred in a CIM implementation. Let us examine briefly some of these issues.

Firstly, and most importantly, the user function represented by a link between two applications must be considered. The way that the two applications are designed to cooperate must model closely the real user requirement of the interface. A line on a system design diagram showing a link between, say, a daily shop scheduling system and a factory controller may in fact conceal a highly complex functional relationship in which data about works orders, priorities, actual shop capacity, tools, NC programs, etc. needs to be exchanged, results monitored and fed back to controlling applications for management information, performance reporting, accounting and so on. All these factors relate to the meaning of the data that is exchanged, and therefore the way in which the two applications must interpret and act upon it.

Secondly the control of the link between applications must be considered. Which application initiates a data exchange, what happens to make it do so, in which direction is data transferred, what happens when it goes wrong, how often does it happen and how quick must the response be? These questions have direct impact, not only on the design of applications and interfaces between them, but also on the network facilities which need to be used to support them.

Lastly the data itself needs to be analysed. The format and structure of the data which needs to be transferred between two applications needs to be compatible in both. If it is not compatible, how can it be translated or converted? In some cases the problems are worse: the same data has different meanings in different applications; is, for example, an operation number the same thing in a process plan, a shop schedule and a part program? Unless these basics have been sorted out, application integration is going to be impossible to achieve.

If you get the impression that the issues of application integration are complex you would be right, but they are not impossible to resolve. Indeed they represent typical problems which are capable of solution using traditional systems analysis and design techniques. The very availability of standards for multi-vendor communications has perhaps removed the principle barrier to integration and thrown these secondary issues into sharper relief.

A practical way forward

I would like to conclude this paper with a brief look at where we are now and some practical steps for moving forward.

I believe that users have a feel for the benefits to be gained from integration, but remain to be convinced by the technology and are sceptical of its promises.

The technology is advancing quickly, particularly communications technology. MAP products are available now, they are improving and we may be confident that they will become cheaper as they are more widely taken up. There are signs too that application integration will become easier as software is designed and developed for interfacting and sandards put in place for data definitions and message contents. Integration, in short, is becoming easier to do.

The challenge to do it rests with management, and the decision to go ahead depends on seeing tangible results. Here are some questions which, when answered, might provide some clues.

First of all, take a critical look at where you are now. Bearing in mind your business objectives, now and in the future, look at your operations. Which are the critical operations you carry out? What are the significant criteria for measuring their performance?

Then look more closely at those functions; how do they use information? What systems are in place to support their information needs? How well do those systems perform? Examine information usage; where is information created, where is it used, how does it get there, is it the right information of the right quality? How much does it cost to get it there and how long does it take?

Is the information you have helping you to run the business? If not, why not; if so, could it be doing better? Bearing in mind what is now technically feasible make a list of projects which, if implemented, would improve performance, and set quantifiable success criteria for each project. Put the list in priority sequence according to those success criteria.

Examine the list to identify any common components, short cuts or projects that could be combined; these count as bounses. Consider the overall direction in which the projects would tend to pull; is this compatible with overall business objectives? If not, something is clearly wrong.

Finally consider the cost of implementing each project against the benefits each would bring, both individually and on a cumulative basis. Those which are individually cost justifiable are clearly candidates for immediate implementation, but consider the overall line of balance first. In this way the high cost, long payback profile normally associated with integration projects, and particularly those needing a network implementation, can be offset against projects which, as a consequence of that initial investment, show a quick return.

The challenge is there; technology is providing an opportunity which must be understood if it is to be exploited successfully. It is down to you.

Proc. 2nd Int. Conf. Machine Control Systems, 17-32
May 1987, © IFS (Conferences) Ltd and authors, ISBN 0-948507-52-7

The UK/DTI MAP strategy

D A Bell and W G Millar
National Engineering Laboratory, UK

ABSTRACT

The paper reports the work that the Department of Trade and Industry is undertaking to
'pump-prime' and underpin the adoption of MAP and TOP technologies in the UK. The
build-up and testing for the recent CIMAP event is discussed, as is the continuing
work in conformance testing, information dissemination and demonstration. The work at
the National Engineering Laboratory, to create a MAP applications Centre is
described.

INTRODUCTION

In 1980 General Motors in the US recorded a loss of $760 million; this was the first time in sixty years in which they had failed to make a profit. As a direct consequence, a major investment programme was started, resulting in a total spend of over $10 billion since 1984. Designed to address the problem of increasing competition, the programme targetted improved quality, increased flexibility and reduced manufacturing costs as key aims. At the outset in 1980, a GM study identified the inability to cost-effectively integrate production equipment as a fundamental problem: the MAP initiative was under way.

The MAP (Manufacturing Automation Protocol) specification is a vertical profile of the ISO Open Systems Inter-connection (ISO-OSI) standard [1]. This is the reference model defining a common architecture for all networks whether local or wide. The functionality of a network is split into seven discrete layers, and MAP consists of the combination of standards, for each layer, which are most suitable for the manufacturing environment. GM have suggested that the benefits of MAP will include: lower project capital costs (10-20%), lower production costs (5-10%) and faster product development (maximum of two years for a new car).

Also in the US, in 1984 a major survey [2] was undertaken to assess the factory local area network market. The survey concluded that by 1989 there would be more than one million connections between factory equipment in approximately 41,000 LANs. In addition, a market value of $51 million in 1984 was predicted to rise, at a healthy growth rate of 35% per year, to $431 million in 1989.

In the UK, the Department of Trade and Industry was tracking the GM initiative and other significant advanced manufacturing events, both in the US and world-wide. MAP, as an enabling technology to allow production equipment to communicate, and thus be part of an integrated manufacturing facility, was clearly an important specification. A national CIM and MAP strategy, to pump-prime and underpin the use of the new technologies within UK industry was essential, and within the aims of the department. Awareness, training, testing, implementation and demonstration were identified as major objectives. However a major focus was vital to stimulate the interest of senior management, and the planning of what was to become an important, and world-beating, demonstration of CIM and MAP was begun.

BUILD-UP TO CIMAP

Towards the end of 1985 plans were made to prepare a small demonstration cell, based on the machining of a diesel fuel injector. The demonstration was to be at Leeds University initally, and then, if successful, it was to be moved to two other sites within the UK. Over fifty companies were canvassed for support and the response was so good that the DTI realised the potential for something much more significant existed. Accordingly, the seeds of CIMAP were sown, with the original plan being extended to include multiple demonstration cells and a full conference programme. Four contracts were placed: Coopers & Lybrand associates, the management consultants were given the task of project management; Findlay Publications Ltd were made responsible for public relations and publicity; EDS (Electronic Data Systems), the General Motors subsidiary, were to manage system integration; and Leeds University were given the duty of MAP conformance testing. It was also agreed that the department would underwrite some of the costs of the event in these areas including the cost of the venue itself. The bill was expected to approach £1.5 million, but part of this would be recovered from entry charges.

The first CIMAP document to be issued was the DAD (Demonstration Agreement Document [3] in April 1986, which described the intended objectives and scope of the event. Descriptions of the fourteen individual demonstration cells, designed to cover all aspects of manufacturing, were included. More importantly, the venue and data had been decided: Hall 2 of the National Exhibition Centre from 1 -5 December 1986. The next major event was a trip to the US by a joint DTI/Coopers & Lybrand team to gain essential support for CIMAP. GM were initially sceptical. How could the UK, with virtually no previous MAP implementation experience, hope to mount such a major event, and take only seven months to do it? Careful planning to date, and the undoubted enthusiasm of the deputation convinced the Americans that it was possible. The team returned to the UK with an offer of help, which included the supply of MAP conformance testing software. At the end of May the CIMAP event was publicly announced.

A pre-staging area, where the network testing and integration facilities and the demonstration cells could be assembled and developed was essential. Gould Electronics donated a major area within one of their warehouses in Basingstoke for this purpose, and from September the cells began to move in. One major benefit of the common pre-staging area was that progress could be seen and monitored, making the essential tight control of such a large project, running to such a stringent schedule, practicable.

A carefully co-ordinated public relations campaign was mounted concurrently with pre-staging. it was essential that such a significant event should be well attended, by the right people. Personalised letters were sent to 55,000 senior managers, and an advertising campaign aimed at a technical readership of at least 500,000 was mounted. By the beginning of November there were already 1000 firm registrations and enquiries were being received at the rate of 500 per week. Overseas interest, in the form of firm bookings had been received from Czechoslovakia, Hungary, Holland and Germany. In all, over 138 publicity items, in magazines and press were printed. The campaign was carefully managed to reach a climax just before the event, and two weeks before the doors were to open, telephone enquiries had reached the rate of 100 calls per hour.

On 21 November the network at the pre-staging area was shut down; there were now nine days left to dismantle and re-build the demonstration in the National Exhibition Centre.

CIMAP

CIMAP was not a trade show, it was the biggest awareness event in the field of CIM and MAP the world has seen to date. It was estimated to have cost over £10 million and to have required more than 100 man-years of effort, all aimed at getting the message of computer integrated manufacturing across to senior industrialists. Judged against that criterion it was an overwhelming success. Officially 5867 attended [4]. Thirty per cent of which were board or senior management level, and 70% of the total came from manufacturing industry. The conferences were fully booked, resulting in 2,500 delegates attending a tripartite programme, specifically tailored to suit senior management, technical management and technical staff.

There were three separate sub-networks implemented; two on MAP broadband sharing the same cable but using different frequencies, and one baseband TOP network. Each sub-network had 18, 9 and 18 connections respectively, and the nodes on different networks could communicate through devices known as routers. The overall network layout is illustrated by Fig. 1. Over sixty UK based companies were involved with the fifteen demonstrations, which were designed to cover all aspects and sectors of UK manufacturing industry such as CAD/CAM, inspection and quality control, flexible manufacturing, assembly and the technical office. For example in cell 3, shown in Fig. 2, the design, machining, transfer and measurement of a desk tidy was demonstrated. Various options, such as where holes were to be drilled were selected by visitors to the stand. A component was then progressed automatically through all stages of manufacture including quality inspection by a co-ordinated measuring machine. The cell was a collaboration between LK Tool, Computervision, Cincinnati Milacron and Deckel with some software developed, under sub-contract, by the Cranfield Institute of Technology.

In order to ensure that attendees understood the importance of CIMAP, and the technology behind it, videos were prepared. On entry to the event, all visitors had to pass through an orientation theatre showing a video which gave a basic introduction to the technology. In addition a bank of screens on the outside of the technical demonstration area constantly played a video outlining the concept of the Open System Inter-connection (ISO-OSI) reference model.

There were fifteen cells giving demonstrations each lasting twenty to thirty minutes, which were so busy that many were running appointment systems. With a marketing forum around the outside of the demonstration proper, CIMAP was a hard, and absorbing, day's work for most attendees.

TESTING FOR CIMAP

Conformance testing cannot be exhaustive, and therefore it does not guarantee MAP inter-working. Nevertheless, the experience of previous demonstrations, particularly Autofact, which was held in Detroit in November 1985, had shown that testing was a vital activity. Leeds University were given the task of conformance testing for CIMAP. A project team of protocol experts was formed with staff from the National Engineering Laboratory, the National Computing Centre, The Networking Centre and PERA. As part of the US assistance, the Industrial Technology Institue (ITI) in Ann Arbor, who were the only accredited MAP V2.1 testing centre, agreed to supply the current MAP conformance test tools. The test system was replicated in the UK and consisted of a VAX 11/750, a UNIX-like operating system called Eunice which was implemented on top of DEC's VMS 3.6 operating system, and the ITI test software [5].

To participate in CIMAP, implementations either had to have ITI MAP V2.1 test certificates for all the pertinent layers, or be subjected to testing. This was a free service to those taking part, but no commercial certificates were issued. A total of nine implementations were tested for CIMAP, at various layers of the OSI reference model, and the event guide [6] provides full details.

Testing was performed on an individual layer-by-layer basis, starting at the lowest layer which did not possess a conformance test certificate and working upwards. The implementation-under-test had to supply a defined test environment which included a scenario interpreter to drive the user's end of the test system, a real-time clock facility, a backing store and a user interface. ITI software was available to test network, transport and session layers, and also the CASE sub-layer of the application layer. Testing, for each layer, was sub-divided into discrete tests. The objective, and specification of conformance, of each particular test being defined, on an individual basis, within the test plans.

For the transport layer, which is the most complex layer, the ITI test plan [7] consists of 272 tests. Approximately 25% of the tests are for normal data transfer, and the rest are designed to test exceptions such as lost, spurious, invalid or out-of-sequence information. In order to enact each particular test, a special piece of software, known as an exception generator, sits below the transport layer and captures, alters or inserts information. The data transfer protocol is monitored and displayed on a device called an EGSCOPE (IBM-PC with ITI software), and a watching protocol expert passes judgement with regard to conformance. The architecture of the ITI test system, for the transport layer, is given in Fig. 3.

A test procedure was devised, with typically three people involved in each session. Each implementation would be subjected to every test for the appropriate layer, on a once-through basis, and a list of passes and failures compiled. It should be noted that no implementation passed, or came anywhere near to passing, on the first pass; surely a manifestation in itself of the value of conformance testing. The implementation would then be put into 'de-bug mode', along with up to three other systems at any given time. The object of the exercise was then to schedule the single test system against the requirements of the implementations-under-test, such that all developers were always busy. Over a period of time, all tests for a layer would be passed, but not on the same version of software. It was then essential to repeat all the tests against one version of the code, and then, very often, tests would fail which had passed previously. By a procedure of iteration, which sometimes took days, and occasionally weeks, a product would pass up to the next layer, until the full MAP stack had been tested.

Passing conformance testing was only the first step in a planned sequence of testing for CIMAP. The conformance testing group had their own sub-networks, dedicated to testing. The next stage was physical connection to the appropriate CIMAP demonstration sub-network, without bringing down the other nodes. Inter-operability testing at the transport and application layers followed, this being checked by the visual analysis of hexadecimal dumps of information transfer by the EDS integration team.

There is no doubt that conformance testing made a major contribution to CIMAP. All implementations tested failed first time, and were improved because of testing. Many problems detected would have been virtually impossible to analyse in the next stages of integration. Also, many systems, although from diffrerent sources, failed in the same areas. These were usually features not implemented at Autofact, and with experience, the conformance test team could often supply vital debugging information to the implementers. Most importantly, inter-operability testing never became a major problem, considering the scale of the event. This is surely the best indication possible that conformance testing has an important role to play in any MAP implementation.

UK CONFORMANCE TESTING

In 1985 Leeds University and the National Computing Centre were jointly commissioned by the Department of Trade and Industry to establish the potential and define the requirements for a UK conformance testing service. As part of the effort they undertook a major survey of potential UK users and vendors of MAP equipment. A total of 3180 questionnaires were sent out, and 296 replies received, of which 42% believed that "MAP would be widely accepted", and only 7% believed the reverse. Just over 17% of users agreed that they had a computer network strategy which included MAP. Significantly, at least 14% of the users and 77% of the vendors would consider using the services of a UK centre. It was thought that the services would include: conformance, inter-operability and performance testing; consultancy; training; and an arbitration service in the event of communication problems. On the basis of the survey it was predicted that the centre would undertake sixteen full conformance tests, and six inter-operability tests, in the first eighteen months of operation.

The report [8], published in early 1986, concluded that such a centre would be a risky commercial venture. It would take around two years to break-even, but was essential if there was to be an indigenous and thriving UK MAP community. Main recommendations were that a centre should be established; it should be operational from the 1 January 1987; and that it should be 100% pump-primed by the Department of TRade and Industry. The Department accepted the findings, and invited tenders.

Consequently, it was publicly announced in November 1986 that The Networking Centre had been given a £1.1 million contract to set up the centre. They agreed to offer a full MAP and TOP conformance testing service from January 1987, based on a SUN workstation, rather than the VAX used for the CIMAP testing. The SUN has enhanced software facilities, and can check additional standards such as the file transfer service FTAM. It also has a new feature called Judge. This is a protocol expert, implemented in software, which monitors the information exchange for each individual test, and passes judgement. This makes the routine testing simpler, but there are still occasions when the human expert has to intervene.

MAP and TOP conformance testing has always been recognised as a world-wide problem; the world confederation of MAP users groups insisting that all testing centres use identical software and procedures. In January 1986 an organisation known as COS (Corporation for Open Systems) was formed with seventeen members initially. One of their declared aims is to "establish a single, consistent set of test methods, test beds, and certification procedures for world markets". COS is not a cheap organization to join, membership is $25,000 per year, and there is a compulsion for larger computer and communication companies to enter into a "research contract" which can cost them up to $200,000 per year. Currently COS has at least forty members, and with an annual research and development budget approaching $5 million they are obviously taking a lead in the development of the next generation of MAP test tools.

NATIONAL ENGINEERING LABORATORY

There is a pressing need in the UK, and indeed world-wide, for MAP and TOP
demonstration sites. The National Engineering Laboratory's considerable experience in
advanced manufacturing is being used to establish a MAP and TOP applications centre.
The centre will emphasise the potential uses and benefits of the technology to
manufacturing industry. This will mean concentrating effort on both the application
layer of the MAP and TOP specifications, and the user applications software necessary
to integrate manufacturing facilities. To minimise effort at the lower layers a MAP
starter kit has been installed, produced by INI (Industrial Networking Inc), with
three IBM-PC nodes initially. A broadband physical network has been supplied and
installed by Ferranti Computer Systems throughout one building of the laboratory.
Fig. 4 illustrates the layout. The most important part of the project will be to
disseminate expertise and experience in computer integrated manufacturing to UK
industry. This will be achieved by demonstration to visitors to the laboratory,
training courses aimed at both senior and technical personnel and by expanding NEL's
consultancy service to industry to cover MAP and TOP technologies.

Within the applications layer, the emerging Manufacturing Message Standard (MMS) [9]
which will replace the GM-defined Manufacturing Message Format Standard (MMFS) in V3.0
of MAP, is obviously an area of interest. MMS defines a message system for
factory-floor devices, and the intention is that companion standards will be defined
by the appropriate industry associations. For example machine tool manufacturers will
specify the sub-set of MMS to be used on their particular types of equipment. Other
application layer standards such as FTAM (File Transfer, Access and Management) are
also of specific interest and NEL contributes to the emerging standards through
membership of EMUG (European MAP Users Group) and the appropriate BSI standards
committees. At present there is very little proprietary software designed to use the
full capabilities of MAP and TOP. The laboratory is examining the idea of a simple
cell controller, which would co-ordinate the activities of a small manufacturing
facility on a real-time basis, and at the same time integrate it into some higher CIM
heirarchy. In the next few years a very significant software development effort will
be required, if the use of MAP and TOP communications is to become feasible, and NEL
will make a contribution in this area.

An in-house feasibility study is in progress to assess the potential of increasing the
efficiency of our central workshop by implementing a MAP or TOP network. One of the
benefits being that part of our demonstration facility will be based on a practical,
and effective, application of the technology. A laboratory-wide baseband local area
network is being installed, and it is envisaged that this would be the media used to
link the MAP sub-network, already installed, with the central workshop sub-network. A
topology of bridges, at layer two of the OSI reference model, has been devised which
will allow the applications centre to access workshop information flow; but for
security purposes, will deny them access to the general laboratory-wide information
flow. This will enable 'real' workshop information traffic to be monitored and
analysed remotely by the existing MAP demonstration sub-network. An ideal facility to
use during our 'hands-on' training courses.

MAP DEVELOPMENT

Since the CIMAP event, MAP has been updated, with version V2.2 [10] now being the
latest specification. Most of the changes were made to accommodate addenda within MAP
V2.1, but there have been two significant additions; the Enhanced Performance
Architecture (EPA) and Mini/MAP specifications, and carrier-band.

As the MAP specification progressed the need was seen for a real-time, speed critical
sub-network, especially within manufacturing cells and for the process control
industry. MAP/EPA satisfies that demand by allowing certain layers of the OSI
reference model to be bypassed, though a loss in functionality is the inevitable
result. Assumptions made in the design of the specification include: a typical access
time of 25ms, a maximum of about 32 nodes within a total distance of 1 Km and an
average message size of 16 bytes. It can be seen that a MAP/EPA node illustrated by

Fig. 5, contains both a full and reduced version of the OSI architecture.. This is because the main reason for the existence of the EPA is to allow full MAP nodes a way of obtaining faster responses on time critical sub-networks. Mini-MAP on the other hand, as can be seen by Fig. 6, only implements the reduced architecture side of a MAP/EPA node. They can therefore only be connected to other Mini/MAP nodes which would normally be part of a cell managed by a MAP/EPA node.

Broadband networking is designed to allow the transfer of multiple channels of frequency multiplexed information simultaneously. For MAP this means nodes transmitting on one frequency and receiving on another, with the frequency being changed by a device known as a head-end remodulator. Carrier-band is a single channel, 5MB/s (half that of speed broadband), technology and therefore is much cheaper and simpler to use. A head-end remodula tor is not required because nodes transmit and receive on the same frequency, but this also means that no other equipment may share the cable. Carrier-band is designed to be used where the number of nodes required is less than 32, and the total distance between them is less than 1 KM. The MAP specification expects that most implementations of MAP/EPA will use carrier-band, but it is not mandatory.

Another major development, though not currently defined within MAP, is the field-bus specification. This is best described as the intelligent sensor network, and is intended to inter-connect devices such as transducers, switches and actuators. Field-bus is designed to sit below Mini/MAP in the CIM heirarchy of networking. There appears to be three main contenders for this standard at present; Bitbus, an Intel proprietary standard; the French state funded FIP (Factory Instrumentation Protocol); and the US MIL-STD-1553B. The MID-STD [11] for example, will connect up to 32 nodes, with a maximum message size of 32 bytes, and at a data transmission rate of 1 Mb/s over twisted-pair cabling.

ENTERPRISE NETWORK

The next major demonstration of MAP and TOP will take place on 6-8 June 1988 in the Baltimore Convention Centre, US. The event will be jointly sponsored by COS and UMUG (US MAP/TOP Users Group) and will be known as 'Enterprise Network'. There are plans for eight cells; one of which will be connected to remote factories, some possibly in Europe. All systems within the event will be bona fide MAP or TOP products, tested and conforming to the latest MAP V3.0 specification, which is currently being defined. US participants responsible for cells include General Motors, Boeing, The United States Air Force, and John Deere. One cell however has been reserved for a European demonstration, and responsibility for this has been given to the Department of Trade and Industry. The cell is presently being planned, but the intention is to emulate a 'jobbing shop' environment.

UK ACTIVITY

The dissemination, and availability, of information on communications standards is vital to the developing CIM and MAP activity within the UK. Consequently, as part of CIMAP the DTI launched the ComCentre. A £1 million contract has been awarded to PERA (Production Engineering Research Association) to operate the centre from Melton Mowbray, in conjunction with the Institution of Production Engineers and the Institution of Mechanical Engineers. Part of their task will be to recreate a data-base of published material, on a world-wide basis. The intention is that users will pay for the services, and make the centre self-financing in time.

The National Computing Centre are also active in this area, they have recently launched a UK MAP Implementors Group (MIG), in conjunction with the Advanced Manufacturing Technology centre, which is the joint consultancy set up by UMIST, Salford University and the Machine Tool Industry Research Association. MIG is aimed at helping small and medium-sized companies to understand and learn about MAP-related products. NCC have also recently published a directory of MAP products [12] which lists 250 products from 150 suppliers.

UK companies are currently participating in two ESPRIT research projects for CIM. The objective of project number 688, CIM-OSA (Open System Architecture), is to publish a series of documents defining a CIM architecture, which hopefully will accelerate the definition of much needed standards in this area. One intention is to define a neutral and modular application interface, aimed at simplifying the job of the system integrator. The UK participants are GEC, ICL, and British Aerospace. European companies involved include Volkswagen, Aerospatiale and Philips. A major demonstration programme is also being funded by ESPRIT as part of project number 955, CNMA (Communications Network for Manufacturing Applications). The plan is to demonstrate computer integrated manufacturing using OSI communication standards. British Aerospace are the prime contractors, and as part of the programme, a CIM demonstrator will be installed at their factory in Warton. This should be available for public viewing in 1987. The project also involves GEC and ICL from the UK, with European representatives including Siemens, Aeritalia and Olivetti.

CONCLUSIONS

One important role of the Department of Trade and Industry is to stimulate the use of advanced manufacturing technology within UK businesses. The Department has been successful in creating an environment which will allow the emerging MAP and TOP specifications to be understood and accepted by industry. CIMAP highlighted the benefits to be gained from using communications standards to implement computer integrated manufacturing. As part of a UK strategy, a UK conformance test centre and communications information centre have been created.

The key contribution the DTI is making, towards the adoption of MAP and TOP technology in the UK and Europe, is being recognised. A European cell, to be included in the next major demonstration event, in the US in 1988, is being planned and managed by the Department.

The Department realises that demonstration of the technology is essential, and as part of this effort the National Engineering Laboratory is developing a MAP applications centre.

REFERENCES

[1]   ISO 7498: OSI (Open Systems Interconnection) - Basic Reference Model, May 1983.

[2]   "The Factory LAN Market", Frost & Sullivan Ltd, Sullivan House, London.

[3]   CIMAP Demonstration Agreement Document, July 1986, Department of Trade & Industry, London

[4]   Findlay Publications Ltd - CIMAP Report, January 1987, Department of Trade & Industry, London.

[5]   Clarke, C. "The story of CIMAP conformance testing", Dec 1986, Leeds University, UK.

[6]   CIMAP Event Guide, Dec 1986, Findlay Publications Ltd, UK.

[7]   MAP 2.1 Transport Protocol Test Plan, ITI, Ann Arbor, Michigan 48106, US.

[8]   "A Report to Define the Requirements and Assess the Benefits of a Comprehensive MAP Conformance Testing Service in the UK", 1986, Department of Trade & Industry, London

[9]   EIA/Draft 5/1393A, "Manufacturing Message Service for Bi-directional Transfer of Digitally Encoded Information", June, 1986.

[10]   MAP Specification V2.2, August 1986, VM Technical Centre, Warren, michigan, US.

[11]   MIL-STD-1533B, "Aircraft Internal Time Division Command/Response Multiplex Data Bus", US Department of Defense, Washington DC, US

[12]   MAP Product Guide, National Computing Centre, Manchester, UK.

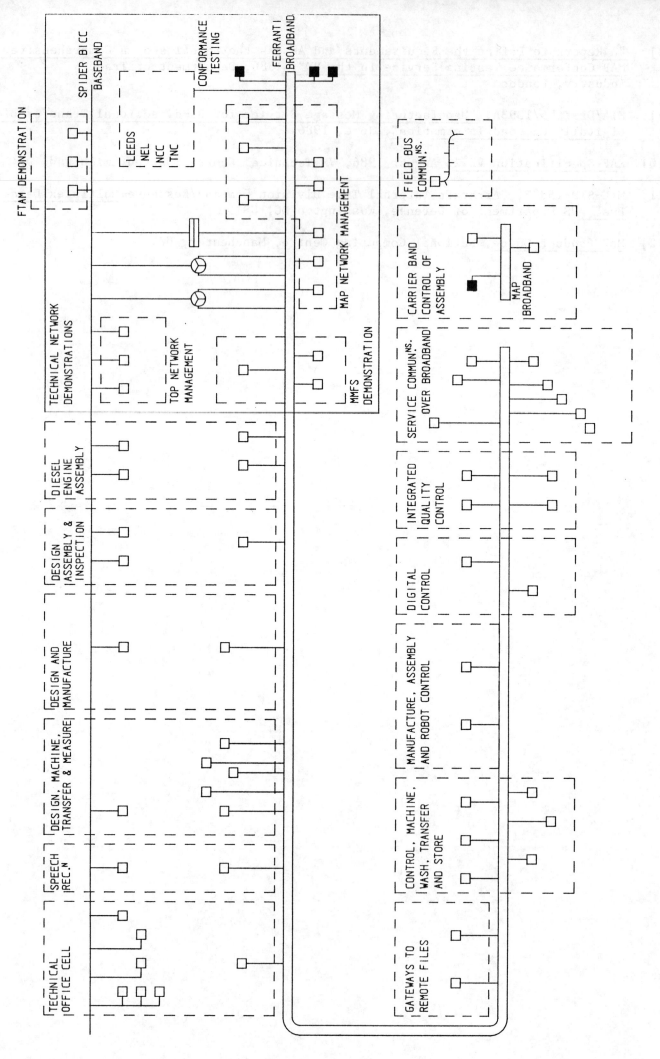

FIG 1 CIMAP - NETWORK DESIGN

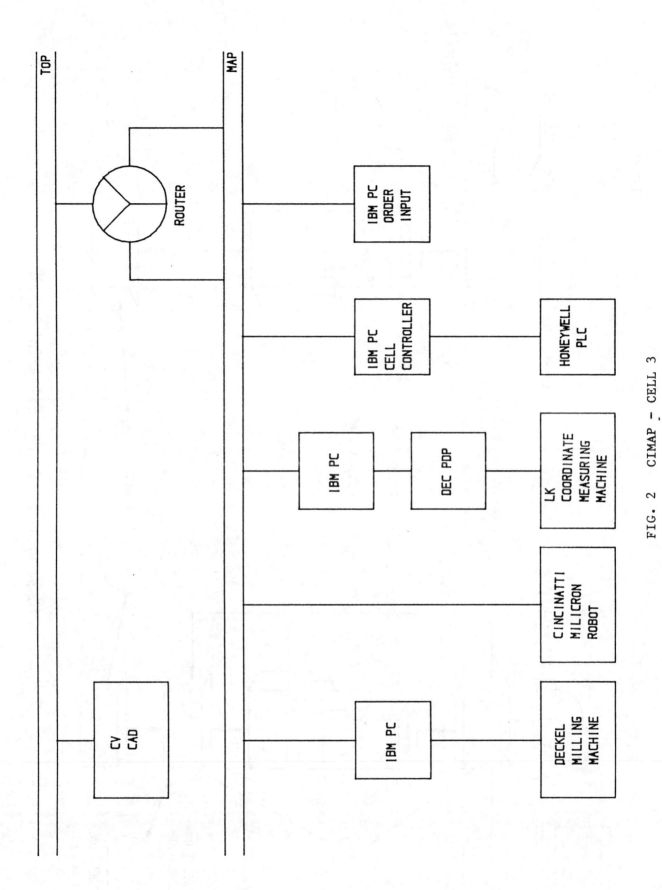

FIG. 2   CIMAP – CELL 3

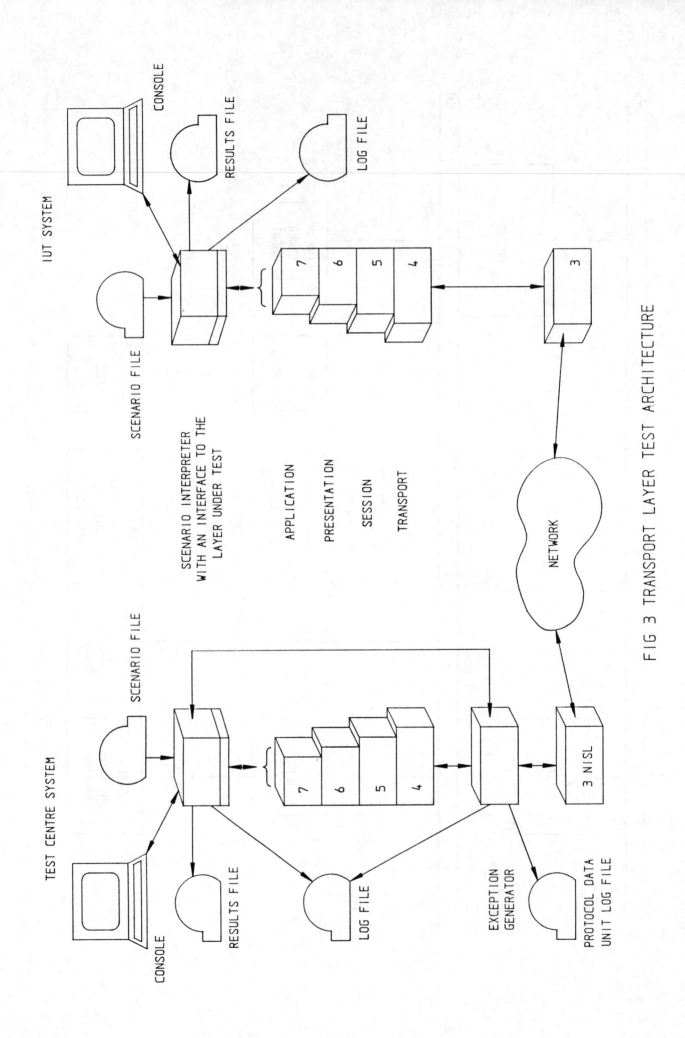

IUT SYSTEM

CONSOLE

RESULTS FILE

LOG FILE

SCENARIO FILE

SCENARIO INTERPRETER
WITH AN INTERFACE TO THE
LAYER UNDER TEST

7
6
5
4

3

APPLICATION

PRESENTATION

SESSION

TRANSPORT

NETWORK

TEST CENTRE SYSTEM

SCENARIO FILE

7
6
5
4

3 NISL

CONSOLE

RESULTS FILE

LOG FILE

EXCEPTION
GENERATOR

PROTOCOL DATA
UNIT LOG FILE

FIG 3 TRANSPORT LAYER TEST ARCHITECTURE

28

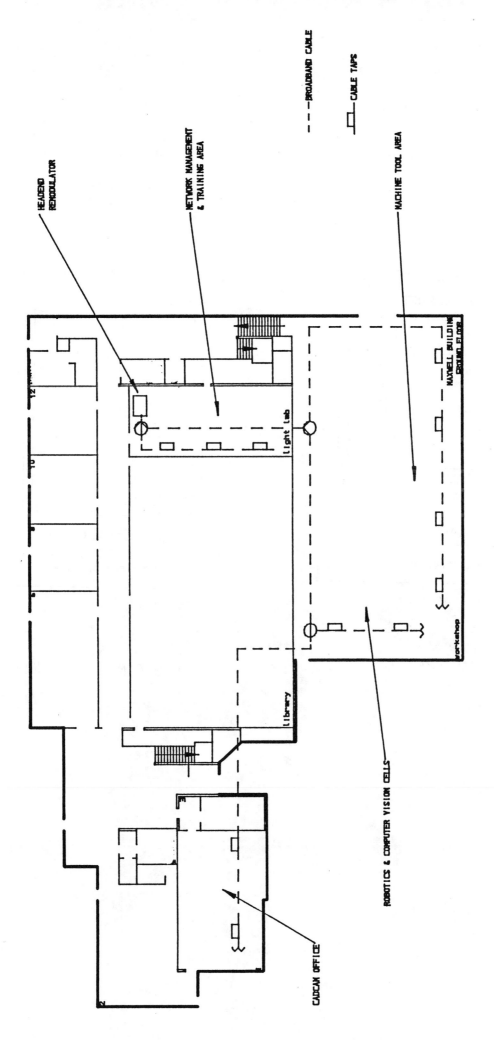

FIG. 4   NEL APPLICATION CENTRE

29

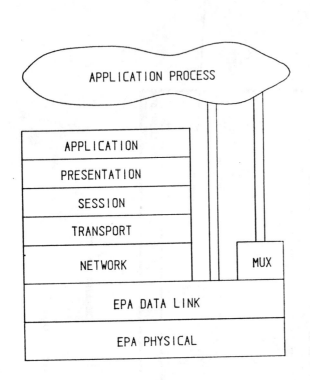

FIG 5 MAP/EPA NODE

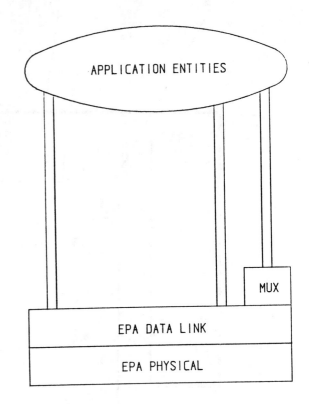

FIG 6 MINI-MAP NODE

Proc. 2nd Int. Conf. Machine Control Systems, 33-44
May 1987, © IFS (Conferences) Ltd and authors, ISBN 0-948507-52-7

FMS under MAP/TOP in under three months . . . how we did it!

I C Cooke

Cranfield Institute of Technology, UK

ABSTRACT

The LK Tools Consortium Cell at the DTI CIMAP event was developed and commissioned in less than three months. Its operation involved use of both MAP and TOP, linking three shop floor machines and a CAD/CAM workstation. The paper describes how this was achieved, and how the OSI-based standards affected the development of an FMS.

INTRODUCTION

The CIMAP (Computer Integrated Manufacturing Automation Protocol) event, organised by the Department of Trade and Industry, was staged at the National Exhibition Centre, Birmingham, during the first week in December. All of the stands were pre-staged in a warehouse site at Gould Electronics, Basingstoke in the three months preceding.

A consortium of LK Tool, Cincinnati Milacron, Deckel, and Computervision was formed to demonstrate MAP and TOP capabilities by exhibiting an FMS cell that embraced design and production functions. The aim was to manufacture components mere minutes after finalising the design on a CAD workstation, transferring part program information, and performing cell control under the TOP and MAP standards.

The cell was to consist of the following machines:

- Deckel FP3NC milling machine
- LK Micro Four coordinate measuring machine
- Cincinnati Milacron T3-776 robot
- Computervision CADDStation graphic workstation.

Previous contacts and collaboration with Cranfield Robotics and Automation Group (CRAG) led the consortium to employ CRAG as systems integrator for the project. Our task was to take the capabilities of the machines, and technical support from the companies, and produce a commissioned FMS in time for the CIMAP event.

Due to restrictions in time, space and manpower, it was decided to carry out the software development, cell build, and commissioning exclusively at the pre-staging site, starting in earnest in mid September. We had experience, commitment, four people full-time, and less than three months to build an FMS.

DESIGN

The functional design of the cell to be exhibited was carried out in the months following CRAG's recruitment to the project. However, due to previous commitments, this design work was restricted to defining only the 'visible' functionality, the component design, physical placement of the major cell items (figure 1), and design of fixtures and fittings subject to long lead times, such as the robot gripper and the machine tool fixture.

So, by the beginning of September this initial design was complete; the representative production component was to be a desktop golf green, with eight standard variations and the facility to redesign the shape of the green itself on-line (figure 2). In order to represent variation at all stages of production, there were two types of raw material, blanks pre-machined with a left or right hand "bunker", two standard green designs, together with custom designs, and two sets of hole positions for the pens to be assembled into.

Thus for any particular order, it was necessary to select the correct material store for loading the milling machine, machine the component with the correct part program, measure it with a corresponding part program on the CMM, and finally assemble it according to the hole pattern which had been machined.

All of these selection procedures, from order entry onwards, and all part program transfers were to occur using the Event's MAP and TOP networks, together with start signals where appropriate. We would be using both of the high level information protocols, MMFS (Manufacturing Message Format Standard) and FTAM (File Transfer, Access and Management).

For safety reasons, we stipulated a PLC (Programmable Logic Controller) and hard-wired connections to deal with safety interlocking and emergency stops. The Computervision workstation could be directly attached to the TOP network, and was supplied with a full complement of software to implement file transfer using FTAM. Similarly, the Cincinnati Milacron robot has a MAP interface, together with the necessary software to implement MMFS communication. The other two machines, however, required gateways to MAP for connection and protocol translation, for which we used IBM PC/ATs. There were two other ATs used in the cell, one for order entry, and one as cell controller, which also had an RS232 connection to the PLC (figure 3). MAP connection was achieved using INI MP400 PC bus/MAP interface cards. With only this elementary design finished did we arrive at the pre-staging area.

PRE-STAGING

The pre-staging allowed the event managers, Coopers and Lybrand, and the technical managers, Electronic Data Systems, to not only convince themselves that the various stands and cells would operate as described in the event's documentation [1,2], but also to allow testing to verify that the stands were all bona fide in their use of MAP and TOP according to the publicity, and that they would all operate simultaneously on the event's network topology.

Deadlines for passing certain testing milestones were imposed on all participants; physical connection to the networks used, full transport layer exercising appropriate to the application, application layer testing, 'interoperability' testing to prove that all applications could run simultaneously, and a final run before stripping down for transport to the NEC.

There were other aspects of the PSA (pre-staging area) which made it an unusual place to develop a networked FMS. Probably most importantly, there was the presence of EDS and the testing group, mainly from Leeds University, both of whom proved valuable sources of standards documentation, knowledge and advice. However, other support facilities normally enjoyed, such as technicians, stores, offices, desks, and even chairs were not available, and had to be imported to the PSA if necessary. In addition, space was severely limited; our allocated area was essentially the size of the working cell itself. Finally, access to the PSA was granted from 7am to 7pm only until the last few weeks before the event. Our particular development schedule demanded that we work considerably more than 12 hours a day, which resulted in moving our computers back to our accommodation daily, giving rise to rumours of a private MAP network in our living room!

DETAILED DESIGN

The detailed design of the software and hardware wiring etc. was carried out in the early weeks of development. Early on, it was decided that identical software should run on all of the IBMs to minimise the problems of debugging and maintenance. This required the

35

construction of a general purpose program, which was configured at run time to perform the specific functions required by each particular node. Moreover, the requirement of each node to respond to at least two asynchronous input 'channels', such as keyboard, MAP, or RS232, demanded a pseudo-multitasking, real time program structure. A scheme was devised to meet these requirements, and a simple algorithm for directing the operations of the cell was worked out.

Again, for the sake of simplicity and to ease design, testing and commissioning, it was decided that each machine would have a single multi-core cable running to the PLC, and therefore, all sensors, actuators, and interlock signals would be routed through the PLC. The robot gripper was the only exception to this rule, actuated directly by the robot.

This scheme had several advantages: all wiring testing could be carried out at a single point, the PLC cabinet, allowing systematic testing to be carried out without error. All sensor inputs could be simulated, via the PLC programmer, for the purposes of program testing, in some cases even before the hardware had been delivered. All actuator outputs could similarly be tested independently of machines such as the robot being active, an indispensable facility when almost all other work was carried out within the workspace of the robot! The cables between the machines and the PLC were connected at both ends by heavy duty multi-pin plugs, allowing easy disconnection and re-installation at the NEC, effectively without disturbing the tested circuitry. Spare wires in these cables allowed late addition of equipment to be easily carried out; in fact, one particular interlock sensor was added to the system after arrival at the NEC. Finally, for the commissioning period, visual confirmation of signal activity was possible with the PLC programming unit, and any signal could be forced remotely.

Sensors to give positive feedback of actuator completion, such as "vice closed and up to pressure", "vice open", were included, together with an operator panel to provide a soft stop and restart function for the robot to allow reloading of the raw materials store. In addition, a hard-wired emergency stop circuit, including strategically placed buttons, was designed to interlock with all of the shop-floor machines.

HARDWARE

The major items of ancillary hardware included:-
 - a hydraulic positive open/positive close vice for the milling machine
 - a vacuum operated fixture for the coordinate measuring machine
 - a pneumatic parallel action robot gripper, capable of gripping both the pens and the component
 - an air blast jet fixed to the Deckel for cleaning the component
 - an air blast jet fixed to the robot gripper for cleaning the Deckel's fixture area
 - a material store/assembly table, with racks for components and pens and a passive fixture for assembly of the pens into the finished component
 - a waste-paper bin to serve for components out of tolerance.

Each of the fixtures was equipped with appropriate sensors to detect correct presence of the component. The m/c tool vice had two pressure sensors on the hydraulic lines, one to detect correct opening, and one for correct clamping force. The vacuum fixture had a single pressure sensor detecting gripping force, and the assembly fixture had a proximity switch confirming correct seating of the component. The robot gripper was equipped with three infra-red sensors to confirm the states fully open, closed and gripping, and closed overtravel, indicating a failure to pick up the part.

After a couple of near misses during commissioning, a hardware microswitch sensor was installed to detect the presence of the measuring machine column in the "home" position, which was then interlocked with the robot motion to pick or place a part on the LK Tool's fixture, preventing either of these actions if the probe arm was not well clear of the robot's travel.

The emergency stop circuit consisted of a 24 volt current loop, connecting all of the mushroom buttons in series with the PLC cabinet and an adaptor box on each of the three machines. Pressing any of the buttons would drop the current in the circuit, de-energising relays in the adaptor boxes. These were wired into the machines own E/stop circuit, and cut power on the PLC output cards. In addition, the voltage in the loop was itself maintained by a similar relay circuit, providing positive feedback to the stop condition. Positive reset was required to restore power to the loop, followed by individual reset of the machines. This arrangement leaves the machines own E/stops local, but overridden by a global stop, which is useful during individual commissioning.

SOFTWARE

The greatest effort in developing this FMS was in software (figure 4). This was partly because of the work involved in utilising an emergent communications technology, for which programmer-friendly interfaces were largely unavailable, but mostly because the essence of tying together machines into a flexible system is a logical, and therefore largely a software problem. The software ranges from the low-level robot and PLC programming, through communications to the highest level hierarchically, the cell control routines, all of which were developed specially for the exhibition (figure 5).

Obviously, there is a vast contribution in man-hours and expense lying behind the existence of the equipment and software packages which were used as building blocks for the FMS, and indeed some of the functions for which we were required to write our own software will become available as off-the-shelf packages sooner or later, but the fact remains that for construction of an FMS in the foreseeable future, the majority of the input required will be software, or software related.

This particular cell was relatively simple in logical terms. The production process could be conceived as a pipe, down which components progressed through the various operations and machines. There are three locations at which a component can reside, other than stores or output positions, and only one component may reside at each of these three. Therefore, the only decisions that must be made are when the robot can perform one of several actions at once. The simplest solution, and the one adopted, is to maintain a queue of waiting jobs for the robot, thus executing them in the order in which they become required. In practice, this queue rarely rises above one waiting job, because parts may only be moved into an empty location.

The robot program was constructed so that the individual tasks, moving a component or assembling the pens, could be performed in any sequence. Each task started and ended by a move from or to a 'neutral circle' locus respectively. Thus the first motion of the robot was always to swing around it's base, clearing all other items, until it was in the vicinity of the action to be performed.

To keep track of the physical part variations, parts were represented by part records held in memory. These identified:-

- part number, 1 to 12 (which includes custom parts), coding for
  * left or right hand bunker
  * hole pattern
  * green shape

- customer identification string, also identifying custom program NC filenames

- job number, which was used for visual information and manual intervention purposes.

When a machine notified the cell controller of the completion of a task, there were in general only a few possible actions that could be taken as a consequence, and only one that should occur, depending on the current state of the cell. For example, if the mill reports completion of the machining cycle, then if the measuring machine location is vacant, a job to move the component is added to the robot's job queue. If the CMM location is occupied, then the component simply cannot be moved at present. Loading the Deckel with the next component's part program is carried out in either case, if a next part exists. No other actions can result from the completion of the machine cycle. Similar logic applied to the entire cell operation; it is not particularly flexible, but entirely suitable because of the small range of possibilities afforded by the physical process of passing components through the cell.

The handling of program transfer was entirely integrated into the same logical structure. Once the system was running, part programs for the standard parts resided on hard disks as close as possible to the machines concerned: on the gateway PC in the case of the Milling machine, and on the CMM's PDP 11 controlling computer. Each of these machines had one extra program filename to hold the 'current' custom part program. The cell controller similarly had two program files, for the 'next' custom programs. By the logic of the physical system, such an arrangement allowed part programs to be transferred from the library built up on the Computervision system just before they were required on the machines, while avoiding a build up of part programs that were rarely used (i.e. only once) at the shop-floor end of the system.

The order entry terminal maintained a queue of components to be produced, keeping the cell controller informed of the next part, and the next custom design part's program names (customer identification) as necessary. The status of each part in process was reported back by the cell controller as it changed, and displayed in real time, together with the current state of the backlog queue. If a custom part was ordered, the order entry program communicated with the CAD/CAM system to check that the design actually existed, before accepting the order.

The PLC program's function was mainly to pass signals from one place to another, performing low level logic such as switching off the hydraulic flow to the milling fixture after it had successfully closed or opened. Additionally, because we were working with a pre-release version of the Deckel controller software, cycle start had to be implemented in hardware connections to the operator console from the PLC. This required a sequence of signals and responses to be processed by the PLC, initiated by a command from the cell controller.

Another major function was the control of the 'soft stop' on the robot when reloading of the materials store was required, which involved the operator working within the normal movement path of the robot. Safety required that the robot be temporarily disabled, which was achieved through a hardware "feed hold" input to the robot's 24 volt I/O. However, to avoid an unnecessary error, while this signal was in operation, no request to move should be sent to the robot by the cell controller. A protocol for achieving this was implemented, so that on pushing the "reload" button, the PLC informed the controller that no more requests should be sent to the robot until reloading was finished. When the robot's current operation was completed, a signal was sent back to the PLC, which resulted in feed hold being applied, and then a lamp indicated to the operator that it was safe to continue. This process was reversed when a second button was pressed to indicate completion of reloading.

Another function of the cell controller was to update a real-time graphical mimic of the cell, which displayed the positions of the various jobs in the cell, and featured an animated representation of robot movements and message transfer across the various networked links. The primary function of this was to illustrate the otherwise invisible utilisation of the network to the audience, but such mimics are an essential part of the tools used to control industrial FMS, giving instant information about the status of the system. It is worth noting that production of this mimic software occupied the majority of the time of one of our three PC programmers.

COMMUNICATION - MAP/TOP AND RS232

The vast bulk of the software that was developed for the cell was concerned with communications. This is partially because the main aim of the CIMAP event was to demonstrate the uses of MAP and TOP communications. Our demonstration was designed to reduce the system's complexity as far as possible, while retaining the ability to show the possibilities resulting from reliable and fast communication. Therefore many important aspects of 'real' FMS installations, such as error recovery and a user-friendly MMI, were only rudimentary. Even so, for large installations, communications form a significant part of the software investment, not to mention hardware costs.

The raison d'etre of MAP and TOP is to reduce the total costs of providing useful and flexible communications links between diverse items of factory equipment. In order to succeed as standards, MAP and TOP must demonstrably ease the burden of communication, while providing more production capability in terms of efficiency, flexibility, and so on. From our experience at CIMAP, can we say that this goal is being achieved?

Machine compatibility

At present, few machines can boast a direct MAP interface, and our cell is a good representation of the kind of solutions that must be sought when implementing MAP in the factory today. However, there are still advantages to be found in using MAP and providing gateways, or protocol translators, to equipment which is not MAP compatible.

There is a range of functions which successful FMS installations use in their communications with machines. Some are restricted to simple NC program management and transfer, relying on VDUs and men to perform other functions. At the other end of the spectrum are totally automated systems, with extensive functionality provided by communications, and hardly a human in sight. The machines themselves present a wide range of functionality which is available through the now almost ubiquitous RS232 port.

It is not necessary, therefore, to implement or use the full range of functions that MAP and TOP specify to gain substantial benefits. It is not even necessary, as we have shown, to be restricted to the functions offered by machines as purchased. It is necessary, however, to justify the use of these standards over and above the interfacing work which must be carried out anyway.

Examining the effort that we put in to develop this FMS, one man worked almost exclusively on providing drivers to communicate with just three pieces of equipment; the milling machine, the CMM, and the PLC. A comparable effort brought forth the multi-tasking system, the cell controller, the order processing, and the MAP-MAP and MAP-TOP software used on all of the PC nodes, which also communicated with two 'external' devices, the robot and the CAD station. The volume of code required for these tasks was much greater than that for the drivers, so where did the rest of the man-hours go?

The real picture is typical of writing drivers for machines. Each machine has different commands, different functions, different 'telegram' structures, different timeouts, different methods of controlling line use, different error procedures, etc, etc. The quality of documentation varies enormously, and for each new driver it must all be digested. Testing is a laborious task, and even with tools such as a protocol analyser, it can be hard to see what is going wrong. Especially since most machines have unhelpful, and sometimes unpredictable responses to errors; one of the machines we were using occasionally had to be powered down for fifteen minutes to recover from a particular error. In contrast, programming for MAP and TOP is well defined, well documented, and a once-and-for-all effort.

MAP Compatibility

MAP is still very much in the process of development, however, and as yet there are still problems, some of which were highlighted in the run up to CIMAP. Perhaps most obvious and best known is the current incompatibility between the two major suppliers, INI and Concord Data Systems (CDS). However, both interfaces can be attached to the same cable, and the two separate networks connected through routers or other devices, so the problem is not insurmountable. The difference is in the lower layers of the seven-layer protocol structure, and they are "working on it".

Other problems occur in MAP-to-MAP communication at the application layer, most commonly in MMFS. However, these are generally fairly minor differences, and should be swept away with the introduction of MMS (RS511) in MAP 3.0, scheduled for the second quarter 88. Neither of these affected our cell, since we used INI MAP exclusively, and only had one version of MMFS, Cincinnati's, to talk to.

MAP/TOP Compatibility

The one major setback that we experienced in MAP software development was inherent in the versions of MAP and TOP currently available, which are not compatible at the application layer. The problem lies in the history of the standards' development; TOP 1.0 was defined before an integral part of the 7th layer, CASE (Common Application Service Elements), was completed, and consequently does not use it. MAP 2.1, on the other hand, specifies CASE as the lowest stratum of the application layer, and hence both MMFS and FTAM, the protocol MAP and TOP have in common, are required to use it.

This fundamental difference is not well publicised, and it came as an unpleasant surprise. Compounding the problem was the entirely reasonable, and otherwise helpful fact that INI implement CASE at board level. Unfortunately, the only way to bypass INI CASE is to interface to the board at the transport layer (layer 4), and build up from there. The task was not impossible, however, as session (layer 5) is relatively simple, and presentation (6) does not currently exist. Because of the restricted time, the approach taken was to effectively incorporate the session layer into the logic of FTAM. The whole incident set us back only one to two weeks. This problem should be eliminated altogether by the next release of TOP.

CONCLUSION

The conclusion to be drawn from this accelerated development of an FMS is that MAP and TOP can contribute significantly to the integration and large scale automation of factory processes, from the office to the shop floor. As with any computer system, there are still bugs to be ironed out and improvements to be made, but the fact is that right now MAP and TOP can make the job simpler, cheaper, and more effective than many alternatives. Moreover, the commitment of the developers of MAP/TOP to minimise the cost of upgrading as new standards are developed enhances the advantage of gaining experience now beyond any drawbacks.

The problems of FMS that remain to be addressed as successfully are adaptation and integration of existing machines and systems, the cost of systems to control and manage flexibility in manufacturing, and the new field of constructing systems to operate reliably and effectively in a networked, distributed environment.

REFERENCES

[1]   Demonstration Agreement Document MAP/TOP Awareness Event (CIMAP) Coopers and Lybrand Associates, (1986)
[2]   System Integration Design Document, MAP/TOP Awareness Event (CIMAP), Electronic Data Systems, Harrow (1986)

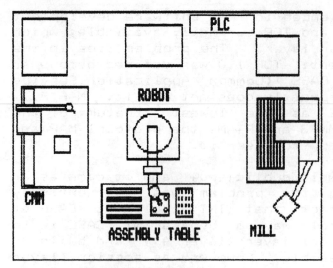

Figure 1. Cell Layout

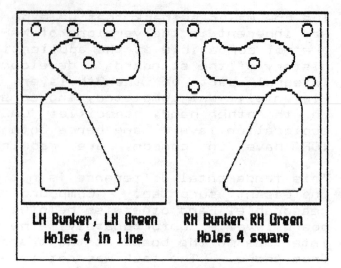

Figure 2. Component Design

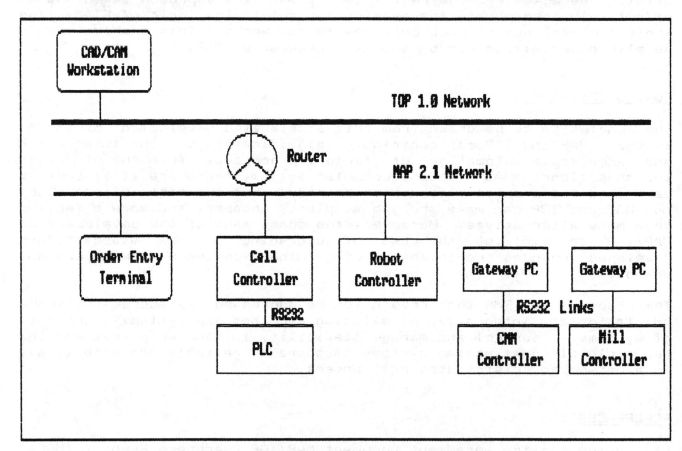

Figure 3. Communications Topology

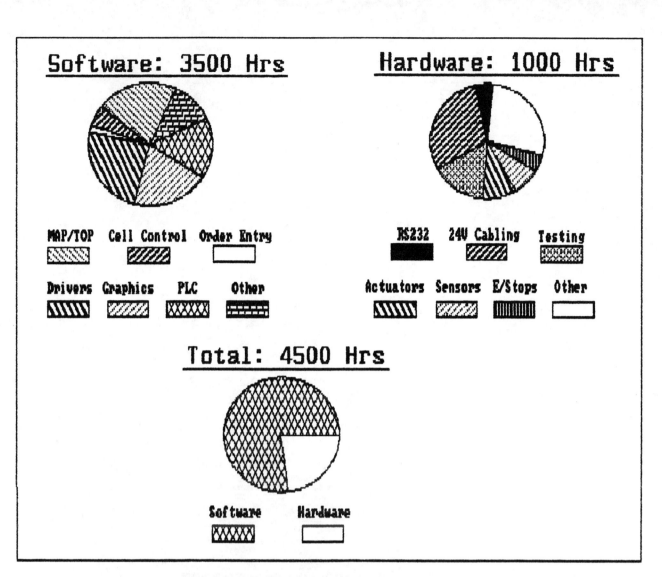

Figure 4. Estimates of Man-Hours

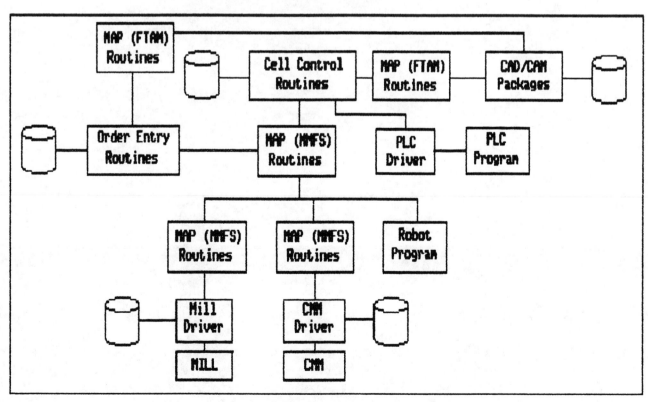

Figure 5. Software Structure

43

Proc. 2nd Int. Conf. Machine Control Systems, 45-54
May 1987, © IFS (Conferences) Ltd and authors, ISBN 0-948507-52-7

CNMA: MAP V3.0 in action

M J Henderson
Siemens Ltd, UK

The first version of the MAP V3.0 standard will be published shortly.

A draft version has already been in circulation for some time. In recognition of the importance that this standard is going to have on factory automation, the EEC decided to part fund, as part of the ESPRIT program, a project to implement these draft standards. Project 955, known as CNMA - Communication Network for Manufacturing Applications - is a multi-vendor exercise led by British Aerospace. CNMA demonstrates Europe's commitment to MAP V3.0 and shows that the five European vendors involved will be well positioned to supply MAP V3.0 products.

INTRODUCTION

Communication has become probably the most significant single factor influencing the technical viability of CIM in the factory of the future. There has been a great deal of publicity about MAP recently. Demonstrations at AUTOFACT in 1985 and CIMAP at the NEC last year showed an increasing confidence that MAP is feasible. The next major demonstration of MAP oriented communication will be the Enterprise Network Event (ENE) which is being held in Baltimore next year. This event will comprise 8 cells, 7 at the exhibition site and 1 remote link to a British Aerospace plant at Samlesbury, as part of the CNMA project. Whereas the cells at the ENE will be demonstrating products conforming to MAP V3.0 for the first time, it may be argued that the Europeans have stolen a march on the Americans with CNMA. CNMA, which was first demonstrated publicly at the Hanover Fair 1987, already uses the RS 511 standard (MMS) for level 7 of the OSI model. It is at this level that the most significant differences between MAP V2.1 and V3.0 can be encountered. This paper described the impetus behind CNMA, the implementation history and CNMA's plans for further development.

ESPRIT PROGRAM

CNMA owes its existence to the EEC's ESPRIT Program. ESPRIT is the EEC's European Strategic Program for Research and Development in Information Technology. This program, launched in 1983, aims to provide the European Information Technology (IT) industry with the technology it will require in order to be competitive in the 1990s. The EEC provides 50% funding of collaborative multinational R & D projects. It is divided into the five key areas shown in Figure 1.

The CNMA project is within area 5, i.e. Computer Integrated Manufacturing, and is also known as Project 955. This project has the aim of furthering the adoption of industrial communication standards with the background objective of elevating the marketing position of European CIM vendors. The CNMA consortium comprises ten companies from France, Germany, Italy and the United Kingdom. There are five equipment vendors - Siemens, Bull, GEC, Olivetti and Nixdorf. Four are IT users, namely British Aerospace, Aeritalia, BMW and Puegeot. The French systems house, TITN, is also involved, as is one of the German Fraunhofer Institutes, IITB from Karlsruhe. The programme of work includes the selection, implementation and demonstration of existing and emerging communications standards, and validating these standards in a real production environment. Acceptance of these standards is encouraged by the publication of implementation guides and the development of conformance test tools.

Implementation is split into several phases.

CNMA has already been displayed at the Hanover Industrial Fair. Preparations are now under way to re-configure the system prior to installation at the British Aerospace factory at Samlesbury, near Preston, where it will be used to produce parts for the A320 aircraft. This phase of the system will be commissioned in May 1988 and will be used as a pilot site for a period of six months, during which time intertested parties will be able to visit the installation. Phase 2 will be installed during 1988 at the new BMW plant in Regensburg, Bavaria and at Aeritalia in Tunis.

CNMA STANDARDS DEFINITION AND DEVELOPMENT

In order to provide a focus for all project activities, it was decided at an early stage to publish 'Implementation Guides' (IG) which would clearly establish which protocols, standards, etc. were to be used at the Hanover demonstration and the Phase 1 facility at Samlesbury.

The IGs also serve to clarify issues where standards are ambiguous. Defining subsets reduces the complexity of the implementation by limiting the protocol options to those which are necessary for the application in question.

The Phase 1 IG has been widely circulated to standards bodies, vendors, users etc. in Europe and the USA and has already had significant impact in the process of protocol specification and standardisation for MAP V3.0. The bulk of the work during preparation of the IGs revolved around the specification for layer 7. Indeed, publication of the IGs was delayed to allow incorporation of the (then) latest issue (draft 5) of EIA 1393Aa (MMS - Manufacturing Message Service). This MMS protocol is likely to become EIA RS511 and one of the CNMA's aims is to encourage this development. Subsets of MMS have been defined for minicomputers, numerical controllers and programmable logic controllers.

CNMA SOFTWARE DEVELOPMENT AND IMPLEMENTATION

Each vendor has implemented communication profiles as specified in the CNMA IGs. Software development continued throughout 1986, layers 1-5 were up-graded in line with the CNMA profile and software for CASE and MMS was written. Conformance testing equipment was installed at the integration centre in Wolverhampton at the end of November and by the end of the year, all scheduled tests had been successfully completed.

CONFORMANCE TESTING OF COMMUNICATION NETWORKS

It is vital for a multi-vendor project such as CNMA to have a common set of tools for testing, protocol verification and conformance checking. The test bed then serves as a reference model for the implementation of the set of protocols.

Existing test architectures were examined, notably the ITI Map 2.1 test system. This was acquired by the Frauhofer Institute (IITB), along with a VAX 11/750 and the VMS/EUNICE operating system. Two configurations were established; one for testing up to session layer and one for testing MMS and CASE. IITB defined an MMS test tool specification which was agreed by all partners. The conformance test bed software was modified across layers 3 to 5 to match the implementation requirements of CNMA.

The Bull SP 37 computer was delivered to the IITB in Karlsruhe in July 1986 and connected a System Under Test. Conformance tests for layers 1-5 were completed successfully by the end of November. The conformance test software was installed at the CNMA Integration Centre in Wolverhampton at the beginning of December and conformance and interworking testing of layers 1-5 (for 802-3) were performed with Bull, GEC and Siemens. The tests on layers 1-5 and the MMS protocol for Hanover were successfully completed. Meanwhile, the Olivetti minicomputer passed conformance tests for layer 5 and MMS in Karlsruhe.

At the time of writing (mid March), all conformance tests on layers 1-5 and MMS on 802.4 broadband with all vendors were being completed at Wolverhampton. For the future, conformance test support will be provided for the British Aerospace Samlesbury pilot.

PILOT 1 FACILITY APPLICATION

Although the ESPRIT programme is fundamentally an R & D programme, participants are encouraged to demonstrate the outcome of their work in a production environment. The need for a Hanover demonstration, which is obviously not a production cell, has necessitated a considerable re-configuring of the Hanover cell to allow it to be used in a production environment.

The Hanover cell is shown in Fig 2 and was used to produce three different designs of 'components'. Visitors were able to select one of these from a VDU on the stand which then passed the selection to the control system. All the mechanical equipment for the cell was provided by Marwin Production Machines of Wolverhampton.

PROVISION OF APPLICATION SOFTWARE

British Aerospace is responsible for the provision of application software in the cell controllers, whilst TITN is supplying application software for the minicomputers to be used for cell control (Kernel). Software for the remaining three minicomputers is being supplied by the respective vendors. This software will enable supervisory access to the cell control mini computer. All the application software was written before the end of December 1986 and was tested and commissioned standalone (and on time) in late December/early January. Integration testing took place from January to March. Inter-networking tests on the various items of equipment were completed before the end of December, i.e. ahead of schedule.

PROVISION OF THE SAMLESBURY PRODUCTION FACILITY

Following an open tender, a KTM FM200 precision boring machine was selected for this facility. Although outside the scope of CNMA, this facility is essential to provide a production platform for CNMA. The FM200 is fitted with a SIEMENS SINUMERIK NC Controller which is interfaced to the CNMA network using a DEC microVax computer.

For production purposes, the machine should be commissioned by the end of October 1987. The transportable system and other mechanical equipment will be installed as required during 1987. The remaining CNMA computers must be integrated by May 1988. (See Figure 3)

Software for the Bull mini-computer will be provided by TITN and a specification for the remaining minis will be provided by British Aerospace and TITN.

PILOT 2 APPLICATIONS

Alongside these frantic activities involved in Pilot 1, a great deal of work is being directed towards ensuring that the Pilot 2 projects proceed smoothly. As stated earlier, Pilot 2 facilities are scheduled for BMW Regensburg and Aeritalia, Tunis. At present, work for the BMW pilot is further advanced and will encompass assembly painting and acquisition of maintenance data.

This application will represent the first implementation of CNMA communication software within the automobile industry and, consequently, is seen as a vote of confidence in the project. (See Figure 4)

CONCLUSION

The most remarkable feature about this whole exercise has been the relative smoothness with which the project has proceeded. Naturally, there have been some very major problems, but all parties have shown themselves willing to provide the resource and effort necessary to overcome them. CNMA demonstrates firstly that the emerging MAP V3.0 standards will allow multi-vendor inter-networking, and secondly that vendors with diverse interests (and cultures) are quite capable of settling their differences for the common good.

These two facts allow optimism that MAP V3.0 is most definitely a viable proposition. The openness of communication which this initiative permits is essential for the successful implementation of the factory of the future.

ACKNOWLEDGEMENT

The author is grateful to British Aerospace for information and material contained in this paper.

M J HENDERSON

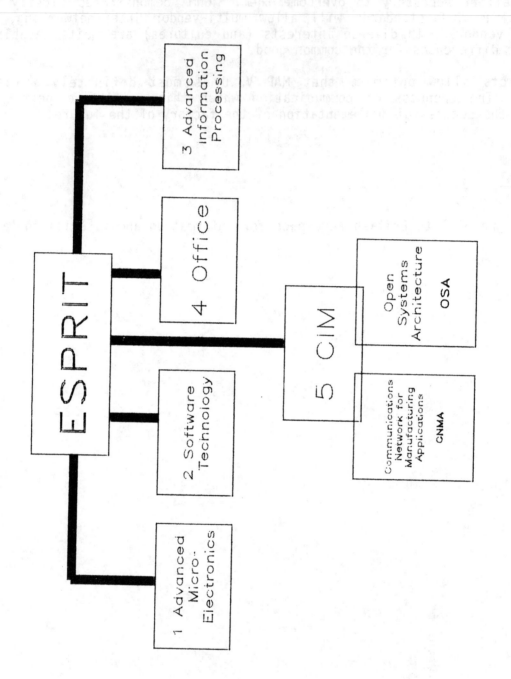

Figure 1: Key ESPRIT Areas

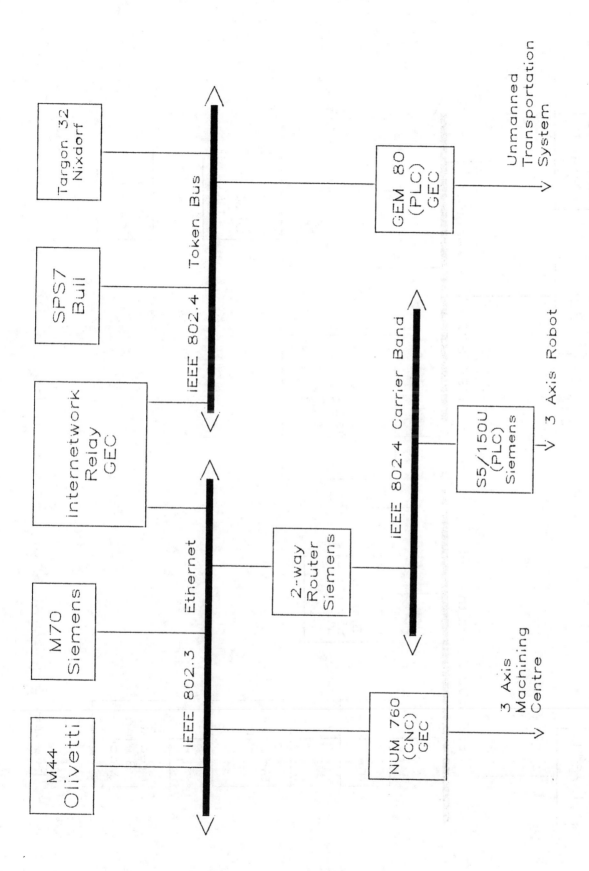

Figure 2:   Hannover Cell Architecture

51

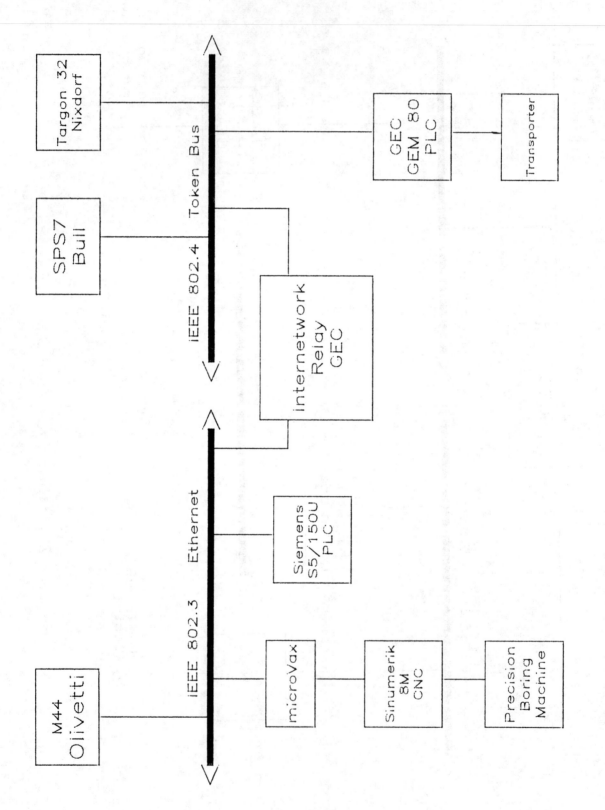

Figure 3. Samlesbury Precision Boring Facility

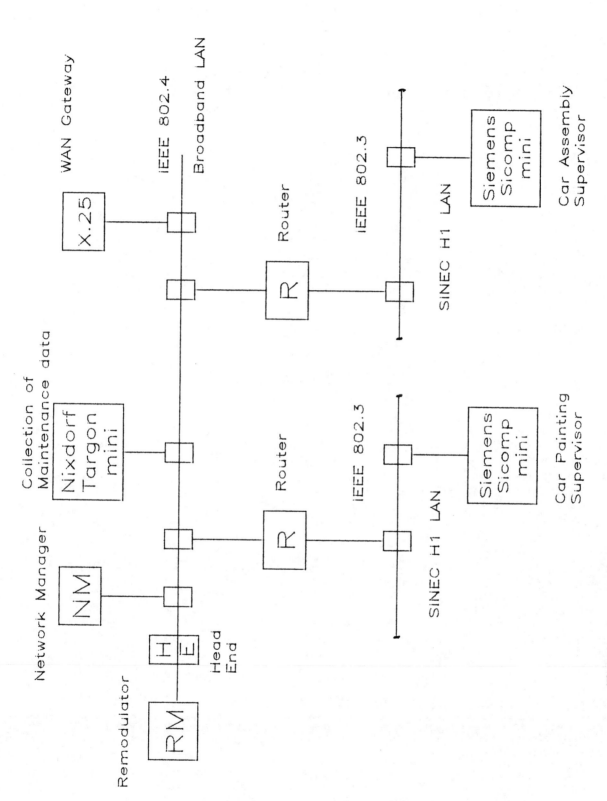

Figure 4: BMW Pilot 2 cell architecture

COMMUNICATIONS II

Proc. 2nd Int. Conf. Machine Control Systems, 55-64
May 1987, © IFS (Conferences) Ltd and authors, ISBN 0-948507-52-7

Cell controllers in action
A Evans
Allen-Bradley International, Europe

ABSTRACT

Cell Control is one of the many concepts that is flooding the manufacturing
world but the definition of what a Cell is and the type of device required to
control it is not so clear. This solution will differ by industry and by
application but some common themes exist by which the Production Manager might
plan his architecture. The paper examines, using the Vista 2000 as an example,
what device architecture is required and what functions a cell must perform to
increase flexibility and lower costs.

1. WHAT IS A CELL CONTROLLER

'Cell control is the answer to our manufacturing need.'

'A Cell controller is in the third level of the Allen-Bradley pyramid.'

The problem with broad brush statements like these is that there is a lot of differing understanding within the manufacturing world as to what they mean. What is a cell controller and what functionality does it add to the automation architecture, to the manufacturing process itself.

What is a cell?
Will not the problems that a Cell architecture solves be different by industry, and even by particular application. The businesses we are automating are different and so will be the problems that Cell Control can solve.

Allen-Bradley has designed a Pyramid automation concept by which we can approach the needs of a diverse market and help define, by industry, by customer, what is required to solve their automation problem.

This five layer structure is an ideal, not to be slavishly followed but used as a model, a tool by which to think automation. In one application the pyramid may have three levels, in another, seven, but some common themes remain, and the process by which the architecture is decided upon will be consistant.

To buy a cell controller, and in the same way to market one, is a difficult task unless the automation architecture is clear. What is more it must be an architecture with a clear direction for the future.

In talking Cell Controllers one cannot simply identify key features and benefits of the product. One must understand what Cell Control is, for each industry and for each application. So before we even start considering products let's begin by thinking about Cells.

Let's start with the Allen-Bradley model, the pyramid (See Figure 1):

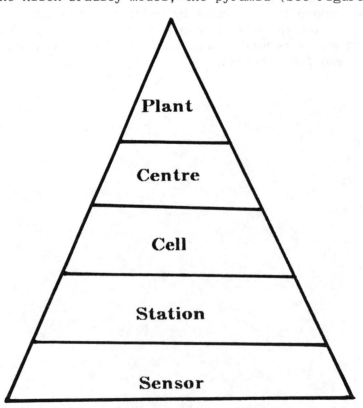

Figure 1.   Allen-Bradley Automation Pyramid

What does Allen-Bradley define a cell to be in our study Industrial Automation Series One. (1).

The Cell:

"Coordinates production flow among various stations. Integrates individual stations into an automated system."

Let us pick out of that phrase, three key words. A cell performs three major functions:

- Coordination.
  The coordination of the diverse activities and orders flowing around the cell.

- Integration.
  The integration of those activities towards a single goal.

- Automation.
  The automation of the whole into a single, structured, system.

Now where does this get us. We now have some general ideas in our minds, broad concepts perhaps of a cell's function but it is difficult to see how it applies in practice, in real customer situations. Also if we look at the definitions Allen-Bradley has published for the other levels of the pyramid. (1).

A Station:

"Performs logic necessary to convert input from the lower levels to output commands based on direction from above."

In terms of three key words again, a station does the following:

- Performs
  Performs the actions necessary. That is, it controls the process.

- Converts
  Converts instructions from above into activity.

- Outputs commands to the machines.

A Centre:

"Schedules production and provides management information by monitoring and supervising lower levels."

In terms of three key words, the centre does the following:

- Schedules
  Schedules the production.

- Monitors
  Monitors in the sense of overseeing the process.

- Supervises
  Supervises the whole, ensuring that its instructions are obeyed.

Now this analysis helps to the extent of giving us concepts to think around, but it does not allow us to apply it easily to a given situation, or to decide what sort of device, in product terms is required at each level and in each application.

It is difficult to understand exactly where one function ends and another begins. At this point in our thinking it is all too easy to fall into an argument about semantics. We argue about when a cell is a cell and a station a station; whether a function can properly be described as Supervising, and we become more confused as the 'buzz' words proliferate and the definitions do not.

The architecture mirrors the human structures involved in production and that helps us to understand, but we must go further and decide what is required to do the job in product terms.

2. THE WORLD OF COMPUTERS

Clearly the device required to automate the process, in a structured architecture will be some form of computer, or will at least use computer technology to solve the problem.

Let us try defining a cell first of all by examinining the <u>functionality</u> of computers. (See Figure 2).

Computer technology

Figure 2

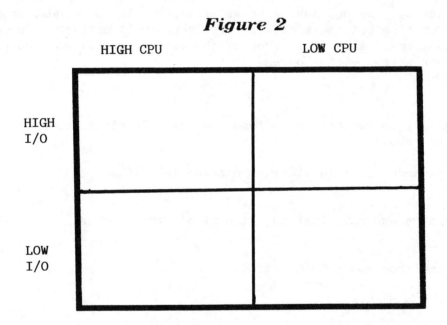

Computers and Controllers

If we consider that all computers, whatever their function always fall within one of these four boxes then in this context, a High CPU device represents a machine which is capable of a large amount of processing, or calculation, and is designed to accomplish that function as well. The Low CPU device handles little, and is capable, by design, of only small amounts, or slow calculation.

High I/O represents the sort of device that handles large amounts of information, be it data or instructions, in whatever form. A low I/O device is that which handles relatively little in comparison with other devices utilising computer technology.

To explain by means of some example the so-called home computer resides in the bottom right hand corner of the Low CPU-Low I/O box. This is the device that we are mostly familiar with through our children. It runs slowly and handles only the input of a single keyboard or joystick. It is designed, for its function, and for its price; low on both counts. (See Figure 3).

The Supercomputer workstation products that are much in vogue in Universities at the present are single user still but wield enormous processing powers to attack theoretical modelling problems, and many other academic issues. These 'super-computers' reside in the bottom left hand box, the High CPU-Low I/O area. We still have relatively small amounts of input/output but now enormous processing power is available to that sole user at his terminal. (See Figure 3).

The Programmable Controllers in manufacturing industry resides in the top right hand box, the High I/O-Low CPU area. The data handling capability of a PLC is enormous, as it should be in a control function. The amount of processing done on the data is however relatively slight. This does increase across the range of available PLCs as does the I/O handling capability. The range of PLCs therefore straddles the top right hand box, crossing it, diagonally as functionality increases with cost.

Microcomputers, specifically the IBM PC and compatible reside in the same box as the home computers, just further up to represent its greater processing power and higher level of I/O capabilities. The RIC card announced by IBM further enhances both of these and places the PC + RIC, somewhat further up the box. (See Figure 3).

The minicomputers and mainframe are in the Low I/O boxes (relative to PLCs) but are designed to do more calculation and trending. They therefore reside on the High CPU side since they may handle less information and data than a PLC and less often, but their capabilities to process it, in whatever form, are much greater.

The Vista 2000 cell controller marketed by Allen-Bradley with the HAM (Hardware Access machine) probably appears as shown in Figure 3.

Computer Technology

Figure 3

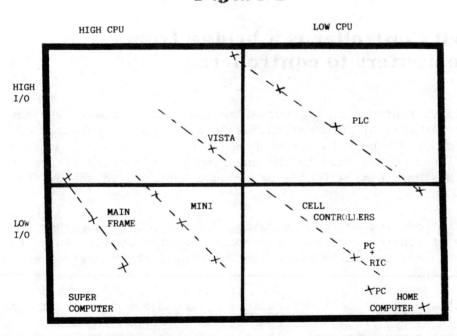

Computers and Controller

So where does this get us. We now know where many types of computer device reside, in relation to each other, as analysed by this four-box representation of computing power.

What does this tell us?

The first interesting thing to note is that there are several diagonal lines crossing the box, representing ranges of computer device: PLCs, minicomputers, and mainframe.

Thus, as shown in Figure 4:

Computer Technology

Figure 4

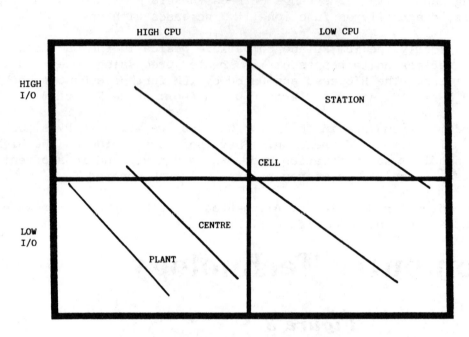

Cell Controller is a bridge from
Computers to controllers

Moving along these lines represents, of course, an increase in power, whether it is used to handle larger amounts of information, as in a PLC, or to calculate faster as with a computer. You would expect to see such an increase across a product range. Moving across these lines corresponds to the changing functionality of Station, Cell, Centre and Plant, and along them is found the product designed to answer the needs at those levels.

The Cell Controller is revealed as the 'bridging' device to link together the worlds of High I/O, that is of control, to general purpose computer world. As a device it will be partially computer, partially controller, living in both environment and linking the two together.

Thus we may represent a range of cell controllers by the diagonal cell line as shown. This is what you would expect, no single product will answer all the needs for cell control in all manufacturing industries. It will, of course require a range of controllers, just as a range of computers and PLCs will be used. We therefore see that the diagram reveals certain devices to be potential cell controllers. These are:

- Personal Computer & RIC
- Vista 2000 & HAM

Now let us examine, across the range, what is common about the functionality of these products for this will reveal the features required in a device to be a cell controller.

We have here a range of products where the I/O handling is increased by adding extra

60

devices to handle the information handling thereby alleviating the main processor of that work. This allows it to process the information gathered from the I/O handlers with pausing to gather it. In Allen-Bradley we call these Main Processors and Access Machines. Schematically we may represent this as shown in Figure 5: (2)

Cell Controller
Architecture

Figure 5

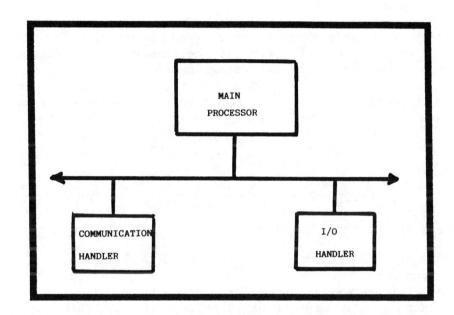

Network of Processors & I/O Handlers

The Cell Controller must therefore be a network of computers and computer devices which divide between them the work of the cell. A central processor, or potentially processors and I/O handlers are structured across a computer network to achieve the task at the speed required. In some cells that will be a LAN, in others the internal bus of the cell controller itself.

No computer that does not have this architecture can truly handle a cell. Of course it can to an extent but the cell demand for timely information will soon overcome it. In very small cells this may be acceptable. As stated at the beginning there will be industries where station and cell, or centre and cell merge, but even there if the customer need for timely information grows beyond that first-identified need, separate handlers will be required or the speed of response will suffer. It is vital therefore to choose a flexible, expandable architecture.

Before we complete this section let me say that this architecture is not unique to Allen-Bradley, and is constructable from competitors' hardware. The extra functionality, and the price of the Vista package compared to those alternatives is where we can gain further advantage.

3. VISTA 2000 AS A CELL CONTROLLER

Let us now examine in more detail the functionality of a cell controller in terms of an Allen-Bradley product with which I am familiar. We will examine it in terms of the three key words regarding a cell, that we defined at the beginning:

- Coordinating
- Integrating
- Automating

Coordinating   By this we mean overseeing a diverse set of functions, and ensuring that their activity is, between them, acting in concert. To do this, several functions have to be performed by the cell controller acting in this way. It must:

- Gain information
- Take action (make commands downwards)
- Store information (the event and the action) in a portable format, for communi-
  cation and reporting upwards.

If the cell controller does these three things, it can see a situation or event in a part of the cell, act on it by commands sent to the same part or different parts, and record that the event has occurred for reporting upwards.

Vista 2000 provides these facilities in the basic software by means of:

- Data acquisition
- Alarm management
- Data definitions

In a way that is directly configurable to the structure of the cell in question.

The optional packages expand the facilities available in this respect to include specialist needs:

- Statistical quality control
- Station level support (to communicate outwards and across the cell)
- Major High Level languages (Fortran, C and Unix development tools) to let the user
  develop more programs specific to his needs.

Vista is also designed that this library of options and extensions can be continually added to.

Integrating   In order to integrate the activities of the cell, the cell controller must enable the coordination activities to be directed towards a set, clear goal, as directed from above. The coordination activity above is expanded into not only reacting to situations that occur but in instigating new activity.

To do this we need:

- Information structured to analyse
- Event processing
- Ability to make commands

The Vista supplies this by means of:

- Database management
- Event processing
- C & Fortran to expand as the users want

And in terms of the optional packages:

- Station level support (upload & download)
- Record Management (Historical)
- 6121/2 support

By this means the Vista can be used to analyse situations and take actions towards its defined goals.

Automating By this we mean the overall effect that the customers will gain by installing cell control. Above we have considered means by which the activities of the station below can be coordinated together and integrated towards a set goal. The structure of this will differ but the customer should always gain an automated system, a system where one of his most valuable commodities is readily available – information.

This is supplied by:

- Trending
- Displays
- Calculations
- Reporting

and Vista 2000 supplies this to a high degree:

- Algorithms
- Real time trending
- configurable graphics

with optional areas, covering

- Report generation
- Plotting, trending on the screen
- Historical Data Collection ... information

With this, the automated system the user himself can alter and set direction, drive the cell towards goals, and change to fit new situations, alarms or events.

4. SUMMARY

This analysis above is an overview and each customer should and will implement it differently, as his business needs drive him.

The key to successful, expandable automation is to identify the requirements first, and to build the automation solution that encompasses them and future needs as well.

Cell Control must not become simply a buzz-word but a working concept, understood in terms of each application, and not only in conceptual, or ideal terms.

This is how Cell Controllers, in action, can aid the manufacturing process, to lower costs and increase flexibility. This must be the aim of CIM, without it the benefits possible will not, and cannot be gained.

REFERENCES

(1) Allen-Bradley Industrial Automation Series One

(2) Allen-Bradley Industrial Automation Series Two

Proc. 2nd Int. Conf. Machine Control Systems, 65-74
May 1987, © IFS (Conferences) Ltd and authors, ISBN 0-948507-52-7

A cell controller product to join the islands of automation
I K Taylor
Cincinnati Milacron Ltd, UK

ABSTRACT

The following paper describes the conception and development of a Flexible Manufacturing Cell Controller. It addresses the problems of ensuring that the product is expandable as the customer's automation capability increases by defining the development steps. The paper also shows how the proposed architecture enables the controller to be linked with other cell controllers and to communicate with higher levels of control in the complete automatic manufacturing hierarchy.

BACKGROUND

Back in the early 1980's when Cell Controllers were unheard of, it was the Flexible Manufacturing System which was being described by the technical press. At that time, a "System" was typically 5 to 25 machine tools controlled by what can now be described as a computer "Room" full of equipment. Government grants and Military Contracts provided the necessary funding for these large installations and enormous efforts and resources were expended to complete these projects. The timescales for completion being measured in years rather than months. Japan and America dominated the world in large system applications where large volume production requirements created the need for "computer control". The requirement for flexibility, although specified as an objective, was rarely needed or implemented.

In 1983 it became apparent that these complex, large systems would not "translate" into a suitable form which would meet the European needs for volume and flexibility. Several attempts to scale down the systems solution for 2 to 6 machine groupings - (let's now call them cells) - failed because the software and hardware architectures were designed to be large. This over-head resulted in an overly expensive control to machine cost ratio and the cost to train personnel and to support the system was unacceptable. There had to be a better way.

At this time, the personal computer was finding its feet and predictions for its future cost effectiveness looked very convincing. During the latter half of 1983 and early 1984, Cincinnati Milacron developed its Flexible Manufacturing Cell Controller (FMCC - see Figure 1) which was exhibited at the MACH 84 Machine Tool exhibition. This first generation Cell Controller coupled a personal computer with a high level language programmable controller to provide a shop floor based product capable of controlling up to six resources. This design has subsequently been put into production at the Cincinnati Milacron manufacturing plant in Birmingham where it controls two horizontal machining centres, a robot wash station, an inspection machine and an automatic guided vehicle. Pallet storage is accomplished by two eight position automatic work changers.

The FMCC has been further developed and reviewed over the past two years. It has enabled us to better understand the control problems encountered in FMS, the computing power required and probably more importantly the operating requirements to keep the cell efficiently utilised. FMCC provided the Cell Controller functional element to create an island of automation. Future developments address the isolated islands and provide an evolutionary path towards much larger automated systems. The following paper describes the basic thinking behind the present development - the Flexible Manufacturing Controller - 90 product (FMC-90) - which provides an update path for those customers with the original FMCC, and introduces the features necessary to realise the complete hierarchical FMS structure.

INTRODUCTION - THE GROUND RULES

There are set steps required in the development of a Cell Controller in order to provide an evolutionary rather than revolutionary approach. The first step is to define a factory wide control hierarchy. The author believes this is a four level structure and FMC-90 is designed to fit into this structure (to be defined later). At each level the tasks must be identified so that a control system product specification can be produced. Data communication between each hierarchical level must be identified such that rigid interfaces can be created. The resultant interface designs and protocols should be communicated within the company, to customers and to the other players in the FMS arena (for example major computer manufacturers, CAD and MRP suppliers). This is necessary to encourage the creation of de-facto standards for everyone to follow.

Once the factory automation products have been specified, the next step is to develop them from the bottom levels upwards. Each product should be defined in detail and then its hardware and software architectures developed such that the solution is Generic. The ultimate confirmation of the adaptability, flexibility and performance of the product will only come when that product is complete and commissioned but this of course is too late. It is for this reason that during the product development the current design should be benchmarked and reviewed against typical applications by way of simulation. In the case of FMC-90, four typical machining cells have been identified and defined in some detail. These are being simulated against the functions of the Cell Controller product to confirm that the eventual performance will be at least adequate with these cell configurations. In addition to this "synthetic" benchmarking by way of simulation, the ability to have a real live test site is of great benefit. In the case of FMC-90, there is a ready made test site presently controlled by its predecessor Cell Controller at the Cincinnati Milacron Birmingham manufacturing plant. This will be upgraded and used to evaluate the new controller product before it is available to customers. The final but vital part of product development is to create the necessary documentation describing the Generic product in order that it can be sold as a demonstrable solution rather than having to create a customer specific alternative. The cost to develop and support a customer special is prohibitive and should be avoided at all cost. Even with the FMC-90 there will undoubtedly be a certain amount of customising required but this should be confined to the interface area where the software languages are those of Programmable Logic Controllers and the customer himself can have an involvement in doing this work.

Once the product has been developed there is an on-going process of massaging its specification and implementation to take account of the changing automation environment. Since the Cell Controller is only one link in the automation chain and other links will undoubtedly be from other suppliers, the expansion and addition of automation equipment will place new demands on the cell controller. An awareness of these changes and demands is of paramount importance. The product must be monitored against its external interfaces, both upward and downward, and horizontal communication must also be considered. Future enhancements and model changes must maintain the product's optimisation within its part of the overall automation picture. This process goes on indefinitely.

INTRODUCTION - THE DON'TS

The world of FMS is very complex and it is easy to become side tracked resulting in the optimal solution possible at a specific point in time not being provided. It is often useful to list the aspects of the overall task which should be avoided rather than accomplished. The following four points should be considered.

(a) Prevent the problems becoming too complex. Simplicity has to be forced, history shows that many of the best ideas are the simple ones. Limiting the available computing power has the effect of focussing the designer to think of solutions within the capability of the processors. There should be no doubt that however much processing power and memory are available at the point in time when the product is developed, it will all get used! Do not forget however that computers have reliably doubled their processing power for the same cost every one to two years or alternatively halved their cost for the same power in the same period of time. A cell controller product developed today which fully utilises its computer processors will have upgrade possibilities tomorrow without any major redesign.

(b) Do not worry too much about customer's preferences. Customers like to dictate which manufacturer's computer to use based on their presently installed equipment. Is it realistic to convert a DEC product into an IBM one to satisfy one customer? The work involved and the support cost is unrealistic when compared with the benefit to the customer. Automation control products should be considered as self-contained black boxes. They must be reliable, provide cost effectiveness, and have adequate performance. Conformance to international communications standards provides the guarantee that these black boxes can be inter-connected without engineering redesign.

(c) Do not compromise the vertical layered structure. The necessary automation products can be created by collaborating with other manufacturers such that their expertise can be realised.

(d) Do not become too secretive. Share ideas; no-one knows all the answers and we need all the advice, help, and encouragement we can get. The need for de-facto communications standards, and the need for collaboration to provide the complete hierarchical chain means we must share ideas before the products have completed development. If any one of the players in the chain fail, the whole of manufacturing industry suffers.

THE FMS HIERARCHY

FMC-90 is designed to fit into the four level hierarchy now being promoted and adopted by many of the large computer manufacturers and industrial FMS users in Europe. The four level philosophy has been the underlying principle behind the architecture of the Milacron European FMS strategy. The four levels are concerned with the decision making strata within factory automation, their level of detail and perspective. The discipline covers parts manufacture and parts assembly and it is a mimic of the human organisational structure from director through managers and supervisors to the manual worker. Figure 2 shows these levels and the distinctions between them.

Level 1 controls the Machines/Robots/Mechanisms etc., and the conventional products from Cincinnati Milacron's Electronic Systems Division. Because of the nature of this business area, we provide the controlling intelligence. Such systems provide a much lower cost to our customers but inevitably without complete standardisation of operation of programming language. International standards have not been able to keep pace with the electronic feature development and no clear de-facto standards have appeared. The Robot world and the Inspection machine world standards have all differed significantly from the Numerical Control (NC) and Programmable Logic Control (PLC) world standards. For this reason it must be Milacron's mission to harmonise the level 1 systems in order that meaningful communication can be made with high levels of the hierarchy - the cell controller provides this harmonising function.

The first generation FMCC explored the machine mechanism data and control communication and provided a sound foundation on which to build the necessary features for further integration. The second generation FMCC - the FMC-90, develops the upward communication in order to progress the integration process for our customers.

Having provided a level 2 cell controller (or supervisor) it is unlikely that Milacron would create a level 3 cell manager or factory controller since this is more likely to be the level to which the computer manufacturers or system houses would be working down from their conventional material requirements planning (MRP) and computer aided design (CAD) mainframe levels. This philosophy has been borne out in our experience to date with FMC where several large computer companies and leading industrialists already have, or have plans to develop, a factory controller or cell manager product. This level 3 product provides the junction for two main factory databases, the manufacturing (schedule) database and the engineering (CAD) database. In most companies these are very separate activities, but for full integration of FMS to be effective they must be brought together prior to the level 2 cell controller.

THE FMC-90 CELL CONTROLLER (LEVEL 2)

FMC-90 furthers the approach to cellular FMS, it provides a control environment enabling our customers to purchase stand-alone cells which when running satisfactorily may be coupled and co-ordinated. Stand-alone cells may include a variety of machine tools, Robots, Transport systems, Inspection and wash stations. Coupling and co-ordinating these necessitates some amount of configuring if only to provide a factory wide rather than local transport system. Any cell controller product must be capable of this adaptation in the customers' premises. FMC-90 has the architecture, in hardware and software, to meet this requirement. The use of modular software packages, closely coupled PLC units and the distributed I/O are the ingredients Milacron is providing to carry out the task.

The first generation FMCC provided machine communication, a basic scheduler and information gathering capabilities. FMC-90 takes these functions further and also adds additional capabilities. Machine communication is improved by incorporating Robot and Inspection machine interfaces as well as widening the communication window to our own Acramatic controls for the purposes of better error reporting and tool management. Scheduling has been improved considerably although for the novice FMS user the basic scheduler is still an option.

At the hub of the FMC-90 is an open architecture IBM Industrial Computer processor supporting high resolution colour graphics, a high speed PLC interface and a variety of processor based high level communication options. The industrial Computer runs with a multi-tasking multi-user operating system utilising dynamic reallocation of memory partition size and priority.

There are four main thrusts with the FMC-90 and these are the human interface, scheduling, tool management and communication.

Colour graphics with controller cursor movement provides a pleasant, friendly human interface. Since the Cell Controller is intended to be within sight of all the cell resources it will invariably be on the shop floor - and indeed is packaged for this environment - and be operated by the shop floor personnel. It cannot be overpowering visually or complicated to operate. Individual machines in the cell must be capable of stand-alone operation under emergency conditions without undue difficulty.

The scheduling function has assumed a prominent role in the FMC-90. As an alternative to the basic priority based scheduler, a multi level scheduler is available providing three levels of scheduling which in turn provide different levels of detail and perspective. Because of the integration possibilities to higher level (i.e. factory controller), the top level FMC-90 scheduler provides interactive order selection and capacity base scheduling. For 50 works orders or four weeks in advance it can schedule a downloaded work to list and communicate the results of this operation. The second level scheduler produces a detailed production plan and provides a list of resources required over a shift or day basis. This is the basis of the third level, the cell real time sequencing. The real time sequencing can be selected to maximise machine utilisation or optimise to the production schedule.

Tool management has been developed to enable tool requirement and replenishment data to be created from the real time tool usage information transmitted up from the machine controllers. A remote tool room work station can be provided to identify the forward tooling needs as well as providing an interface for future tool gauging equipment.

Utilising the results of collaborative projects now under way with several companies, upward communications to a variety of processors used in factory controllers can be provided. In each case a common standard of data structure has been implemented in order that a de-facto standard link can be established. Our present experience in this area together with our planned development should enable the FMC-90 to be easily integrated into established factory systems. Previously, considerable effort has been required and without the interactive nature required of data transaction, self optimisation has been virtually impossible.

THE FACTORY CONTROLLER (LEVEL 3)

Over the past few years as factory automation has become a reality, it is noticeable that there have been two major driving forces working towards each other. The large computer companies with their traditional mainframe products have been moving down from the corporate processing levels (CAD/MRP) towards the shop floor. The machine tool and process control companies have been moving their levels of control upwards in a direction away from the shop floor. The question is have they met yet? It is analogous to starting the channel tunnel from each end and hoping to meet somewhere in the middle, and we all know the possible results of this scenario. It is the author's opinion that there is a gap in the centre at present (not two tunnels!), a void which the Factory Controller must fill.

The Factory Controller fulfils the role of a manager, as stated earlier, it arbitrates between Cell Controllers (or supervisors) and is able to balance the workload between Cells. It can also take on factory wide responsibilities which individual Cell Controllers cannot perform. For example, a single Cell may control its own transport and tool management systems. A Factory Controller when linked to several cells may be used by these cells to provide transport and tool room management as a central facility. Figure 3 shows a typical cellular FMS adopting levels 1, 2 and 3.

The main functions of the Factory Controller include Scheduling, Tool Management and Communications in a similar manner to the Cell Controller, the difference being that for the Factory Controller the planning horizon is longer (weeks to months). The interaction between levels is important in order to balance resources (cell activities) and the ability to provide local data storage is necessary such that a system like Figure 3 can operate for a reasonable period of time should the mainframe link fail for any reason.

The Factory Controller is not just a post box between the mainframe (Plant or Corporate) level and the Cell Controller. It has intelligence in order to carry out the same mental processes as a manager distributing the work to the appropriate supervisors (cells). It has to monitor and evaluate responses to a proposed work plan and modify the demand to balance the workload. It has to report problems to higher levels of management and provide a workload input when the boss (mainframe) is on leave. Without the Factory Controller, a single cell performs adequately but several Cells cannot balance or co-ordinate their activities. The Factory Controller is required in the evolutionary process after the Cell Controller has been established.

Cincinnati Milacron are collaborating with a large computer manufacturer to enable them to create a Factory Controller which will bridge the gap between Corporate and Plant levels (level 4) and the Cell level (level 2). Figure 4 shows the gap which this is filling in the automation pyramid. At the Factory Controller level the communication demands and the number of supplier possibilities are probably at their greatest. The need for suppliers to meet internationally agreed standards is paramount. Since the level 3 control is at the intersection of the upward and downward forces it could create the largest communication mismatch.

COMMUNICATIONS

Can we ensure that the two Channel tunnels meet in line and if they do are the railway lines and rolling stock compatible? The answer has to be yes, but not without some preparation work. For example, who decides at which end of the tunnel the cars drive on the "wrong" side of the road?

In the factory automation world, General Motors began to worry about this in 1980. They decided that it would probably cost them several million dollars to develop a Manufacturing Automation Protocol (MAP) but it would cost them a lot more if they did not develop a standard. The need for a communication protocol standard on the shop floor where no other candidate standards existed was mandatory for the future success of factory automation. All the major players in the FMS arena are involved in MAP and must be for long term security and success. But care must be exercised, MAP is not for everyone, it depends on the amount of automation in place since MAP is nothing more than a tool that allows users to connect the products together. The automation intelligence is separate from the communication and will always be so. Good communication does not rectify bad management.

MAP is presently expensive although the price will drop as it becomes established, but so will some of its presently lower cost counterparts (not necessarily competitors). The final position for MAP in the automation hierarchy will depend entirely upon its cost and cost effectiveness. We are now moving out of the MAP mania era into the real world of products and their appropriate price tags. More and more we read about a hierarchy of networks, not a MAP only factory, and this surely is more realistic. Standards such as MAP help mesh the myriad of automation products available into a single distributed control system. Although these standards will offer large scale connectivity, a hierarchy of networks including Mini MAP and possibly some proprietary networks will be necessary to satisfy the response and throughput requirements of many devices. Figure 5 shows the automated manufacturing pyramid with its corresponding networks as considered by the author.

It must be appreciated that today many groups throughout the world are striving to develop and demonstrate MAP, TOP, Field Buss, etc. These networks are new and they are developing, they are changing in order to improve their performance. Today MAP is at version 2.1 but later this year it will be at version 3.0 and this is in pursuit of improvements. Working in the field of factory automation tends to be like walking on shifting sand. A period of stability is needed when network performance is adequate and the FMS players can get on and play a tune together. We are close to the point where how we communicate is no longer the problem, it is what we communicate and how we use the information that really counts.

THE FUTURE

One numerically controlled (NC) machine is estimated to be as productive as four manual machines. An NC machine with a carousel work changer coupled to it capable of storing eight pallets is four times more powerful than the stand-alone NC machine and this is consequently 16 times more effective than the manual machine.

This single NC work changer machine can only expect a single human operator to supply all the necessary machine needs i.e. tools, fixtures, parts, etc. Sixteen operators catered for those manual machines! Superimpose a twilight shift with no manning, just in time batches of one component and the single operator is quickly submerged. Couple six NC machines together with a common transport system, automatic tool delivery, just in time operation, three shift working and abide by the Health and Safety rules outlawing people in the working area, and the overall problem becomes clear. There is work to be done, we have seen the size of the mountain range and although much development is in hand we are only in the foothills. There is a vast amount remaining and the peaks tower above us. The potential gains in productivity are enormous (16 x N) and the rewards are high but there are also great risks. The FMS players must think clearly, work hard, work together as a team and scale the peaks, we owe it to manufacturing industry.

Figure 1

HEIRARCHICAL AND DISTRIBUTED FMS CONTROL ARCHITECTURE

LEVEL	FUNCTION	PLANNING HORIZON	HUMAN EQUIVALENT
LEVEL 4	MAINFRAME (MRP & CAD)	1Q ⟶ 2YR HORIZON Batch Processing	Director
LEVEL 3	FACTORY CONTROLLER (Cell(s) Manager)	WEEK(S) ⟶ MONTH(S) Transaction and Batch Processing	Manager
LEVEL 2	CELL CONTROLLER (Cell Supervisor)	SHIFT ⟶ WEEK Transaction Processing	Supervisor
LEVEL 1	MACHINE / MECHANISM CONTROL (NC and PLC)	M Sec response time Real Time Processing	Operative

Figure 2

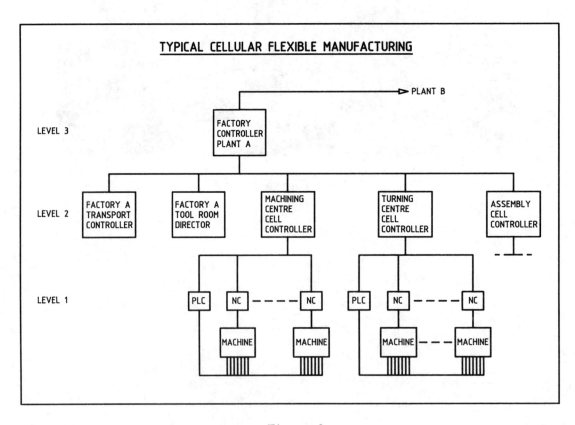

Figure 3

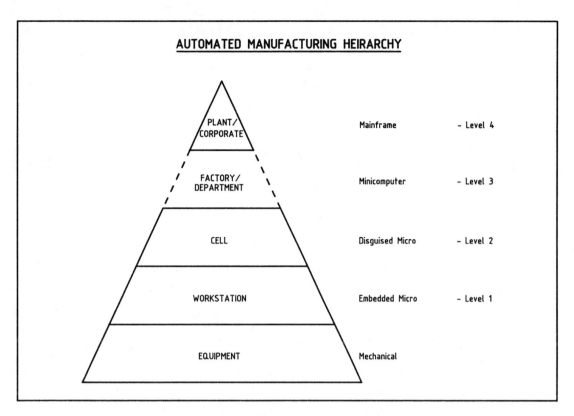

Figure 4

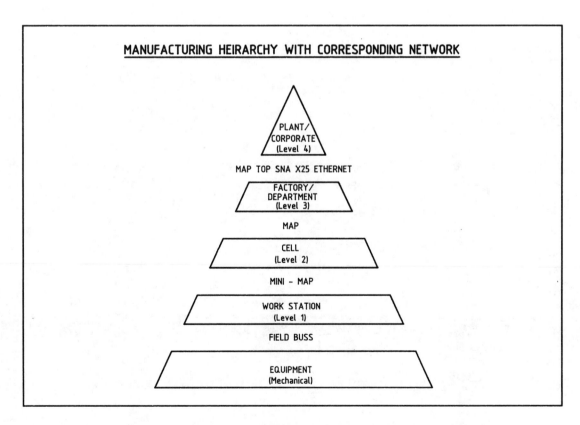

Figure 5

Proc. 2nd Int. Conf. Machine Control Systems, 75-90
May 1987, © IFS (Conferences) Ltd and authors, ISBN 0-948507-52-7

Implementing manufacturing strategies through the application of programmable control

D F Kehoe and U S Bititci
University of Liverpool, UK

ABSTRACT

Modern manufacturing systems rely increasingly upon the use of distributed programmable controllers to implement real-time process control in a CIM environment. In general, however, the important relationship between the applications strategy for such devices and the company's manufacturing philosophy is poorly defined and under utilised.

This paper describes the work currently being undertaken at the University of Liverpool to implement top-down manufacturing control strategies through the application of industrial programmable controllers and includes an industrial case study. An approach to the use of proprietary local area networks such as TIWAY 1, Data-Highway and Token-Ring to integrate these distributed control systems is also discussed.

INTRODUCTION

The past decade has seen a steady increase in international competition in the markets for manufactured goods. Manufacturing industry's response has been to develop strategies for reducing operating costs through improved productivity, lower WIP, better quality control and faster customer response.

Many companies have sought to improve their competitive position through the application of advanced manufacturing technologies. Typically the stages in the application of computers have been;

- process automation
- factory information and data collection systems
- manufacturing control systems

In terms of the industrial application of programmable logic controllers (PLC's) this has in the main been focused on the first two of these stages. The introduction of PLC's in the early 1970's was primarily used to replace the conventional relay or fluidic control of industrial processes [1]. The widespread use of this form of control coincided with the reducing cost of semi conductor processing power.

The 1980's has seen a development towards the integration of distributed PLC's through the use of communication networks [2]. In addition to providing a sophisticated hierarchical control facility these networks can also provide the manufacturing manager with essential process data.

Today most suppliers of PLC equipment provide systems which conform to the model shown in Figure 1 in having both signal and message level interfaces. At the signal level real-time control activities such as sequence or PID tasks are performed whereas at the message level peer to peer or peer to host communications are implemented to provide manufacturing information and control.

What has been more difficult to identify, however, has been the role of PLC systems in the implementation of manufacturing strategy. The adoption of a flexible or just-in-time (JIT) approach to manufacture has implications at the controller level which need to be appreciated by the applications programmer.

The view proposed here is that in designing both the process control and data communication applications of PLC's, the systems engineer should be aware of the higher level manufacturing strategies in order to configure the control software most effectively.

PROCESS AUTOMATION

In terms of the structure of modern PLC systems, process automation is implemented at the signal level. Increasingly the new generation of controllers have the processing power to integrate previously discrete automated process elements. Typically in batch production environments this process integration is occuring together with a fundamental change in the way manufacturing is controlled. Pulling material through based upon sales driven requirements rather than inventory led push is fundamental to the JIT strategy adopted by many major industrial companies. Similarly in the process industries, integrating the control of discrete elements to improve overall production efficiency forms the basis of modern manufacturing strategy.

The application of manufacturing strategy at the signal level has recently been illustrated in two separate projects involving the implementation of industrial PLC's.

The first case study involves the work of the University of Liverpool's Advanced Manufacturing Systems and Technology research group in establishing the operational flexible manufacturing system shown in Figure 2a) [3]. In terms of the control configuration, this facility comprises of two sub-systems;

- A machining cell in which a prosthetic robot loads and unloads two CNC machine tools and delivers the components to a SCARA robot assembly area.

- A materials handling cell which transfers pallets from a robot load/unload area to the machining cell.

Each of the two sub-systems is controlled at the signal level by its own PLC. The sequencing of events within the machining cell (load/unload instructions, machine starting/stopping, initiating assembly etc) is controlled by means of ladder logic programs executed on a Texas Instruments PM550 PLC. Each of the "intelligent" devices within the machining cell interfaces with the PM550 sequence controller via 24v DC I/O ports. These are addressed during the execution of the CNC or robot part programs. Other devices such as conveyors or clamping equipment are also connected to the PLC's I/O ports.

The signal level control for the materials handling cell is undertaken by an Allen-Bradley PLC 2/-05 controller. The control software for materials handling is in two parts:

- dedicated sequencer logic for the movement of the pallets between stations.

- adaptive logic to instruct the PUMA 560 robot to select the correct material load or assembly unload routine.

The two sub-system controllers are integrated at the signal level via I/O interfaces which enables the two cells to operate together.

Initially the manufacturing control strategy was for the system to produce components in a fixed sequence governed by the scheduled machine work-to-lists. This approach, however, led to a build up of buffer stock between the machining and assembly operations brought about by imbalances in the milling and turning processing times. A more effective strategy was to consider the performance of the manufacturing system as a whole (i.e. the convension of raw materials into finished assemblies) rather than the utilisation of individual machines. This approach involved "pulling" material through the system based upon the demand from the subsequent operation - commencing with the requirements of the assembly station.

In terms of the PLC control software the implication of adopting JIT assembly meant a greater degree of flexibility was required in selecting the appropriate material routing (Figure 2b). In turn, the machining centre sequencing programs were required to indicate component demand. This process is illustrated in Figure 3a) and b).

Through the application of the PM550 controller in this way the work
in progress within the cell has reduced and the overall system
efficiency improved.

The significance of implementing manufcturing strategy at the signal
level has also been demonstrated in an industrial context at the Van
den Berghs & Jurgens Limited production unit at Bromborough, Wirral.
The company manufactures a range of margarine products at the
Bromborough site on production lines arranged as shown in Figure 4a.
Each element of the production process occurs in-line and has
traditionally been controlled by either discrete PLC devices or
hard-wired logic.

An approach to improving the operating efficiency of these production
lines involves integrating the individual elements and thereby
reducing the machine stopping cycles. The existing control logic for
any given element of the production line (votating, filling or
packing) can only respond at the signal level to other elements by
either running or stopping.

A new control system currently under development utilises a TI 565 PLC
(Figure 4b) and software configured to balance the production flow
between the filling and packing machines. This approach is to be
implemented by using I/O data from one machine in the controlling
algorithms for the second machine. In this way the company are
seeking to reduce operating costs and improve product quality.

MANUFACTURING INFORMATION SYSTEMS

The development of peer to peer communications between distributed PLC
devices represented the precursor to factory wide information
networks. With the facility to communicate to a range of
microprocessor based and software configurable process machines (CNC,
robotic, PLC) a degree of flexibility can be engineered into modern
manufacturing systems.

The move towards more flexible production facilities was brought about
by the need to reduce batch sizes (and hence stockholding) and to
create a more responsive industry capable of satisfying demanding and
changing markets. These new information networks provide
manufacturing companies with a far more versatile facility than the
traditional DNC link. In addition, to programme uploading and
downloading, today's shopfloor communications systems provide a range
of message level utilies which allow distibuted devices to both send
and receive information. Most modern proprietory networking systems
support command codes which enable:

    - bit status reading
    - bit setting
    - memory data read/write
    - program upload
    - program download
    - diagnostic status reporting
    - discrete node identification

The application of industrial local area networking systems to
implement a flexible manufacturing strategy had also been illustrated
at the two installations described above.

Within the University based flexible manufacturing system each of the
component cells has a separate communications network. This situation
was deliberately created to mirror the experience of many industrial

companies who have installed a variety of manufacturing cells supplied by different vendors. The machining cell at Liverpool utilises the Texas Instruments TIWAY 1 hosted local area network (LAN) to communicate between CNC machine tools, PLC's and the IBM host microcomputer as shown in Figure 5. This industrial LAN is configured using a multidrop topology with a data rate of up to 115K baud and empolys HDLC data link control protocols [4]. Each of the devices on the network utilises an interfacing adaptor to convert the TIWAY 1 protocols to a form compatible with the particular machine interface (normally RS 232C). The IBM host computer communicates with the devices on the network using a high level Universal Command Language which facilitates:

- status updating
- data read/write
- program upload/download

It is through the use of these command codes and the configuration of the process level software that enables the implementation of the flexible manufacturing strategy. This requires that the components to be manufactured can be quickly reconfigured (in terms of the downloading of part programs) and also that the batch sizes can be flexible programmed (performed by writing manufacturing data messages to the controllers). In addition the communications system also provides real-time status information, cell output and machine utilisation reports. The PM550 PLC software has therefore to be structured in such a way as to utilise and respond to the information exchange provided by the communications network.

The materials handling cell also uses an industrial LAN in Allen-Bradley's Data-Highway. This network again employs a multidrop topology with a baud rate of 57.5K and uses an advanced Token Passing access control protocol [5]. The materials handling PLC and robot together with the supervisory IBM computer each has an appropriate interface adaptor to communicate with Data-Highway. The Data-Highway command set provides the same degree of flexibility in terms of material selection as is present in the machining cell.

To fully realise true manufacturing flexibility and integrity at the system level the requirements of individual cells needs to be communicated via the supervisory controllers. This facility is provided by the Token Ring IBM PC networking system which allows distributed microcomputers to share informaion and storage devices. The relationship between the three proprietary LAN's is illustrated in Figure 6. Each of the networks operates under the Disk Operating System (DOS) and requires an initial configuration to define the number of nodes, address, status and access. The command codes to provide the variety of network facilities are written as driver subroutines and are called through the applications software which communicates directly with the PLC's on the TIWAY 1 and Data-Highway LAN's. The Token Ring network is used for file transfer (part programs) and message (data) transfer. In this communications environment the PLC software engineer has to accommodate information received and required at both signal and message levels.

At Van den Berghs & Jurgens the same philosophy is being applied in an effort to improve the flexibility of the finished product packaging hall. Traditionally cases of margarine have been palletised at one of two stations according to a preconfigured routing (Figure 7). To make the packing hall more responsive to changing product volumes and variety, the PLC's which control case routing need adaptive software which can utilise information from other controllers in both the production and packing halls.

This new flexible manufacturing strategy is to be achieved through the application of both peer to peer and peer to host communications systems. TIWAY 1 communications networks provide operator and management information systems whereas the peer to peer links allow the message transfer associated with product routing. The applications software is being configured in such a way as to respond to instructions at both signal and message interfaces.

CONCLUSION

The application of programmable logic controllers to process automation and to factory wide information networks is a well established discipline within manufacturing systems engineering. This paper outlines through a number of case studies how today's industrial PLC systems can be used to implement manufacuring control strategy at both the signal and message level. It is this important relationship between controller software configuration and the overall production objectives that needs to be exploited if these devices are to realise their full potential in improving manufacturing performance.

REFERENCES

[1] P. Clark "Programmable Controllers Versus the Relay", Control and Instrumentation Magazine, pp.28-29, (January 1985).

[2] A. Leach "Distributing PC's Via Local Area Networks", Control and Instrumentation Magazine, pp.51-55, (January 1985).

[3] D. F. Kehoe "Control Elements within an Operating FMS" FMS Magazine, pp.46-48, (January 1986).

[4] TIWAY 1 Host Software Programming Manual, TI Publication No. 8105, August 1985.

[5] Allen-Bradley Communications Interface Module User's Manual, A-B Ref 1770-6.5.13, April 1986.

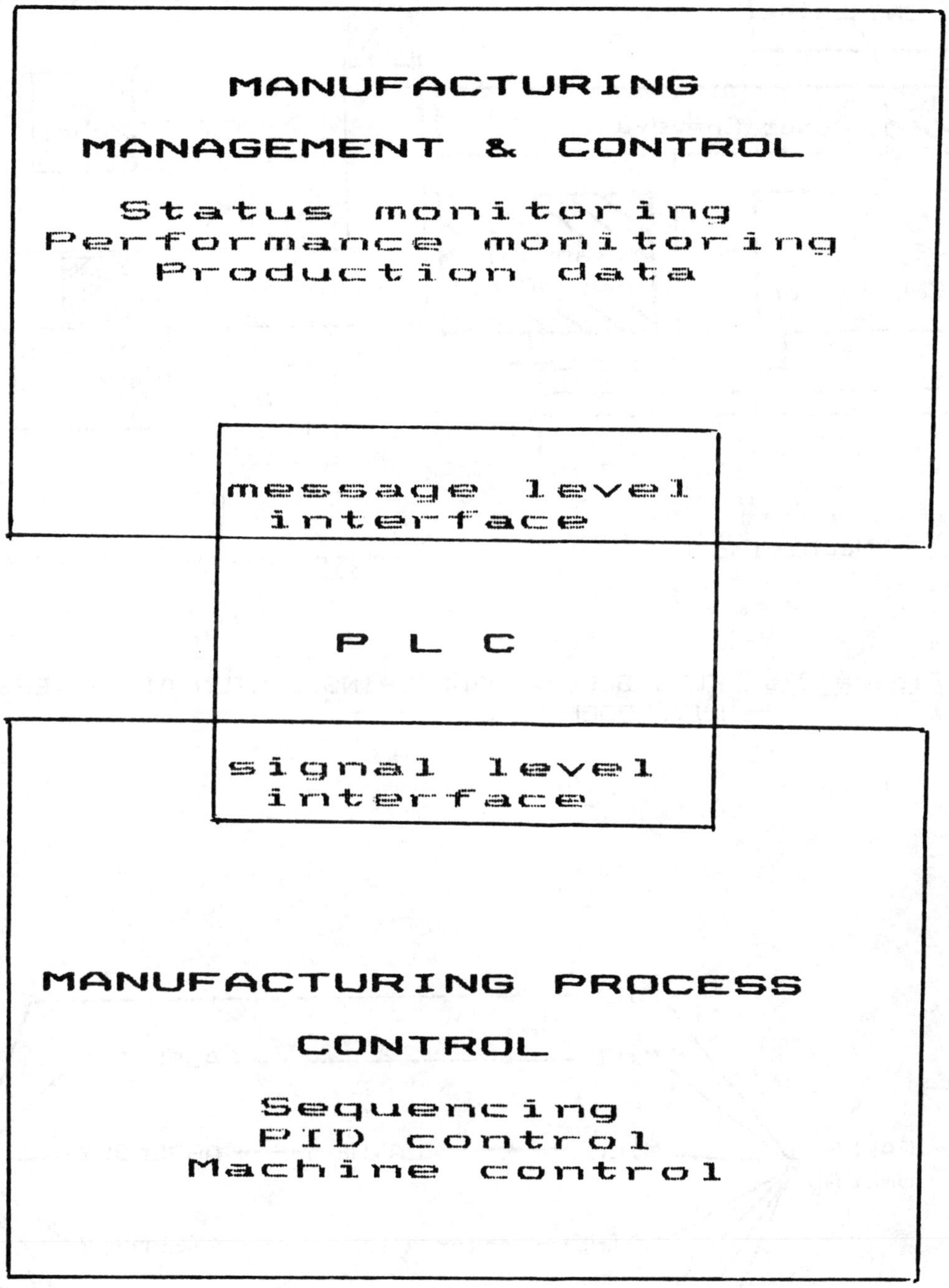

MANUFACTURING

MANAGEMENT & CONTROL

Status monitoring
Performance monitoring
Production data

message level
interface

P L C

signal level
interface

MANUFACTURING PROCESS

CONTROL

Sequencing
PID control
Machine control

Figure 1   THE INTERFACING CAPABILITIES OF MODERN
PROGRAMMABLE LOGIC CONTROLLERS

81

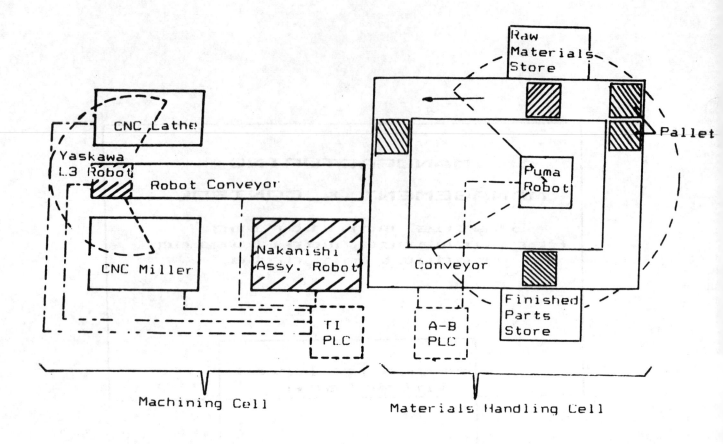

Figure 2 a   FLEXIBLE MANUFACTURING SYSTEM AT UNIVERSITY OF LIVERPOOL

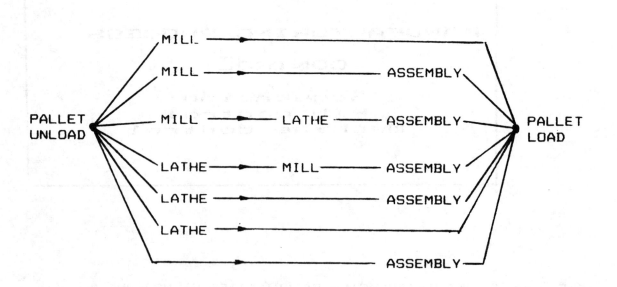

Figure 2 b   ALTERNATIVE MATERIAL ROUTES THROUGH THE MACHINING CELL

```
I     X5            X14           X12                                CR2        I
I----I I-------I I-------I I------------------------------( )------I
I mill         mill          mill part                    collect part    I
I idle         empty         on pallet                    & load mill     I
I                                                                         I
I                                                                         I
I     X8            X7                                            Y7        I
I----I I-------I/I------------------------------------------( )------I
I mill         program                                   execute mill   I
I loaded       not executed                              program        I
I                                                                         I
I                                                                         I
I     X5            X8            X7                              CR3        I
I----I I-------I I-------I I--------------------------------( )------I
I mill         mill          program                      unload mill     I
I idle         loaded        executed                                     I
I                                                                         I
I                                                                         I
I     CR4           X1                                            CR7        I
I----I I-------I I-------------------------+------------( )------I
I mill         mill output              I                deliver part  I
I unloaded      #1=on                   I                to pallet     I
I                                        I                              I
I                                        I                X14           I
I                                        I------------( )------I
I                                        I                reset mill    I
I                                        I                output        I
```

Figure 3 a   SAMPLE PROGRAM MACHINING CELL SEQUENCE CONTROL

```
I    CR2         X6          X3                              Y4          I
I----I I-------I I-------I I--------------------------( )------I
I Mill load   robot    locating pin          I    raise locating I
I request     idle     down                  I       pin         I
I                                            I                   I
I                                            I      CR100        I
I                                            +----------( )------I
I                                                   flag1        I
I                                                               I
I    CR100       X3                              YO             I
I----I I-------I/I--------------------------------( )------I
I test flag1   locating pin               I       Y1          I
I             not down                    +----------( )------I
I                                         I    move to pallet  I
I                                         I      CR101         I
I                                         +----------( )-------I
I                                                flag2          I
I                                                               I
I    CR101       X2                              Y5             I
I----I I-------I/I--------------------------------( )------I
I test flag2   robot at pallet          I     lower locating  I
I             station                   I        pin          I
I                                       I      CR102          I
I                                       +-------------( )------I
I                                                flag3          I
I                                                               I
I    CR102       X3                              Y9             I
I----I I-------I I--------------------------------( )------I
I test flag3   location pin             I     select & start  I
I             down                      I     robot program   I
I                                       I       CR103         I
I                                       +-------------( )------I
I                                                flag4          I
I                                                               I
I    CR103       X6                              Y4             I
I----I I-------I I--------------------------------( )------I
I test flag4   robot idle               I    raise locating pin I
I                                       I        CR104         I
I                                       +-------------( )------I
I                                                flag5          I
I                                                               I
I    CR104       X3                              Y2             I
I----I I-------I/I--------------------------------( )------I
I test flag5   location pin             I       Y3            I
I             not down                  I-------------( )------I
I                                       I    move to mill     I
I                                       I       CR105         I
I                                       +-------------( )------I
I                                                flag6          I
I                                                               I
```

Figure 3 b   MILL LOAD SUBROUTINE OF THE MACHINING CELL PLC
              PROGRAM

84

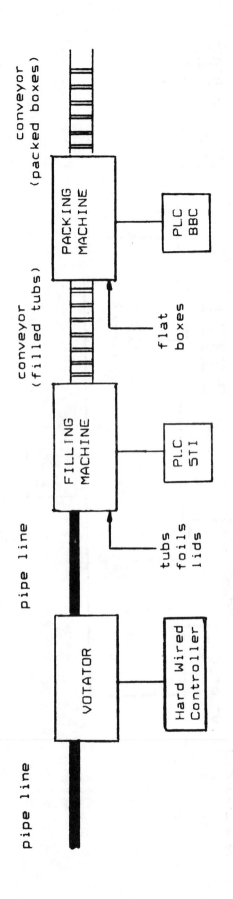

Figure 4 a TRADITIONAL PRODUCTION LINE CONTROL AT VAN DEN
BERGHS & JURGENS

85

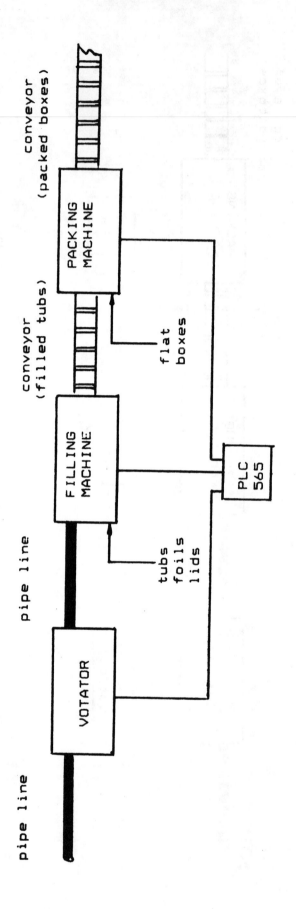

Figure 4 b   INTEGRATED PRODUCTION LINE CONTROL AT VAN DEN
BERGHS & JURGENS

86

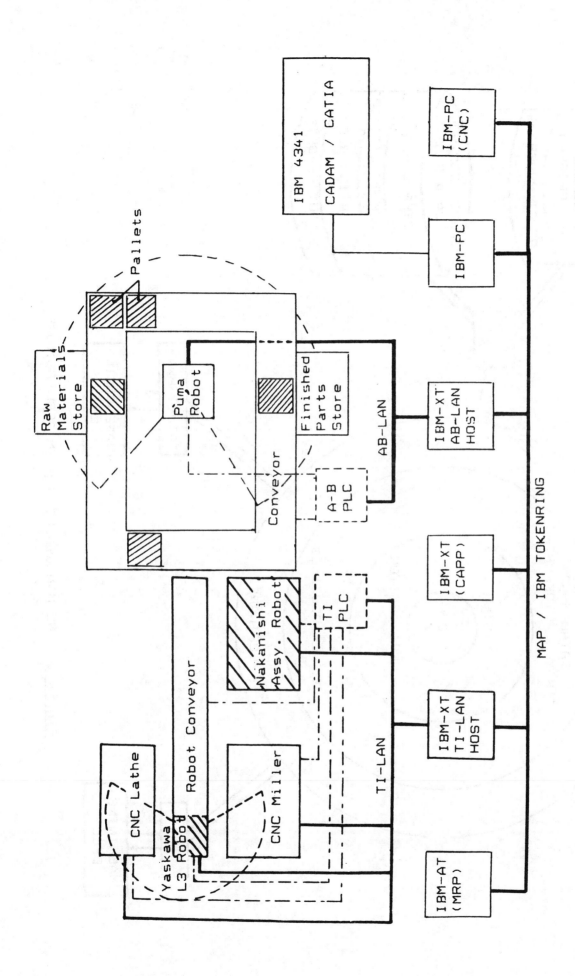

Figure 5   THE MANAGEMENT STRUCTURE OF THE UNIVERSITY'S FMS

87

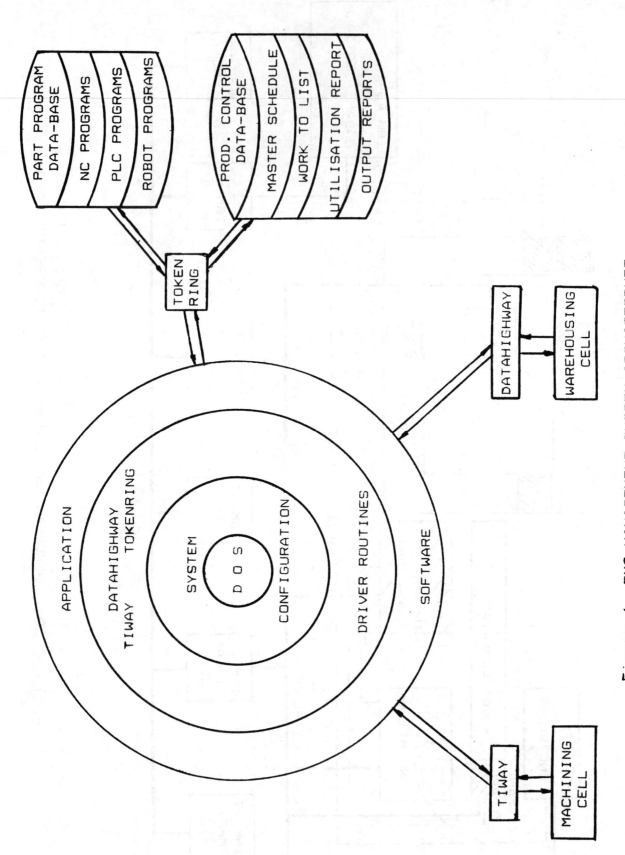

Figure 6 FMS MANAGEMENT SYSTEM ARCHITECTURE

88

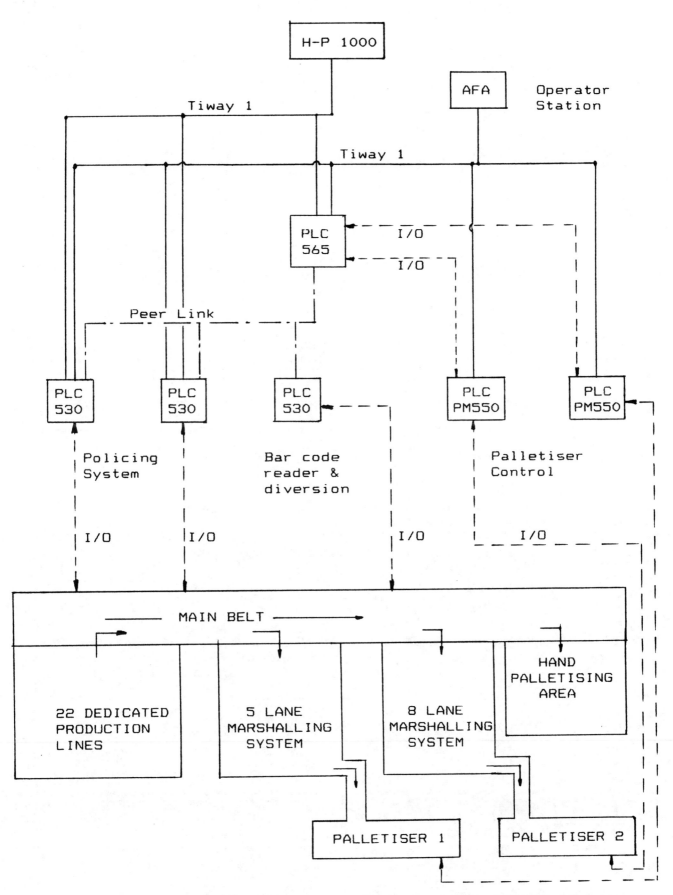

Figure 7   INTEGRATED CONTROL & COMMUNICATION SYSTEM AT
VAN DEN BERGHS & JURGENS

Proc. 2nd Int. Conf. Machine Control Systems, 91-102
May 1987, © IFS (Conferences) Ltd and authors, ISBN 0-948507-52-7

The connectivity problems associated with carrier band when used in industrial networks

W Cargill

Texas Instruments France, France

Currently Industrial Networking is receiving a great deal of attention as our industries move towards integrated systems and flexible methods of manufacture. At the forefront on this interest is the Manufacturing Automation Protocol which proposes standards for Factory and Cell Industrial Local Area Networks. This paper looks at the problems of connectivity currently with us and proposes a way forward via incremental automation and a migration path to MAP once the standard becomes stable. The perspective taken is from the plant upwards and the benefits of adopting the approach proposed are discussed.

INTRODUCTION

There are many factors which influence the use of Industrial Local Area Networks (ILAN's) in Process Control and Industrial Automation Applications. The issue consuming most effort at present is the introduction of standards for communication in a manufacturing environment : "The Manufacturing Automation Protocol" (MAP). The objective is to have multiple vendor inter-connectivity between applications. More recently an addition has been made to MAP which recognises the need for small, dedicated and more responsive networks for use in batch and cell control or even small factories or processes. The MAP cell architecture adds the carrier band physical signaling option to MAP. The carrier band network carries only one data channel, it is less complex and no expensive equipment or experts are needed to instal and maintain the network. Network speed is a function of cable quality. Carrier band MAP networks use baseband coaxial cable and transmit data at 5 Mbps. It is likely that twisted pair networks will also use carrier band but at slower speeds, perhaps 1Mbps. The question is not one of speed or of electrical interface requirements but what does the application design require in terms of network performance. There are many design alternatives. It is cell and batch control networks which are discussed in this paper.

PERSPECTIVE

The remainder of the paper is concerned with the practical applications constraints of industrial automation. It concentrates on the shop floor perspective. An equally valid approach is from pre-production to manufacture. Both must be considered when dealing with the application of Advanced Manufacturing Technology (AMT) but time precludes discussion on both approaches here.

The issues break down into four categories :
. Investment in new plants and factories
. Incremental automation
. Application requirements
. Technical constraints.

INVESTMENT IN NEW PLANTS AND FACTORIES

One reason put forward at the moment for the sluggish performance by companies active in the general field of Process Control and Industrial Automation is that very few new plants or factories are being started. Indeed there has been much in the news of plans for new plants being stopped and even where work has begun, it is then cancelled. It looks as if this trend is set to continue at least in the foreseeable future.

If one is going to invest in an enabling technology, like MAP, this area offers the best opportunity. The MAP broadband cable spine can be installed, baseband cables can be laid for individual manufacturing and process cells. All new equipment can be bought with MAP interfaces.

At present this is somewhat difficult as the standard is still evolving and there is no clear upgrade path from present MAP 2.1 to MAP 3.0. However, I doubt that companies are waiting for an enabling technology before implementing investment plans which significantly impact their future. Indeed there are many stories around which tell of the difficulties some companies have had going too far too soon with automation. It will be some time yet before we see fully automated, fully integrated plants being built from green field sites.

The main issue to be addressed by suppliers is what interface should they have ? From the shop floor perspective we are discussing should robots, PLC's, machine tools, weighing systems, heat treatment plants, painting systems, test equipment etc... link into the main MAP network or the dedicated carrier band network.

As usual, the issues are dependent on the system design. The question to be asked include :
- Does the plant require remote ontrol operation either now or in the future ?
- Is the data held or needed by the local controller key to a further feedback loop ? e.g continuous quality monitoring, very small batch manufacture etc...
- Is the local controller itself able to operate a distributed batch process or manufacturing cell ?

Current trends are that dedicated, if flexible, equipment will link into carrier band MAP while computer systems like CADCAM, Production Control, Process Planning, Commercial Systems etc... will use broadband MAP. The gateway between the two systems will be the Batch Process or Cell Controller.

The medium term future is likely to see equipment suppliers offering at least carrier band MAP while suppliers involved in Integration will have both the ability to go up to broadband MAP and down to carrier band MAP.

As the initial premise is that for now and the foreseeable future investment in new plants and factories will be slow this route will provide a slow growth for MAP standards. As volumes remain low, costs will be high. There have to be other ways forward.

INCREMENTAL AUTOMATION

So, if there are no new plants being built, and standards are not yet agreed, do we simply wait. The answer must be NO. We work in increasingly competitive times for all our industries. We are continually looking for ways to improve productivity, improve quality, enhance reliability, obtain faster response and cut costs just to remain competitive.

As already discussed, if we look at the problems of total automation and integration to build our "Factory of the Future" we probably wouldn't start. The technical problems, assuming they could be solved with present technology, at present have no cost effective solution.

The way forward is, therefore, to have an overall plan which identifies priorities, recognises current technical limitations and shows the best return on investment by project. This may involve investment in some new equipment to be used in islands of automation. It will certainly mean using a lot of what you've already got. It will involve some integration of plant and systems. It may be of interest that some of today's most successful, cash rich companies refurbish existing plant to allow them to move forward when faced with the astronomical costs of complete replacement.

A sensible approach to your networking requirement is to instal the cabling in line with your overall plan. A broadband spine can be used for audio, visual and other networking as well as MAP. Your more dedicated cabling such as for MAP carrier band can wait for project justification. But remember, the network on its own does nothing and shows no payback. It's what you do with it that counts.

At last we've got down to cell level. The project is specified, planned and looks like providing a satisfactory payback. In many cases today the specification calls for some level of integration as the only way of achieving the necessary benefits which lead to the required payback. The network may have to cater with extremes of electrical noise, intrinsic safety and distance. The network must also be able to connect a mix of equipment from different suppliers, some old, some new and some refurbished. This same problem was faced by companies in the early days of Flexible Machining where conventional machines were integrated with more recent Computer Numerical Control (CNC) machines. Existing machines which have some form of programmable control are likely to support RS232 serial interfaces as their link to the outside world. At present your new machines may support a form of MAP probably Rev. 2.1. Discussion is still taking place on how Rev. 2.1 products will be upgraded to Rev. 3.0. It is generally agreed that not until we get to MAP Rev. 3.0 will the difference in interpretation be removed from the standard so ensuring that product from different companies will communicate without the need for special software. Your overall plans call for a much fuller level of integration in future years when a stable MAP standard will be available.

However, if the type of network architecture proposed in this paper is adopted and provided multi-vendor connectivity can be supplied using today's technology, the only change required will be the addition of network driver software to connect the cell to the MAP broadband network. The remainder of the cell remains unchanged protecting current investment in machines and software.

New equipment can be linked into the existing network in the same way as all of the other devices. The Section on Technical Constraints will discuss a way of solving this problem.

APPLICATION REQUIREMENTS

So far we have considered the overall structure of our network, how this will meet a system design requirement and the problem of connectivity to existing controllers. The next point to consider is what are the typical applications the ILAN will have to cater for.

We have already stated our objectives which are worth repeating :
. Increased productivity
. Better quality
. Enhanced reliability
. Fast response
. Cut costs.

The next thing we have done is to prepare a system design which shows our application requirement. We have a MAP broadband network already installed but the project we are working on now will have its network installed as part of the project, with a future gateway to MAP broadband.

What techniques are available for us to meet our objectives.

Increased Productivity

This means keeping our machines running, optimising performance and catering for fast changeover between batches. It can also mean developing predictive techniques which warn of possible problems before they stop the plant. It certainly means fast response to machine stoppage. The kind of things the network will handle are :

Performance monitoring
Ensure plant and machines are run to specification

Condition monitoring
Continuous monitor of plant and machine operation

Product tracking
Where we are in a production run at any time with forward warning of when changeovers will occur.

This will provide us with the basic data to achieve our objectives. The batch or cell controller can then provide warning, alarm, trending, status, performance etc... displays and reports. This type of data transfer requires very low network throughput especially if we consider that we only need regular status updates other than when a plant deviation is detected i.e deviation reporting minimises data throughput and also provides operators and management with the information they need - not vast lists of displays and figures which they must interpret.

The only activity which requires heavy traffic on the network is re-configuration of the plant between batches. This may require upload and download of lengthy new programmes for robots, CNC, PLC etc... There are two points to consider. Firstly, it is likely that at this stage there will also be mechanical work to be carried out e.g re-setting, re-fixturing, material changeover etc... Secondly, that in more up to date systems local controllers will have the ability to hold several programmes and the network will simply select the next programme to be executed. This type of system may have automated setting, multiple fixturing and palletised material handling so changeovers will be very quick indeed.

Better Quality

More and more in-process gauging, condition monitoring and quality control system are being built into equipment and production lines. Again exception reporting techniques are used. The only change to this is the feedback of variables for subsequent trend analysis. No significant increase in network throughput is experienced.
However, when problems do occur they can be responded to quickly and effectively so minimising scrap and getting the plant running again as soon as possible.

Enhanced Reliability

This area shows least direct benefit from the techniques we are discussing. It is more dependent on basic design. However, by close control we can ensure that products are made within design tolerances, repeatability is guaranteed and fast and effective information feedback to design is assured.

Fast Response

So far we have talked about the direct impact of ILAN's. This includes preventing maintenance, machine and condition monitoring and fast changeover between batches. Another valid ILAN application is to allow operator input of his requirements once machines have stopped. This is variously known as operator status or help calls. The automatic system will know the machine has stopped, the operator will either confirm or inform the manufacturing control system of the reason e.g waiting material, electrical fault, quality problems etc... Again no great increase in network throughput is generated.

Cut Costs

Again the benefits here are more indirect. However, they are significant and quantifiable :

Improved utilisation of equipment
This is particularly important where new plant is bought which only shows acceptable payback when high utilisation is achieved, much higher utilisation than has ever been achieved in the past.

Longer plant life/reduced cost of spares
Keeping the plant running at optimum performance and carrying out planned preventive maintenance will ensure increased life.

Reduced energy usage
Optimum use is made of the services required to run the plant be they electric, hydraulic, pneumatic, hot water, steam etc...

Reduced scrap and re-work
Immediate response to any quality related problem minimises the amount of scrap made and re-work which has to be carried out.

The even more intangible benefits I have seen in certain projects are reduction or even elimination of sub-contract work and postponed or, at least, put back investment in new plant.

And the final point to be made is that management have the information available on which to base decisions and gain control of manufacture.

TECHNICAL CONSTRAINTS

Incremental automation is the only safe way ahead when investing in AMT. Management can see the result of their investments before moving to the next stage. It is vitally important to functionally specify each element within an overall plan probably phased over a number of years. The need for networking both at company, plant and cell level has been discussed. We know the types of things we want to do at the cell level.

Standards in communication are the way of the future. However, they are not quite with us today and timescales keep going back. What is needed is, therefore, a solution today with a migration to MAP tomorrow. There are few carrier band networks installed in the batch and cell control areas. If we decided to install carrier band using baseband cable the problem we would immediately encounter would be interfacing to the mix of programmable control devices, most of which support RS232/20 mamps current loop type serial interfaces. What are available are interface products which allow ILAN's to link into these devices. The best known of these applications is Direct Numerical Control (DNC) where several CNC controllers can be linked to a cell controller. However, this is only part of the problem because at the beginning we defined the need of communication between applications. The need is for a device, similar to a DNC interface but which can interface to robots, PLC's, ATE, weighing, mixing and all of the other shop floor control devices. The definition and understanding of this problem has led to TEXAS INSTRUMENTS developing the UNILINK Secondary Adapter(S/A). This allows any programmable device which supports the RS232 serial standard to be interfaced to TIWAY1, an ILAN which utilises the HDLC protocol for bit-oriented independent data transmission.

Clearly this secondary adapter interfaces to a wide range of machines. There is a huge installed base of machines which needs this connectivity. In addition, until MAP standards are available and vendors are supplying interfaces, this type of interface will still be needed.

Two other functions are required from this type of device. It must operate as a protocol translator to the wide range of machines we have discussed and it must offer a migration path to MAP in the future.

There are alternatives to this approach. By far the most widely tried is to write network drivers for every single controller to be interfaced and run these in a host machine. This type of solution can only be achieved by point to point connection and the benefit of the ILAN is lost. In addition the software complexity of such an approach has ment high cost, many problems and difficulties in maintenance of the system.

By utilising the UNILINK S/A a standard well proven ILAN can be used, host software requirements are minimised and interface problems simplified. The whole problem is broken down into small, manageable modules.

The last problem is in the cell computer. How do you protect your investment in software so that when you are faced with the MAP upgrade you are not faced with a re-write of the software you have developed. Firstly, TIWAY provides a Universal Command Language (U.C.L.) which has some synergie with MAP 3.0 and especially the Manufacturing Message System, RS511. This should be no surprise as they were written with the same overall goal in mind. Consequently a straightforward conversion of commands via a technique similar to a look up table will allow upgrade in a co-ordinated manner. In addition the S/A provides a uniform appearance to the host regardless of the protocol used by the attached machine. This significantly reduces host software complexity again because the host doesn't have to be aware of the physical layout of the machine it is talking to.

CONCLUSIONS

Industrial Automation is a vastly complex field involving many technical disciplines with an infinite amount of overlapping technology. One area receiving widespread publicity at the moment is Industrial Networking. For anybody who has looked at factory control requirements it is obvious why this seemingly, enabling technology, should become a key module in achieving successful automation. You don't get very far in planning automation without running into the problems of systems integration. To date significant, if not insurmountable, problems have been experienced with integration of multi-vendor equipment. Hence, the current moves towards standards and MAP.

However, there is still some way to go before these standards are stable. In addition we must utilise the investments we have made and are making. This can be achieved by Incremental Automation.

Step 1
System design and forward plan

Step 2
Machine control refurbishment where necessary and fit interfaces to existing plant

Step 3

Install cell or batch process control host software to control integrated facilities

Step 4

Migration to MAP broadband factory network when it becomes available.

A further step may be to go back to your cell when MAP-EPA becomes available and retrofit a standard network in place of you proprietary network. There is no cost justification for this but it may be seen as adding some future potential for development of the cell.

In this way the benefits and payback objectives can be monitored as projects are installed. Projects can be broken down into manageable pieces and lessons learned can be re-applied. Further investment by management can be monitored and controlled against actual results.

TEXAS INSTRUMENTS
EUROPEAN INDUSTRIAL SYSTEMS DIVISION
INDUSTRIAL NETWORKING

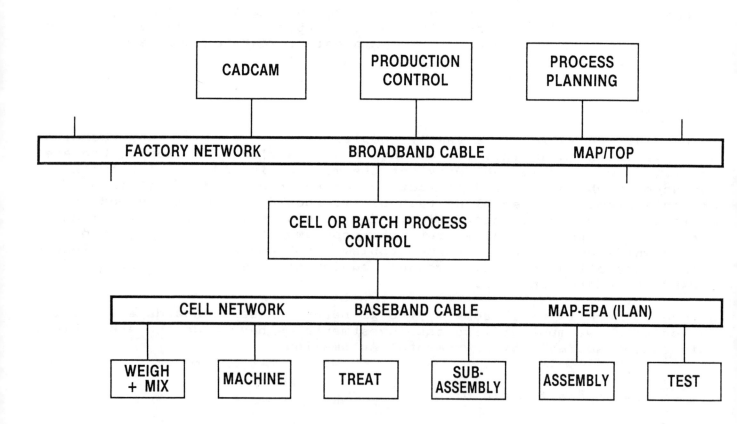

- Figure 1 -

TEXAS INSTRUMENTS
EUROPEAN INDUSTRIAL SYSTEMS DIVISION
INDUSTRIAL NETWORKING
ARCHITECTURE

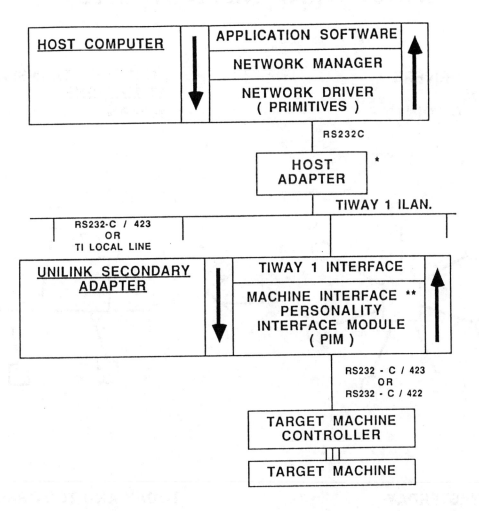

* REPLACE BY NETWORK COMMUNICATIONS MODULE FOR DIRECT INTERFACE WITH HOST COMPUTER BACKPLANE - WHEN AVAILABLE .

** DUAL TRAGET MACHINE PORTS FOR ATTACHED EQUIPMENT AND OPTIONAL TERMINAL / DISPLAY .

NOTE : THE S/A SUPPORTS REDUNDANT NETWORK MEDIA .

- Figure 2 -

TEXAS INSTRUMENTS
EUROPEAN INDUSTRIAL SYSTEMS DIVISION
INDUSTRIAL NETWORKING

**NETWORK DRIVERS
FROM HOST
= POINT TO POINT**

**PROTOCOL TRANSLATOR
AT MACHINE
= ILAN**

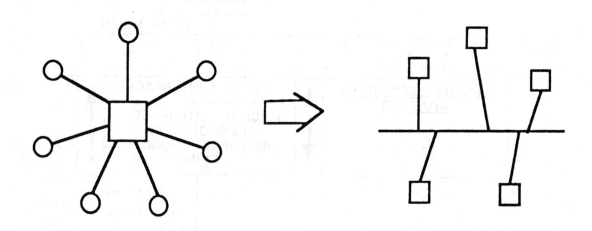

YESTERDAY

TODAY AND TOMORROW

- Figure 3 -

TEXAS INSTRUMENTS
EUROPEAN INDUSTRIAL SYSTEMS DIVISION
INDUSTRIAL NETWORKING
CONNECTIVITY

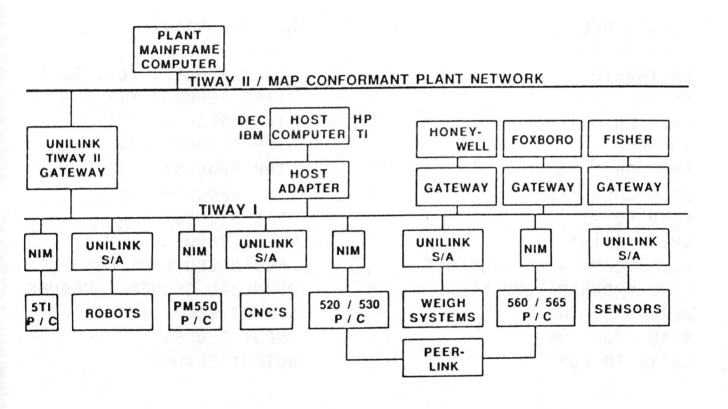

- Figure 4 -

INDUSTRIAL NETWORKING

UNIVERSAL COMMAND LANGUAGE TO MAP

T.I.'s UCL	MAP 3.0 RS511
CALIBRATE	START REQUEST (0); SCEK
BEGIN	START REQUEST (1)
PROCEED	START REQUEST (2)
SUSPEND	STOP REQUEST (1)
ABANDON	STOP REQUEST (2)
EMERGENCY STOP	STOP REQUEST (0)
READ POINT	READ REQUEST
WRITE POINT	WRITE REQUEST
RECEIVE PROGRAM SEQUENCE	UPLOAD SEQUENCE REQUEST
SEND PROGRAM SEQUENCE	DOWNLOAD SEQUENCE REQUEST
RETURN STATUS	STATUS REQUEST
READ FROM PORT	INPUT REQUEST
WRITE TO PORT	OUTPUT REQUEST

- FIGURE 5 -

Proc. 2nd Int. Conf. Machine Control Systems, 103-110
May 1987, © IFS (Conferences) Ltd and authors, ISBN 0-948507-52-7

Broad band networks: installation experiences

A J Domenico
Electronic Data Systems, UK

Abstract

There has been an increase in the number of broad band networks installed in factories due to the vast data handling capability and flexibility of message handling provided. This paper discusses the experience of installing two networks; one for the new Vauxhall Cavalier paint shop, the second for CIMAP, the DTI MAP awareness event.

This paper discusses the experiences in installing two braod band cable systems and their relevance in an overall automation stategy. The two that have been installed and are operating are for the GM Vauxhall new paint shop and for CIMAP.

GM has invested 90 million pounds Sterling in building a new paint shop in Luton to give the Cavelier perhaps one of the best paint and body protection schemes in its class. This not only increases the value of the Caveliers' now being built but also positions GM for the eventual Cavelier replacement. For those not familiar with the process, I will give a brief, over simplified view of the automotive assembly process.

Cars are scheduled for assembly from the sales orders on hand and the plant capacity. The first process is to make a "body-in-white". Basically, this process is to weld together the bellypan, sides and tops of the vehicle to form a shell for painting and trimming out. This is a continuous process that requires a certain mix of body types to keep the line flow even. (i.e. no more than 1 estate car in 5). When the "body-in-white" gets to the paint shop, they would like to paint as many of the same colour as possible in a row. So the order of the bodies may change to provide for this. The new facility provides for flexibility in scheduling for painting so it is necessary to know what bodies are where in the paint shop. When the bodies go to be trimmed out, they may again have to be sorted to provide for the proper mix on the trim line. (i.e. don't put two cars with the quad speaker radios closer than every 6th car). Thus through the paint shop it is necessary to know the location of the bodies, and by the use of body banks change the order that they are presented to the various paint processes. We used Philips PREMID for the Automated Vehicle Identification (AVI).

This system collects the information on vehicle identification and brings it back to the central plant computer via the broad band cable. Because it is on the cable it will be relatively easy to change the reading points should more information be required for routing decisions. We used a system built by F & H controls with multiple HP1000's and Gould controllers for the sorting and used TDS digitizer and Laser Scan bar code reader on the QC deck. These are also connected via the broad band cable thus providing resilience and flexibility for change to the process.

There are 48 DEC VT200 series terminals in use at various points in the plant connected to a VAX 11/785 cluster via the broad band cable. The diagram shows the cable from the EDS plant computing room through the paint shop and extending into an adjoining office block. EDS used a sub contractor for the cable plant design and installations but EDS did the network design, installation and is doing operation. The use of a sub contractor for the cable plant design was neccessary to insure that not only would the cable provide for all the connections required for the paint shop, but also it would be easy to extend the cable to the "body-in-white" and trim shop as the automation plans require. Also in designing the cable EDS chose to put 4 way taps at convenient intervals rather than just taps where they were required for the present paint process. Thus the cable has 81 4 way tap points but is presently only using 40 drop points from the cable. EDS elected to use a sub contractor for the installation because there is a substantial amount of special tooling required for installation and balancing the cable. Once this had been completed EDS provided extensive training to the GM maintenance staff so they could perform repairs and maintenance as required. The bulk of the devices run under Ungermann Bass Net 1 software, which is a CSMA/CD system. This was the perfect method for handling the terminals and printers, and because the network is lightly loaded gave acceptable performance with the AVI. It did not however perform consistently rapid enough to give the response required for Gould Modicon Controllers in the sorting and control

This system was installed in March of 86, before CIMAP and before GMT 400 was operational, therefore Ferrantti point-to-point modems over the broadband cable were used for that application, not MAP connections. If the paint shop had been installed 6 months later, the decision may have been different. The system has been operational since last summer and is in use daily to produce the Caviliers we are proud to drive.

The cable system was installed to both meet the communication needs of the new facility (paint shop) and also to provide the bases for future automation within the Vauxhall plant. The cable plant provided the base for installing the automated systems within the paint shop so it was quite important to test the facility prior to bringing up the systems so that communication problems could be isolated from application systems problems. Thus the cable plant was first installed, balanced and tested before any network functions were added. Then each of the NIU's were tested with local loop back prior to being put in the plant. Once in the plant they were retested in loop back mode to make certain that they operated prior to adding any devices. This management control built a solid network as the foundation for successful manufacturing automation.

The second broadband network to be discussed was used for CIMAP. In truth it was really physically two different networks for one was used at the staging area and the second for the actual event at the NEC. The networks were physically different but logically the same so I will not make a distinction. For those not familiar with CIMAP it was DTI sponsored event that was the largest demonstration of MAP and TOP applications ever assembled. The diagram shows the topology of what was put together. The important things to see on this diagram are the division of the applications into cells and the fact that the main network is really three subnetworks joined by two Intel/GEC routers. There are also other networks, in which EDS had involvement. Allen Bradley put up a MAP broadband plus a Vista net carrier band cell. EDS did testing to make certain it was a MAP 2.1 network. ERA technology put in a MIL-STD-1553B field bus cable. EDS tested the cable for interference. Intel put in "Bit bus", its field bus candidate, which again EDS tested for interference with the main network.

There were 5 remote links, EDS got very heavily involved with the X.25 router between the MAP network at Birmingham and the MAP network in the GM Technical Center in Warren, Mich. USA, less heavily involve with the remaining links, although these were also tested.

The main EDS role for CIMAP was to make certain that it all worked and that it was an honest representation of what is possible in manufacturing communication at that time. Leeds University had a team that was responsible for conformance testing of the products to be joined to the network. EDS was responsible for interoperability testing, or for making certain that the devices communicated with each other and did not interfer with any other device on the network. Our plan for accomplishing this was very straight forward but also very thorough. First the cable plant was installed by Ferrantti for the broad band and BICC for the base band sections. These were thoroughly tested prior to we proceeding to the network design.

We did the network design function in the summer of 1986 and had to accept the fact that at that time INI and CDS would not support operation of their devices on the other vendors network. Officailly they still do not, however, since that time there has been many unofficial mixed networks. So if we were starting again we might be tempted to just us one MAP network and reduce the amount of internetwork routing. The Enterprise Network Event in June 88 will use a single MAP network for all vendors.

After the network design we individually check each network prior to putting on any application load. For the MAP networks we used the CDS token scope to both generate tokens and monitor their passage around the logical ring. For the TOP network the Spider Monitor generated a test packet and we could then look for an 802.3 standard response. Once satisfied that each network was operational, we then installed the internet routers and tested them. This was done by establishing a Transport level connection from the Spider monitor on TOP to each of MAP networks, then using the INI test programmes for MAP to MAP connections.

Only after EDS was satisfied that the full network, the 3 main sub networks and the internetwork routing was operational did we start the application testing. It is interesting to note, that although all the products on the network were conformance tested, the major portion of EDS's work was sorting out the interoperability problems between equipment.

The interoperability testing was carried out by establishment of 6 milestone events with a highly visable status load showing the progress of each partnership. Each milestone event built upon the work of the previous, so failure to meet 2 milestones in a row evoked the process to move to the sales forum. The milestone events were as follows :

(a)   Arrival at the pre-staging area with conformance certificate
(b)   Physical Connection to the networks
(c)   Transport Connection Establishment
(d)   Heavy Kit Connection
(e)   Application Testing
(f)   Final Performance Testing

The EDS team used simple but effective management tools to monitor the completion of each milestone. For instance conformance to the physical connection was monitored by the Spider monitor on TOP and the CDS Token Scope on MAP then posted on the visible status board for all to see.

EDS tends to de-emphasis the management controls imposed to insure cooperation between multiple companies working on the same project, because this is what we do for a living and it is very familiar to us. However, the skills and management controls to make the project work are considerable.

My experiences with installing broad band networks leads me to the following conclusions:

(a)   They are not as complex as they first seem.
(b)   The cable plant requires professional design and installation.
(c)   Connections to the cable are expensive so should be planned to get maximum use.
(d)   Installation of the cable must be part of an overall plan to meet business needs.

It is my opinion that broadband cables do provide a very good backbone communication service for industrial application. However the high cost of connection may cause other solutions to be adopted. The most promising solution right now is to use broadband for the back bone, then carrier band for area connections and field bus within a cell. This gives a hierachy of communication facilities that may more closely match the requirements within a manufacturing plant.

BROARDBAND CABLE PLANT DESIGN — LUTON PAINT SHOP 1st. FLOOR

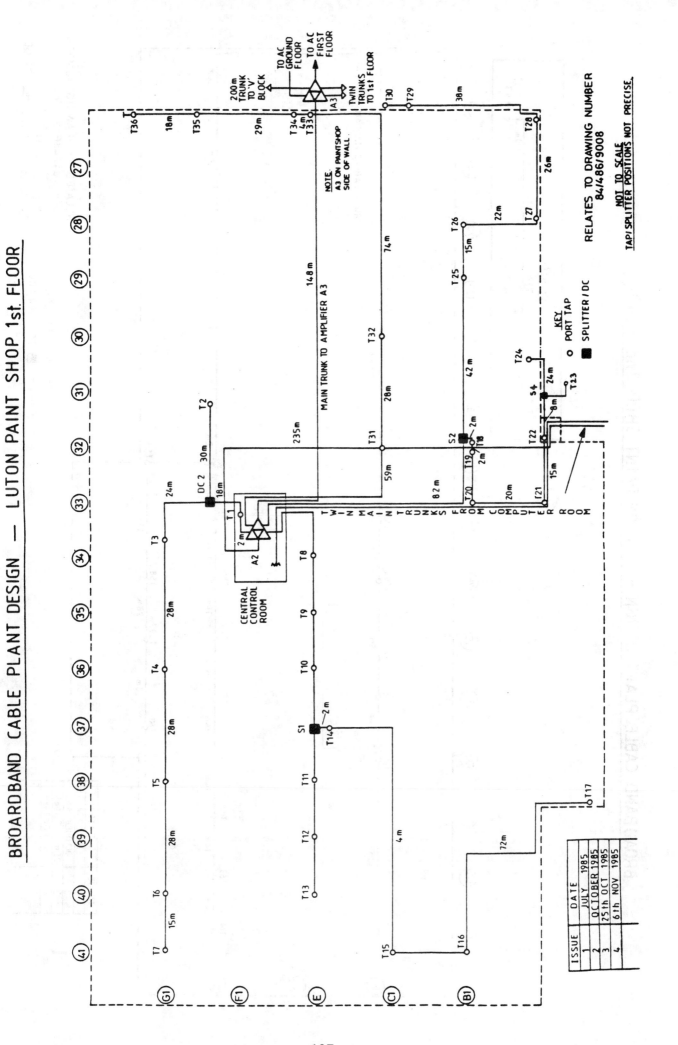

BROADBAND CABLE PLANT DESIGN — LUTON PAINT SHOP 2nd. FLOOR

'V' BLOCK

TO A3

RELATES TO DRAWING NUMBER
84/486/9009

NOT TO SCALE
TAP SPLITTER POSITIONS NOT PRECISE

○ 4 PORT TAP
■ SPLITTER / DC

TRUNK CABLES FROM AMPLIFIER A3

ISSUE	DATE
1	JULY 1985
2	OCTOBER 1985
3	25th OCT 1985
4	6th NOV 1985

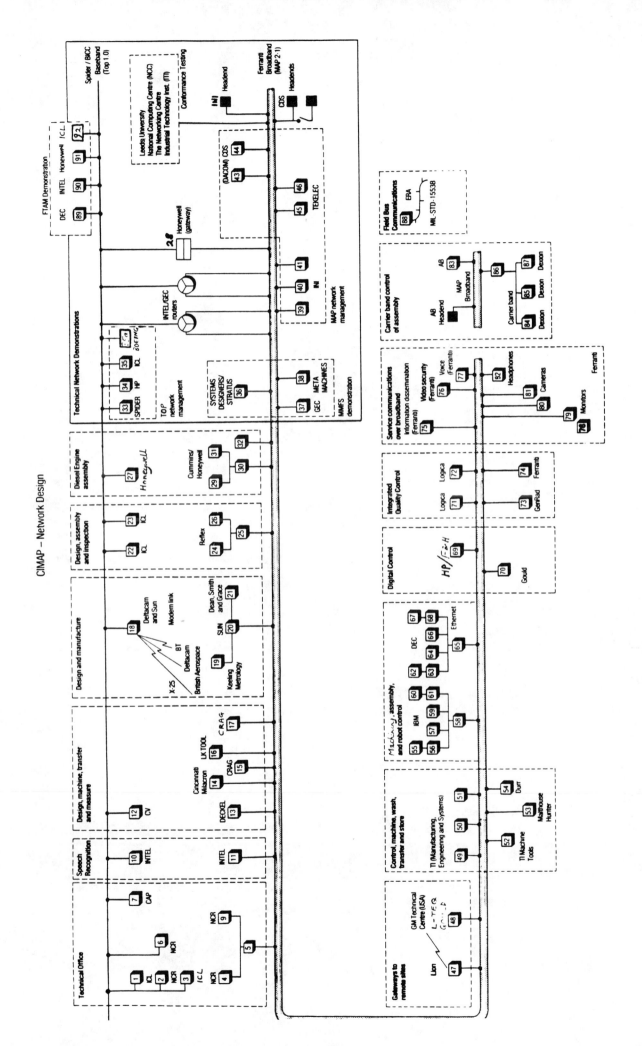

CIMAP – Network Design

Proc. 2nd Int. Conf. Machine Control Systems, 111-120
May 1987, © IFS (Conferences) Ltd and authors, ISBN 0-948507-52-7

Introduction of communication software based on relational technology on the shop floor

R Pietrzak
University of Hannover, West Germany

The increasing expansion of flexible manufacturing in practice even in production of single parts and small series gives tool management great importance in further considerations on rationalization. This guides to introduction of a tool data base as first part of a workshop communication system (WCS).

The tool data base was demonstrated and discussed in different interested firms. The impulses of this procedure were integrated into a second release. A simple, low-cost graphical editor to create tool drafts was added according to the results of interchange with practice.

Possibilities and limits of Relational DBMS concerning practice on the shop floor are discussed.

INTRODUCTION

Considerations on rationalization in the field of tool management aim at shortening set-up times and optimization of tool inventory concerning variety of different tools, effort in disposition and investment in tools and equipment.

The restrictions to computer aid in tool management and disposition are in particular characterized by the circulation principle [1], figure 1 and its close connection to the workshop in operation [3,4,5]. The circulation principle corresponds to multiple use and reconditioning of complete tools and components. Short dated events and co-workers oriented to manufacturing describe the close connection to the shop floor. From this point of view computer aid makes the information flow on the shop floor more efficient and less susceptible to disturbances [1,2] and tool inventory can be optimized [1]. Success in these aims depends on a software architecture that fulfils the requirements described below.

TOOL CIRCULATION AND ITS REQUIREMENTS TO INFORMATION PROCESSING FROM THE FUNCTIONAL POINT OF VIEW

The main functions of the tool circle are described by the stations stock, preparation, use and reconditioning in the physical tool flow and coordination as an additional main function of the information flow. Tool management covers the fields of production: design, process planning, manufacturing and assembly as well as the logistic fields: procurement and storage. Manufacturing and assembly are those fields that require all functions of the tool circle and thus require the largest variety of function assortments in different firms and describe the most complex requirements to information processing concerning tools.

The main functions of the tool circle are roughly determined. The functions within these main functions may be located in one place together with subfunctions of other main funtions or they are devided because of grown tasks.

Information requirements and input of new data depend on the function to be executed. Figure 2 desribes an example. To edit the tool data sheet the NC-programmer must be supported in search of tools. Search of tools is possible by name of the tool, classification code, ident number and adapter system. With respect to human factors during software engineering the NC-programmer must be able to get information about these possibilities and how to use them during the whole process of search. At the other hand he must be able to ignore this information when he is accustomed to the system. The resulting guidelines of software architecture can be described as follows:

- function oriented structure of software and presentation of information
- easy input and update of data
- easy adaptability to different firms (standard software)
- graphical support the user is accustomed to from paper work.
- support of the user according to his qualification.

Commercially available data base management systems (DBMS) even concerning relational technology support the first three aims. Graphical support is only poorly developed. Function oriented linkages between different parts of the data base within an dialog are also poorly supported by those DBMS or integrated software tools. According to this situation the approach of collecting and structuring data, possibilities and limits of different DBMS in tool management and the development of a low-cost graphical editor will be desribed. An example of practical introduction of a DBMS-based communication system will be given.

112

THE APPROACH OF COLLECTING AND STRUCTURING DATA

Information to fulfil tasks in the factory is generated from tool and order data. Information leads to new data e.g., coordination is done by information generated from some classification and geometry data, the choosen tool with its set-up data will be put onto a tooling sheet, figure 3. Central filing of data to support all those functions is of great importance. No data must be held multiple and thus no updating of parallel data systems is necessary.

For structuring data of real world objects, like tools, the structure and relationship of the whole set of those objects must be transparent, figure 4 [6]. On one hand we work with individuals, e. g. a presetted tool with its individual preadjustment data, on the other hand we work with groups of equal individuals, e.g. cutting inserts of one order number with data describing all group members. It is possible for times, that there exists no real object of a group, e.g. if all cutting inserts are worn-out or if a choosen tool is not yet assembled. Sets of similar groups are collected in classes. An essential function of a companies numbering system is to connect real or possible objects with their image in a data base.

Structuring of data is committed in a data base schema. Actual attributes of individuals ar stored in tables for individuals, attributes of groups are stored in tables of groups an so on. Storing characteristics for tools makes the schema widely independent of the configuration of the workshop. E.g. "stock" or "milling center" is stored for an individual tool in the tool location table. If there is a new possible location in the tool flow, like a new machine tool, only an additional word is necessary but there are no consequences for the data base schema. This is called an object-related schema design [6].

DATA BASE MANAGEMENT SYSTEM (DBMS) – POSSIBILITIES AND LIMITS IN MANAGEMENT AND DISPOSITION OF TOOLS

The users degrees of freedom in definition of applications and in integration of application programs based on DBMS characterize the possibilities and limits of diffenrent DBMS from the users point of view, figure 5.

The definition of columns in files/tables is possible in different ways concerning data type and size of single data and records. More different data types influence susceptiblity to faults in user dialog.

The quantity of definable files/tables influences use of memory. Both, the definition of columns and the quantity of definable files/tables limit the possible function assortment of the application software, its adaptability to different workshops and their equipment and the upgrade compatability in step-by-step introduction.
Comfort of definition and quantity of definable input/output forms mainly influence the adaptability of application software to common practice and the acceptance as well as the susceptiblity to faults by the co-workers.

Linkages between different files/tables within a data base are limited concerning
- the possible quantity of different files/tables open at the same time and
- the possible choice of columns from different tables that can be accessed by one input/output form (view).

Both characteristics influence the consistency of the data and the use of memory as well as the adaptability of application software to the content of information needed by the co-worker in the special workshop within his special function.

There are different ways to integrate application software based on DBMS into existing computer applications, figure 6.

The access to external data can be limited to files in a special format, e.g. text files. In that case external software must be modified to create files in this special format. But its always necessary to transfer the data from external files to files/tables in the data base before data can be accessed by application software based on the DBMS.

Access to external software may be conducted by starting a second process and return to the first process with transfer of data or by calling a subprogram within an application software that uses the programming interface.

The portability of application software depends on the portability of the DBMS and its tools as well as of the application software when using the programming interface.

These explanations are based on experiences with three different DBMS in development of tool management software and contiguous applications, figure 7. From the users point of view ORACLE is the most efficient DBMS concerning its characteristics in query language and data base tools except for definition of input/output forms and linkages between forms not bound to hierarchical menues. A further drawback for application of comfortable ORACLE tools in the workshop area is the lack of a programmable graphics interface. As regards application programs using the programming interface the rwt tool data base, developed with the cooperation IFW, sets standards other applications will have to cope with.

APPLICATION OF A DATA BASE MANAGEMENT SYSTEM IN FUNCTION PROGRAMS IN THE WORKSHOP

The following figures demonstrate the information flow in the workshop area with regard to one shop order. The NC-programmer selects the tools from the data base according to the part to be manufactured. The application program enables the programmer to create a note with all ident numbers of necessary tools, figure 8. All data concerning the manufacturing process can be transfered to the tooling sheet by automatically reading the created note. The simple, easy to edit graphical description enables the co-worker in the workshop in order to assemble and preadjust the tools, the NC-programmer collected in the tooling sheet.

The concept of the tool draft editor (TED), shown in figure 9, enables the user to create tool drafts on low-cost equipment. This solution realizes an optimum between necessary information and fast enough display on the monitor. The tool drafts can be created by makros according to components of real tools. The created drafts are transformed into a compressed representation that can be tansfered to the data base. This concept meets both aims, reduction of necessary storage capacity and fast display on the monitor.

The tool data in the tooling sheet must be completed by pre-adjustment of tools. The correctional data are transfered to the central data base. A list function enables generation of the complete tool data block in a format necessary for the special machine control. The tool data are transfered to the machine control together with the NC-program data via DNC, figure 10.

Another function supported by the tool data base is creation of set-up plans during NC-programming, figure 11. The list function mentioned above may also be used to transfer technological data like cutting speed, to editing NC-programs. Functions like these were realized in cooperation with two german manufacturers in the field of metal cutting.

REFERENCES

[1] Balbach, J. Rechnerunterstützte Rationalisierung des Werkzeugwesens in Betrieben mit spanender Fertigung kleiner Serien, Dr.-Ing. Diss. University of Hannover, 1983.

[2] Ley, W. Integrierte Fertigungshilfsmitteldisposition, Dr.-Ing. Diss. RWTH Aachen, 1984.

[3] Granow, R., Schmiedeskamp, R. and Balbach, J. "Werkzeugverwaltung – Einstieg in die rechnerunterstützte Werkstattkommunikation" VDI-Z Vol. 126, No. 17, pp. 617-623 (August 1984).

[4] Diehl, W., Hellberg, K. and Schmiedeskamp, R. "Werkzeuggrafikkonzept für rechnerunterstützte Werkzeugverwaltung und Bearbeitungssimulation" Zeitschr. f. wirtsch. Fertigung Vol. 80, No. 5, pp. 195-199 (May 1985).

[5] Hammer, H. and Potthast, A. "Grafisch-dynamische Simulation für die Bohr- und Fräsbearbeitung" Zeitschr. f. wirtsch. Fertigung Vol. 80, No. 9, pp. 372-378 (September 1985)

[6] Petersen, W. and Schmiedeskamp, R. "Tool Management – a Point of Main Effort in Computer Aided Communication in Heterogenous Automated Workshops" Proc. of the 18th CIRP MFS-Seminar Vol. 18, (July 1986).

FIGURES

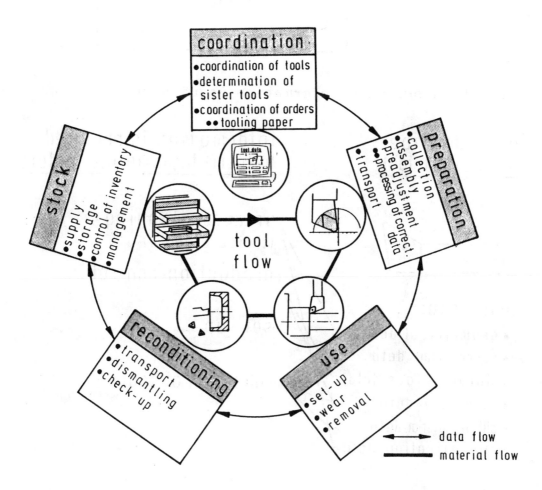

figure 1: Main functions of tool organisation

115

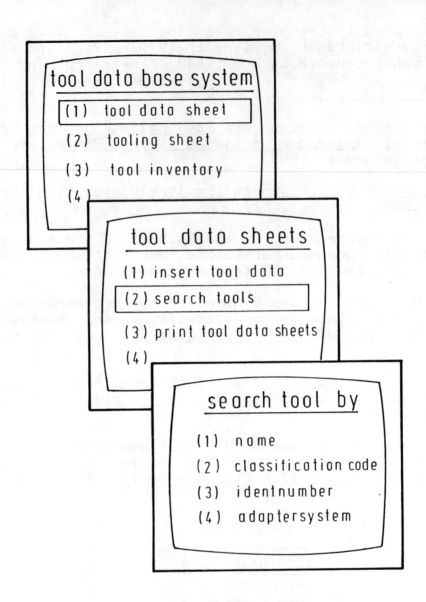

figure 2: Function oriented information requirements

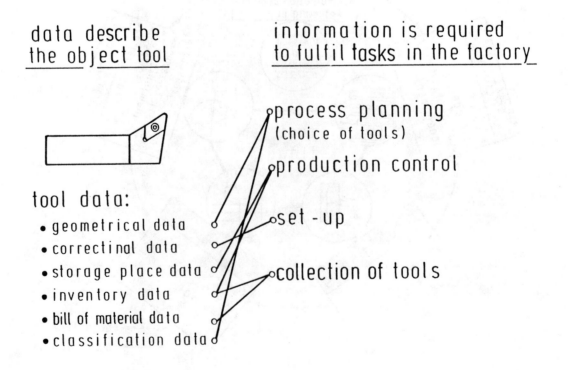

data describe
the object tool

information is required
to fulfil tasks in the factory

tool data:
- geometrical data
- correctinal data
- storage place data
- inventory data
- bill of material data
- classification data

process planning
(choice of tools)

production control

set - up

collection of tools

figure 3: Coherence of information and data

data according to	classes	groups	indivi-duals
● complete tools	class # | tool syst.	group # | reamer	ind.# | correct.data
		group # | drill	ind.# | storage place
		group # | bill of mat	ind.# | state of set-up
● NC-tools	class # | name	group # | inventory	ind.# | state of ass.
		group # | fault data	ind.# | fault data
	class# | graphics	group # | character.	ind.# | state of wear
		group # | cutting d.	ind.# | magazine pl.
	class # | cutting d.	group# | stand. tool	ind.# | reservation
● tool compo-nents	class # | ⋮	group # | ⋮	ind.# | ⋮

objects

figure 4: Structuring data according to a companies numbering system

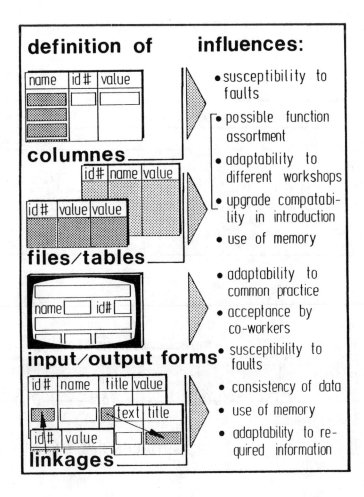

figure 5: Users degrees of freedom concerning definition of data structures in DBMS

117

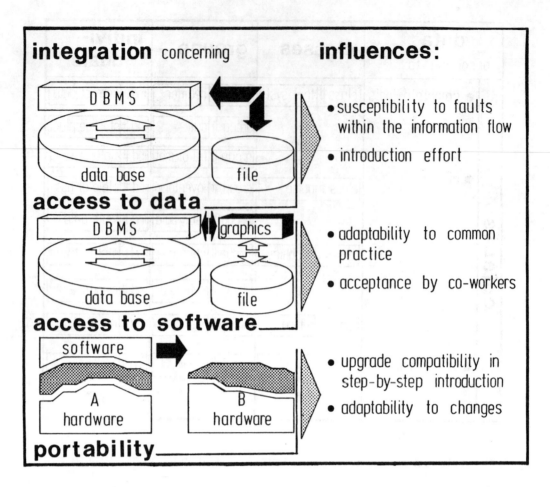

<u>figure 6:</u> Users degrees of freedom concerning integration of external applications into DBMS applications

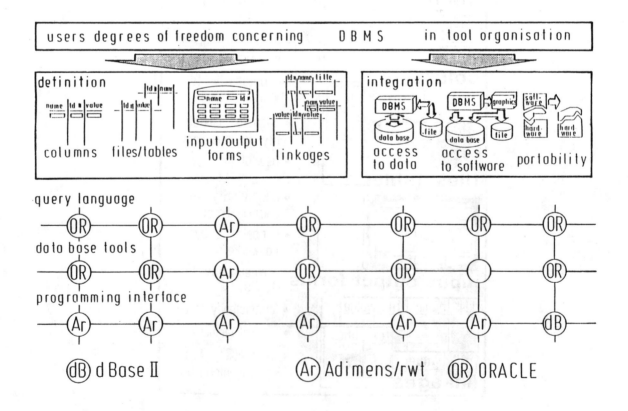

<u>figure 7:</u> Different DBMS in tool organisation from the users point of view

118

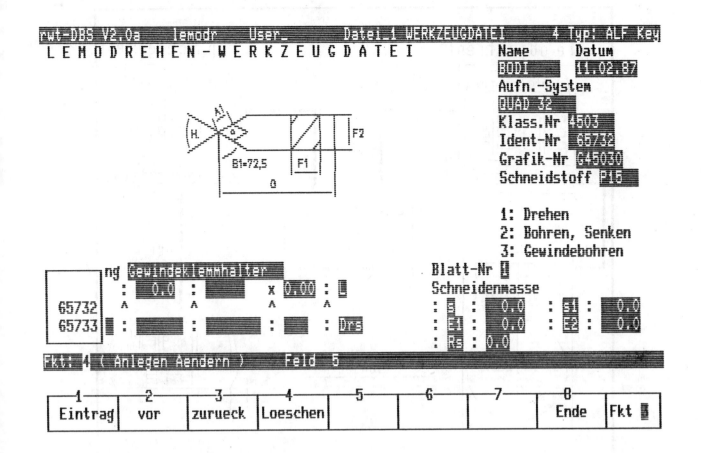

figure 8: Selection of tool data

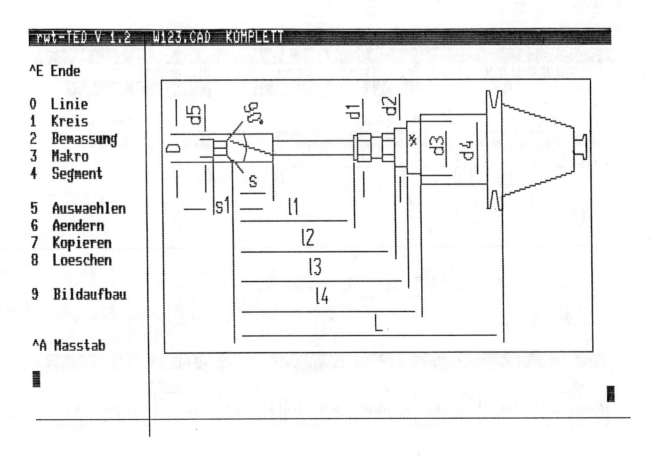

figure 9: The concept of the low-cost tool draft editor

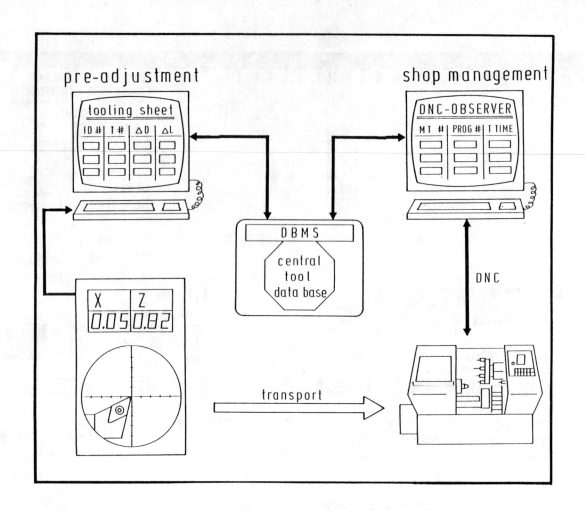

<u>**figure 10:**</u> Information flow between pre-adjustment and machining

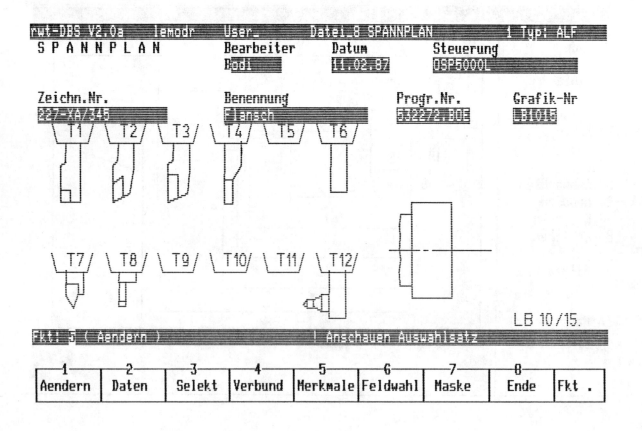

<u>**figure 11:**</u> Set-up plan from the tool data base

CONTROL SYSTEMS

Proc. 2nd Int. Conf. Machine Control Systems, 121-128
May 1987,© IFS (Conferences) Ltd and authors, ISBN 0-948507-52-7

Rule based control, a new tool

I H Darius
Texas Instruments Inc, USA

ABSTRACT

Both in traditional process control and in line or cell level optimization and
scheduling in the manufacturing industries, forcing all problems to fit the same
mathematical model has proven tedious and in most cases unsuccessful.

This paper describes a method for using the more flexible techniques of rule-based
knowledge representation to improve the chances of closing previously uncontrollable
'loops' by making full use of the accumulated knowledge about the process.

A technique for improving control performance using grouping and hierarchical
structuring of rules is described.

KEYWORDS

Rule-based control, Industrial control systems, Artificial Intelligence.

INTRODUCTION

Ever since the wide spread use of the P.I.D. algorithm, research in the area of self-tuning control loops and adaptive controllers has been very active. In general the principle is to devise a method to dynamically modify or predict the parameters used by the traditional P.I.D. algorithm. Some of these methods proved to be so efficient that they are now being used in real applications and products (1).

Recently people have used symbolic techniques to try and combine some of the benefits of embedding knowledge into systems and the classic P.I.D. by using so called 'Expert Systems' to modify (adapt) P, I and D coefficients (20). Others have gone further and used the inference method itself to perform the actual control (3). This article describes a method for combining 'general' control knowledge, used in a rule based controller at the low level, and more specific knowledge about the process in supervisory type rules at a higher level.

The goals were twofold. The first was to prove that closed loop control of a process is possible using a rule based and the appropriate inference mechanism. For the method to be successful, the control achieved would have to be comparable with classic implementations of P.I.D. control and be usable on 'classic' processors such as the ones used in the current generation of personal computers. The second and most important aim was to demonstrate that capturing simple knowledge about the dynamics of the system in rules that can be created, manipulated and understood by control engineers and operators is possible.

WHY A SYMBOLIC APPROACH?

Symbolic languages have inherent advantages in terms of their development environments. Although imbedding knowledge in computer applications has been around as long as computers have been, only the advent of symbolic languages has provided an application independent and formally developed framework for knowledge representation. One of the earliest and simplest knowledge representation techniques is the expression of knowledge in rules. The implementation of this technique is more easily handled in a symbolic environment and several existing packages can be used. An important side benefit from this is that it will make interaction with higher level systems easier when these systems start using artificial intelligence techniques in assisting operators while handling upsets (6).

A major concern when using implementations of symbolic environments is whether they can be applied to 'real-time' problems. An additional goal of the project was to verify whether this concern was valid. Just as microprocesssors and their use in control systems facilitated the use of more (then called) non-traditional control (4), the author believes that the new implementations of symbolic environments on the state-of-the-art processors will make the use of heuristic control feasible.

Traditionally, new techniques penetrate the industrial control market slowly. Much of that sluggishness has been due to the complexity of the proposed innovations and their reliance on models of the processes to be controlled. In industry segments such as food, the complexity of the processes, the lack of reliable sensors and the economics of the problem have kept the implementation of the highly complex control strategies, such as the ones used in the petro-chemical industries, to a minimum. Neither the models nor the people to produce them are available, although a wealth of operational process knowledge has been gathered (5). Recently however, this industry has been the center of gravity for the implementation of some of the newest Artificial Intelligence techniques.

IMPLEMENTATION

Figure 1 shows a block diagram of the functions used. The simulator was a simple time delay feedback loop. The complete system was developed, tested and run inside the PC SCHEME (7) system for the TI Professional Computer (7). Although not currently used by the system, provisions have been made to allow the system to accept rules created using a standard Expert System shells such as Personal Consultant Plus (7).

Simple inference mechanisms, such as exhaustive search of the rules, executed every computational cycle do not provide an adequate solution to the problem of keeping the computation time as constant as possible and small. The rule searching mechanism will always be process situation dependent but only when the computation time is of the same order of magnitude as the desired sample time, will the change in execution time influence control behavior. The goal then becomes to keep the inference chain length as constant as possible. In this implementation this was approximated by dividing the rules into groups and by structuring them so unnecessary rule parsing could be avoided.

Most control methods are based on monitoring and minimizing the error, the difference between the process variable (PV) and the setpoint (SP). The other parameter than can be used to control the process variable is the loss, anything that counteracts the control signal (output). These losses can be proportional to the setpoint (i.e. heat losses) or caused by such uncontrollable (from the closed loop standpoint) factors as production speed, etc. Although it is usually impossible to measure the loss parameter, for any given sample losses occurred during the last sample period will be proportional to the difference in the measured process variables at the sample boundaries and the control signal action during that period. Similar to the integral (I) part of the P.I.D. controllers this technique used in the anticipatory rules described below and accounts for some of the robustness of the controller when cyclic variation of the losses is simulated. The controller as a whole uses a combination of this loss estimation and error minimization techniques.

STRUCTURING RULES

As indicated in Figure 2 the rules are functionally grouped, therefore naturally providing an inherent sensitivity analysis basis. This method also provides a natural way of limiting the inference chain. The rule groups form a hierarchy which primarily reflects the control and safety precautions one would normally expect. This hierarchy drives the inference mechanism and therefore actions involving primary control and safety will take priority. Let us take a closer look at the groups involved.

Two of the rule groups are optional if their functionality is not needed or the knowledge for them is not available. They are hierarchically equivalent:

1. Optimization rules, intended to moderate or avoid sharp peaks and other undesirable control behavior by controlling the shape of the output curve versus time. Specific equipment performance knowledge and availability predictions expresses in selection or preference rules are in this category.

2. Adaptive or supervisory rules are used to embed the process specific knowledge discussed above. This group of rules is responsible for the inclusion of certain low level control rules or for the modification of the parameters within them. This group should allow for the 'tuning' of the rule based controller without intimate knowledge of the control rules and their functionality.

The other groups are concerned with the actual control. Although none of them are actually optional their influence can be tempered by the above optimization or supervisory rules. Figure 2 shows where rules take effect as a function of the error. In the first category, safety and alarm rules, a slightly different implementation of the standard absolute and relative (to setpoint) level alarming are used at the extremes of the control interval.

Environmental rules are the kind used by operators and engineers to achieve proper regulation control. Effective in the area where the output has a visible (large) effect on the PV, they are essentially expressions of the rules of thumb (3) used by these professionals when tuning control loops. These rules are implemented using the 'fuzzy set' concepts described in (3). In the case where the control action (output) only has a one way effect on the PV (e.g. temperature control with heater only) return of the PV to the controlled position is ensured by the anticipatory rules. These rules suggest an output proportional to the losses as computed from two (or more) adjacent PV values.

Convergence and encircling rules, consist of a class of rules that attempt to progressively 'trap' the PV in a small error zone around the setpoint. The rules used here are of the following general format, and are grouped into a family like:

```
IF Error > p1
    THEN Action is p2
    ELSE IF Error > p1'
        THEN Action is p2'
        ELSE IF error > p1''
            THEN Action is p2''
            ELSE.......
```

Where p1 (p1',p1'') and p2 (p2', p2'') are the rule parameters, p1 being the error parameter determining the distance to the setpoint at which the rule is going to the 'fire', p2 the rule-coefficient, subsequently used to determine the control signal. A family of encircling rules is generated by using pairs of parameters (p1,p2) located on the s-shaped curves in Figure 3. The number of pairs used in a family depends on the dynamics of the process and the control requirements. The selection of the family can be done by the engineer while configuring the system or automatically by a set of supervisory rules that contain the knowledge about the process response characteristics. This particular method may be instrumental in achieving operator configurability by offering a method allowing configuration at a level not requiring intimate familiarity with the low level control capabilities but rather general principles and macro process behavior.

Deadband rules are used to avoid continuous control action or asymptomatic effects. They eliminate any control action change whenever the controlled variable is within a specified interval around the target.

REALTIME PERFORMANCE AND MULTI-VARIABLE CONTROL

Performance of a knowledge based control system will of course depend on the amount and structure of the knowledge used by the system. The test performed indicates that when using a personal computer class engine, 2 to 3 control loops can be run with update frequencies up to 5 Hz. This is slightly inferior to what most microprocessor based digital controllers achieve, but probably quite adequate for most loops that are difficult to control.

To date, multi-variable problems have not explicitly been addressed. The control concept used however deals with the very similar problem of what could be called multi-level control. In this framework, the eventual control signal (output) is not determined by a single selected rule. All rules that 'fire' make a contribution or suggestion for the output and the final result is determined by the highest level rules. These mechanics can also be used to reflect contributions to the control signal from different process variables.

In the area of manufacturing these multi-level control techniques could be effective in 'controlling' overall material flow much like classic flow control but using the scheduling knowledge.

Both these aspects of rule based controllers are currently under study.

CONCLUSIONS

The feasibility of using rule based techniques for direct control has been demonstrated by this and other programs. The grouping of rules, the designation of rules to a certain control area and the idea of supervisory and optimization rules have increased the possibilities of easy implementation and higher quality control. Knowledge about a certain process or its control peculiarities can now be used to either improve the control or reduce operation costs. The technique of combininb the classical error minimizing techniques with a loss prediction method adds robustness to the overall controller performance.

Some of the techniques developed while addressing the classical control loop problems may turn out to be very helpful in providing a new approach to some of the control and scheduling problems in the discrete manufacturing area.

REFERENCES
[1] Kraus, Thomas W.: "EXACT - An expert system: From concept to commercialization" Advances in Instrumentation, Vol.40, Part 1, 1985

[2] Arsen, Karl-Erik: "Use of expert systems in closed loop feedback control", American Control Conference June 1986.

[3] Taunton, Chris: "Expert systems to go on-line at Blue Circle", Sensor Review, April 1986.

[4] Pearson, Ronald K.: "Obstacles to the practical application of nontraditional control", Advances in Instrumentation, Vol.39, Part 2, 1984.

[5] Drius, Ivan and Marien, Michel: "Artificial Intelligence": Potential applications, example of an expert system in the food industry", Journal de l' APRIA, Nov 1986.

[6] Moore, R.L., Hawkinson, L.B., Knickerbocker, C.G., and Churchman, L.M.: "A Real-time Expert System for Process Control". Proc. First. Conf. on AI Applications 1984, IEEE Computer Society, Denver Co.

[7] PC SCHEME, TI Professional Computer and Personal Consultant Plus are trademarks of Texas Instruments Incorporated.

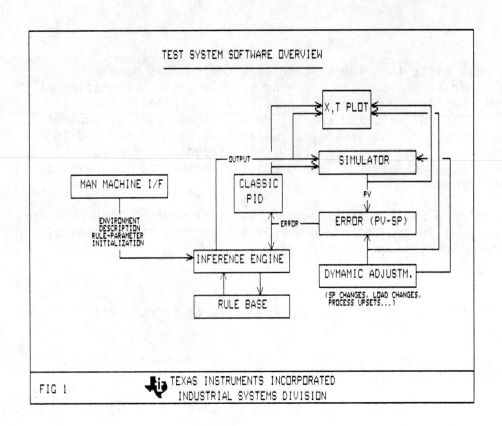

FIG 1   TEXAS INSTRUMENTS INCORPORATED
        INDUSTRIAL SYSTEMS DIVISION

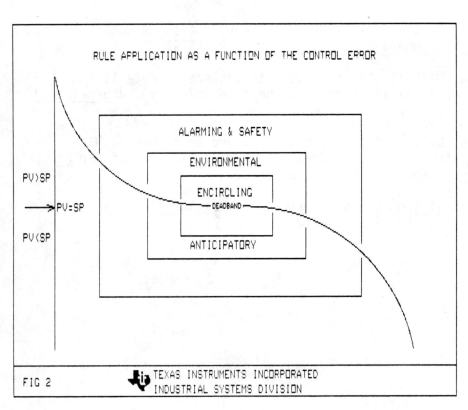

FIG 2   TEXAS INSTRUMENTS INCORPORATED
        INDUSTRIAL SYSTEMS DIVISION

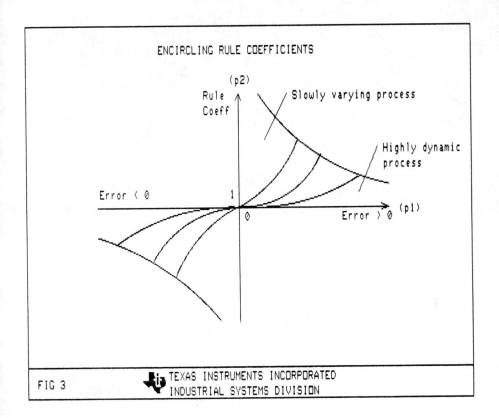

ENCIRCLING RULE COEFFICIENTS

FIG 3   TEXAS INSTRUMENTS INCORPORATED
INDUSTRIAL SYSTEMS DIVISION

Proc. 2nd Int. Conf. Machine Control Systems, 129-138
May 1987, © IFS (Conferences) Ltd and authors, ISBN 0-948507-52-7

Traditional information technology: PLCs vs PCs

D T Bonner
Istel Automation Ltd, UK

ABSTRACT

The organisational and strategic issues involved in choosing between using a PLC or a computer for real-time Control and Monitoring are discussed. The paper looks at the history and application of the two type of devices and super-imposes this onto the requirements of todays user. The conclusion being that from a technology viewpoint the choice may be immaterial, however from a company strategy and organisational viewpoint some fundamental questions need to be considered.

INTRODUCTION

The theme of this paper is to define the issues involved in deciding whether to use a Programmable Logic Controller or a Computer in a facility control and supervisory function. In developing this theme it is necessary to:-

a) look at the history of these two quite separate devices,

b) to understand their evolution,

and

c) to have some kind of view as to where they are going.

This, I believe, will help people to understand the prejudices that exist and why the decision between a PLC or PC can be emotive.

Hopefully, I will show that the choice is not a simple, straight forward technical issue and that some of the underlying issues affect fundamental company strategies and organisations.

COMPUTERS

Computers have been with us for some time now and the speed of their evolution has been incredible to say the least. To get a feel for the speed of the progress, one of the first electronic computers in the late 1940's, ENIAC, was made up of more than 19,000 valves, had less than one K of memory and dissipated some 200KW of power. Today we have more processing in a hand held calculator.

The size, cost and environmental needs of these computers limited their general applicability and the market for them was very definately in Data Processing, at the company level. The newness of the technology was also reflected in the reliability of these machines and generated the DP department as a whole new part of the organisation, with members of this new profession looked upon in awe by mere mortals. The skills of the members of this new profession were obviously specialist and very scarce.

Figure 1 shows the level within a company where these computers were applied.

This description has hopefully given you a picture of these early computers, they were physically large, expensive and required scarce, specialist skills to both operate and maintain them. This, therefore, is the starting point from which computers have evolved and this starting point has affected significantly how computers are perceived by the world at large.

Programmable Logic Controllers (PLCs)

PLCs started life in the 1960's, as an "intelligent" replacement for Hardwired Control Panels. The reason for this was simple:-

Companies had been automating some of their shop floor control equipment. The control of this equipment had been designed into the wiring installation and this meant that any changes to the facility or it's control sequences required wiring changes which were both costly and required an intimate knowledge of the installation. The need for flexibility, within the controlling equipment, generated the PLC. In this context, figure 2 shows the application area of the PLC at the opposite end of the business to where computers were applied. In this scenario, there was no choice or conflict between PLCs or Computers.

The PLC was fundamentally different in it's origin from the computer in that the computer was new and could be designed starting with a blank sheet of paper. The PLC, however, was a replacement of existing technology and therefore had significant constraints placed upon the design. Some of these constraints were:-

a) There already existed trained and skilled Control Engineering and Maintenance departments. These people worked with, and designed control sequences, using Relay Logic Techniques.

b) Control Panels were situated on the shop floor near the equipment. The environment was generally dirty and electrical noisy.

c) The equipment to be controlled varied in terms of voltage and power rating and interfaces between the PLC, the equipment and operators needed to be both safe and reliable.

d)   Control Panels did not require specialists to operate the "controller". The people were used to operate the manufacturing process.

e)   The space on the shop floor was at a premium and so the control panels had restrictions in terms of physical size and power consumption placed upon them.

It should now be clear that although computers and PLCs relied upon the same electronic technology to work, the way in which that technology was used was, by necessity, completely different.

Current Situation

Market

Before proceeding, it is worth while considering the current needs of the Market Place because this is influencing how this technology is being applied.

Users are looking to automatically control and monitor more and more areas of their business. This is generating more complex applications. In addition to this, when new equipment is installed flexibility is being demanded as a means of safeguarding the investment against the need for future changes and, hopefully, helping in the payback. This flexibility and the related control complexity generally requires that sophisticated scheduling and sequencing rules are applied to the equipment.

Companies are looking to get better control of the Business by collecting accurate information about achievement against schedules and feeding this into the planning cycle, so the schedules that are produced are in-line with the reality of the situation. This requires facility controllers to provide information relating to Production, Quality and Facility performance.

The trend is away from 'Islands of Automation', towards large, integrated and synchronised manufacturing units and the technology is here to support this trend.

In addition to this there is a move towards pushing accountability for manufacturing achievement down towards the shop floor. This means that all the 'tools' needed to achieve must be available to, and under the control of, the person accountable.

132

Technology

If we look at the current state of electronic technology, this has advanced to the stage where significant amounts of processing power and storage can be placed in very small boxes. Reliability and resilience to harsh environments has improved so that computers and PLCs are similar. Interfaces have been developed which allow computers to be connected to shop floor equipment, so that direct computer monitoring and control can be achieved. Finally the cost of the two different pieces of hardware are similar.

In this environment we see that the application of computers in industry has moved progressively from the corporate, centralised mainframe environment (as shown in figure 1) down towards the shop floor by the use of mini-computers and distributed processing techniques. The advent of the input/output interfaces for computers has enabled computers to be used to directly control plant equipment, a role normally associated with PLCs. Figure 3 shows the application of computers in this environment.

The same advances in technology have allowed PLCs to do more than just control equipment. The increased power and storage has enabled PLCs not only to control more complex plants but also to provide information and data normally associated with computers e.g. Productivity and Quality reports, Trend analysis, Facility Breakdown recording, etc. This, together with the improvements in inter-PLC communication, allows PLC to be used to co-ordinate and control several PLCs. Thus, as shown in figure 4, the application of the PLC has moved up from the shop floor into the cell control level. From this it is clear that there is no longer a clear breakpoint, or even a gap, between the areas where computers can be applied and those where PLCs are to be applied.

Organisation

The overlap and blurring of the application of this equipment now raises the question of "who is responsible for this control equipment?"

Traditionally computers have always been procurred, operated and maintained by the DP department. PLC's on the other hand have always been looked after by the Control Engineering or Maintenance departments. Therefore, organisationally, who is responsible for and has the skills to maintain equipment situated on the shop floor and used for real-time control?

This question raises both organisational and strategic issues relating to the Procurement and Maintenance of systems. If a policy of accountability at the shop floor is also adopted then this equipment is controlled by and maintained by the "Production Unit Manager."

Therefore to summarise the current situation, we have:-

1) Computer and PLC technology and standards which can equally be applied in real-time control and monitoring on the shop floor.

2) Vendors of control equipment who are fighting hard to sell their equipment into the facility and cell level control environment (see figure 4).

3) The organisational policy of a company and the relative strengths of the internal departments impacting how the two types of control equipment are viewed.

How do you choose?

I hope that I have now shown that the choice between a PLC or a Computer as control equipment is not only a technical issue. If we accept the technology is capable then some of the standard questions to be answered are:-

1) Does it fit with my standards?
2) How reliable is the equipment?
3) Is vendor support adequate, how long will it be needed?
4) Spares requirement?
5) What is my maintenance strategy?
  - In-house or contracted out?
  - must the available maintenance skills match the equipment or the equipment match the available skills?

However in times of change, especially where an Integrated Manufacturing Strategic approach is being adopted, additional questions arise:

1) Who is accountable?
2) Do they have the skills?
   - Electrician.
   - Technicians.
   - DP Staff.
3) Do I want them to have these skills?
   - Grading and Personnel issues?
   - Retention?
4) If change is needed from what we currently do, how do we migrate?
5) Can it be integrated into the "Information Network"?
6) Is the equipment used for control or information processing?

CONCLUSION

In my view the choice is made easier by keeping things simple. In doing this I would anticipate that a distributed approach would be adopted, with a recognised hierarchy of computing power. This approach:-

1) allows the "system" to be built up of small modules interconnected using interlocks, data networks or direct data links. It is my opinion that there are longer term benefits to be gained by implementing two or three small boxes rather than one big one.

and

2) allows the control and information processing functions to be separated and therefore solutions to be chosen dependant upon the need e.g. a PLC may be more suitable for the control, whereas a Micro-computer may be better for information processing and integrating into the Information Network.

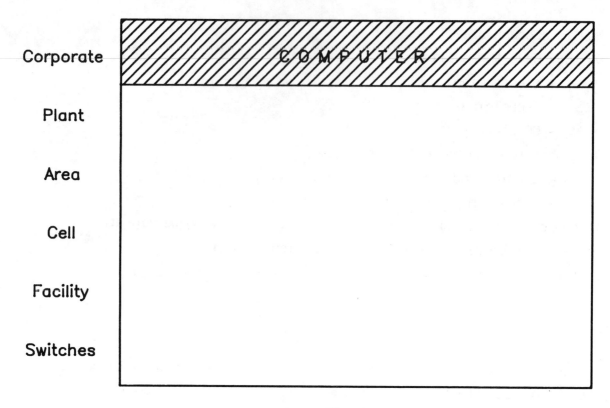

Corporate

Plant

Area

Cell

Facility

Switches

Fig 1.

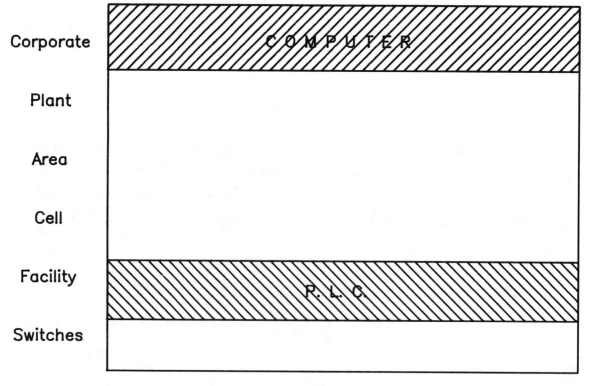

Corporate

Plant

Area

Cell

Facility

Switches

Fig 2.

Corporate

Plant

Area

Cell

Facility

Switches

Overlap

Fig 3.

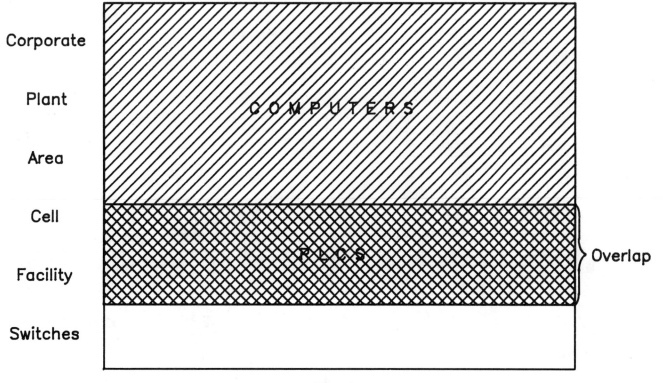

Corporate

Plant

Area

Cell

Facility

Switches

Overlap

Fig 4.

Proc. 2nd Int. Conf. Machine Control Systems, 139-164
May 1987, © IFS (Conferences) Ltd and authors, ISBN 0-948507-52-7

Industrial computers in machine control

H Stringer
IBM United Kingdom Ltd, UK

ABSTRACT

The Industrial Computer is a relatively new device. It has recently been
described as an "information exchange for the factory floor" because of it's
ability to transfer and redirect all forms of data, thereby enhancing factory
communications.
This paper describes in detail the design and function of an Industrial Computer,
the environment in which it operates, it's use in machine control and finally
it's position in relation to factory communications and CIM.

INTRODUCTION

A major challenge for the modern industrial company is to improve productivity and reduce manufacturing costs in order to remain competitive, especially in a climate of intense foreign competition and slowed production growth. Many forward looking companies are turning to new technology, in particular computer technology, to help streamline their manufacturing processes.

Until recently, standard computers systems were not generally considered suitable for use in industry. Indeed, few people believed that modern data processing equipment would ever be capable of surviving in harsh industrial environments. The basic architecture and physical construction often appeared too fragile to operate reliably alongside heavy industrial machinery.

Of the few non-ruggedised computer systems actually installed in hostile situations, most require a high degree of care and service in order to remain functional. Special precautions are taken wherever computers of this type are interfaced with the "real world". They need protection from quite small variations in temperature or humidity. Further, housing equipment of this kind in special air-conditioned computer rooms, free from vibration, shock and supply voltage fluctuations, often proves restrictive and, perhaps more important, represents an unacceptably high cost, when considering any first steps towards Computer Integrated Manufacturing.

Increasing demand for the automatic control of many manufacturing processes was met, almost exclusively, by customised micro-computers and Programmable Logic Controllers, forced higher and higher in complexity to satisfy the growing need for high speed, versatile, computing power.

With recent advances in computer technology, particularly in the commercial sector, it is now possible to produce computers with much greater resilience; machines which will mount directly into standard equipment racks and which have the processing power of earlier Main-Frames.

When housed correctly, these computers can withstand very hostile conditions. The development of bubble memory and industrial specification disk drives has further removed concerns about durability, with the result that relatively inexpensive computer systems, toughened to a very high degree, may now be used throughout the factory as supervisory machine controllers or gateways to large computer networks and corporate hosts.

With regard to the Industrial computer's position on the factory floor; It is now generally accepted that in order to achieve total integration of computers into manufacturing, there must be a distribution of processing power throughout the factory, at the same time linked with a positive movement away from the "know-all", "be-all" central processing source. The Industrial computer has evolved naturally to meet that demand.

The idea of siting processing power where it is needed most, where the action is, has several distinct advantages over previous arrangements; Real time control of equipment, along with error logging and alarm trapping, to name just a few. Of greater importance is the ability to connect these localised "centers of control" together to form a network so that a supervisory cell or plant control computer can manipulate and monitor the entire manufacturing process, while each local device is left to handle the real events occurring under its immediate control. In this way, the machine operator is provided with direct access to the mainframe and at the same time is given a user friendly interface to complex industrial equipment.

This paper presents the Industrial Computer under the following headings:

a. **THE INDUSTRIAL COMPUTER**

A detailed description of the Industrial Computer's design and function and the environment in which it is intended to operate.

b. **THE INDUSTRIAL COMPUTER IN MACHINE CONTROL**

The specific use of Industrial Computers in machine control with particular emphasis on operator interaction, instrumentation support and shop-floor interfacing.

c. **INDUSTRIAL COMMUNICATIONS**

Shows where the Industrial Computer fits into the factory communications hierarchy. Topics covered are: Local Area Networks (inc MAP), Transmission techniques, protocols, proprietary systems, internetwork strategy and CIM.

THE INDUSTRIAL COMPUTER

The prime function of any ruggedised micro-computer or Industrial computer is to act as an information exchange for the factory floor. This implies having the power to transfer and redirect all forms of data, often between dissimilar devices which use incompatible protocols.

In order to fulfil this role, and also to meet the special interfacing and connectivity requirements of the factory environment, Industrial Computers should be designed with an "open architecture".

The term "Open architecture" means that the infrastructure of the computer - it's electronic design - supports and encourages the integration of other devices manufactured to the same standard. The advantage of an "open architecture" is clear when we consider that the industrial marketplace is "Multi-Vendor" - for any piece of computing equipment to be successful it must offer the end user a great deal of flexibility.

The freedom to enhance the base product with various "add-ons" and "add-ins", benefits both the end user and the system manufacturer.

Closed architectures are often intended to "lock" the customer into a particular vendor's proprietary solutions.

The range of computers referred to in this section are all designed with an open architecture.

The IBM 7531: is a floor standing computer designed for use as an intelligent computer workstation

The IBM 7532: (FIG 1) is a rack mounted computer, designed for operation in light industrial conditions

The IBM 7552(*): (FIG 2) is designed as a stand alone or rack mounted, multi-option, machine, cell or line controller for operation in harsh industrial environments

SYSTEM ARCHITECTURE

The IBM Industrial computer functional diagram (Fig 3) reveals a standard micro-computer configuration. Each functional block effectively exists as a separate stand-alone device. They are attached to the Central Processing Unit (CPU) by three common bus structures: Address,Data & Control.

While each individual unit has sufficient on-board intelligence to handle specific I/O tasks, the distribution of data across the busses and the sequencing of microprocessor control is performed exclusively by the CPU under the guidance of a memory resident program or operating system.

The Direct Memory Access (DMA) facility allows each sub-systems to halt CPU operations momentarily to perform their own high-speed data transfers to RAM.

The intelligent sub-system strategy, another feature of "open architecture", provides a further base for the development of third party/OEM attachments.

THE MICROPROCESSOR (Fig 4)

The Intel 80286 Microprocessor has a 24-bit address, 16-bit memory interface, an extensive instruction set, DMA and interrupt support capabilities,a hardware fixed-point multiply and divide, integrated memory management, four levels of memory protection, 1-gigabyte of virtual address space for each task, and two operating modes: the 8086-compatible real-address mode and the protected virtual-address mode.

(*) The IBM 7552 Industrial Computer is a product that has been announced in the US. It must not be construed that it is IBM's intention to announce this product in the UK.

* REAL ADDRESS MODE ALLOWS THE SYSTEM TO EMULATE THE INTEL 8086
In real-address mode the microprocessor's physical memory is a contiguous array
of up to one megabyte. This mode enables most Personal Computer operating systems
and software products to transfer effectively between the Intel 8086/8088 and the
Intel 80286 microprocessor family.

* PROTECTED MODE REVEALS THE TRUE POWER OF THE 80286
The protected mode offers extended physical and virtual memory address space,
memory protection mechanisms, and new operations to support operating systems and
virtual memory.
The protected mode provides a 1-gigabyte virtual address space per task mapped
into a 16-megabyte physical address apace. It is the task of the operating system
to utilise and manage these powerful features.
The INTEL 80286 was designed specifically for use with multi-tasking operating
systems

ADVANCED PROTECTION MECHANISM:
a. Automatic integrity checks (code,data type, size & privilege)
b. Task Isolation Control (user/user isolation and sharing)
c. Multi-level Protection (up to 4 levels: user/operating system
   isolation and access control)

OPERATING SYSTEM PERFORMANCE ENHANCEMENTS:
a. Multi-tasking (Integrated task switch)
b. Ability to provide direct access to Operating System functions

SYSTEM HARDWARE DESIGN
The design criteria (Fig 5) employed in the development of an Industrial Computer
must include the following:

*   EXTENDED TEMPERATURE
*   VIBRATION AND SHOCK
*   POWER AND VOLTAGE FLUCTUATIONS
*   CONTAMINANTS AND PARTICULATES
*   OPERATIONAL SECURITY

These criteria are reviewed in the design of all computer systems, including
those designed for commercial use.
For the factory environment however, they are of primary importance.

"ENGINEERED TO WITHSTAND THE INDUSTRIAL ENVIRONMENT"
A comparison can be drawn between the design of a computer intended for the
commercial office environment and a computer of the same power intended for use
on the plant floor. Industrial computers require: (Fig 5)

*   FILTRATION SYSTEM
*   COOLING SYSTEM
*   POSITIVE INTERNAL AIR PRESSURE
*   DESIGNED TEMPERATURE RESISTANCE
*   INDUSTRIAL POWER SUPPLIES
*   INDUSTRIAL SPECIFICATION FRAME CONSTRUCTION
*   RUGGEDISED END USER INTERFACE
*   OPERATIONAL SECURITY
*   DATA AND CONTROL INTEGRITY
*   NEMA COMPATIBILITY

Designed temperature resistance

Any device expected to operate alongside heavy industrial machinery should be able to withstand temperature extremes. In the case of the IBM 7552 Industrial Computer a range 0 to 60 degrees centigrade is specified. Intelligent computer workstations or data collection computers, usually positioned in less harsh situation, will require an operational range a little lower, for the IBM 7532 Industrial Computer a range of 0 to 50 degrees centigrade is specified. These specifications are valid for a fully configured machine excluding temporary storage media such as diskettes used for diagnostics or "boot-up" purposes.

Power supplies

Voltage fluctuations and power outages are common place where the Industrial computer is powered on the same supply as industrial machinery. Special components must be added to smooth out fluctuations and prevent small outages from reaching internal DC power rails. In certain applications it may be desirable to have an internal backup battery which would allow the computer to terminate critical applications in an orderly fashion, recording error status and important data to disk or non-volatile memory, prior to a complete shut-down. Some systems may further provide circuitry for the connection of an independent external DC supply for permanent operation when the main supply fails. Additional factors to contend with are electromagnetic and radio frequency interference which produce spurious signals throughout the microprocessor causing premature system failure. These effects can be minimised by incorporating special RF filtration networks.

Ruggedised end user interface

Probably the most difficult component to adapt for industrial use is the user interface device. Such devices are needed to enable the system operator to enter commands or instructions, which interact directly with the process being controlled. These interfaces will more often take the form of a keyboard or touch panel.

Touch panels are suitable where the operator is required only to select an option or menu choice or return a simple reply, but if the application calls for extensive interaction with the system or the data retrieved is to be manipulated, to extract statistical information for instance, then a full size, full function keyboard will have to be employed. Until recently a keyboard of this type would have represented a very weak link in the protective armour of an industrial computer. There are now available, typist quality industrial keyboards designed with concealed membranes to prevent the ingress of dirt and moisture.

Operational security

*   SYSTEM BATTERY BACKUP
    a. Short term supply for orderly shutdown (>10 secs)
    b. Facility for extended operation with user supply
*   MEMORY ERROR CHECK/CORRECTION
*   AUTO-START
    a. Orderly start-up
    b. Application program dependent
*   WATCHDOG TIMER
*   MALFUNCTION ALARMS
    a. Catastrophic/non-catastrophic/program
    b. Optical isolation
        (typically 5-30 vdc, 30ma EXTERNAL SOURCE)

Corrosion

All exposed surfaces, both internal and external must withstand a certain degree of attack by corrosive elements. Even in areas of manufacturing not designated as "Hazardous Corrosive" there may exist small quantities of gaseous contamination. These typically would include:

* REACTIVE SULPHUR
* SULFUR DIOXIDE
* NITROGEN DIOXIDE
* OZONE
* ACIDIC GASEOUS CHLORIDE

It is essential that the correct choice be made of the materials used in the manufacture of printed circuits, functional units such as disk assemblies and exposed areas of keyboards and enclosures.

Other environmental factors

* PARTICULATE CONTAMINATION
  a. Suspended particulates
  b. Settleable particulates
* VIBRATION
* SHOCK
* ALTITUDE

APPLICATION AREAS FOR INDUSTRIAL COMPUTERS

Application areas for the Industrial computer are best divided into two distinct categories:
1) By Environment (Fig 6)
2) By Product   (Fig 7)
(Note. In all cases, communications are a fundamental requirement).
Specific application areas:

* NC MACHINE TOOLS
* ROBOTICS
* AUTOMATION
* INSTRUMENTATION
* SUPERVISORY WORKSTATION
* INTELLIGENT COMPUTER WORKSTATION
* UNATTENDED OR REMOTE OPERATION

COMMERCIAL CONSIDERATIONS

For commercial classification and analysis purposes, Industrial computer products may be shown in a two dimensional matrix.
One axis represents the computer's operating environment and the other axis the type of Industrial computer and the degree of ruggedisation. (Fig 8) The relevance of developing any particular product in the matrix will, in essence, be decided in terms of it's market potential. (ie.. is there a demand for a corrosive/portable computer) For some of these configurations, clearly the demand already exist, judging from the number of standard commercial microcomputers currently being employed on the factory floor.
The two dimensional matrix is only valid for one technical definition of "ruggedised micro-computer". For completeness, the graph requires a third dimension - that of price/performance. Where prices fall or performance increases, Industrial computers may be specified for an increasing number of applications.
Independent surveys, commissioned to analyse the role of the ruggedised micro-computer in manufacturing applications, reveal the potential European market size.(European Engineering Industries Only) Fig 9 (Figures represent Ruggedised Micro-Computer units).

THE INDUSTRIAL COMPUTER IN MACHINE CONTROL

In some instances the industrial computer may simply be regarded as a "front end" processor in factory communications, providing nothing more than data consolidation for mainframes. Increasingly though, through the development of new and powerful industrial software, the Industrial computer is being employed as an intelligent machine interface, not only to perform the important task of machine control but to simultaneously provide an interactive, "user friendly", communications tool for the machine operator.

Dedicated machine tool controllers and programmable logic controllers are of course traditionally concerned with controlling the important manufacturing process at very close quarters and are therefore linked directly to the movement of machinery or materials. The exchange of information with other devices usually takes the form of bits and bytes of binary data relating to real-time events occurring under their immediate control. User friendliness and versatile communications are not the highest priorities in the design of such systems.

Having higher level status, the Industrial computer is free to provide effective supervisory control of the whole process. Work can be assigned to robots and PLC's in a coordinated fashion while the operator is presented with a more simplified picture of work in progress. Also a computer positioned this way can still act as the traditional "buffer" between low level control devices and an upper level main-frame.

ADVANTAGES OF USING INDUSTRIAL COMPUTERS IN MACHINE CONTROL

* Operator interaction
* Application Flexibility
* Improved Communications (Industrial Interfacing)

OPERATOR INTERACTION (Fig 10)

Machine supervision and control:

Application software available for the Industrial computer can provide the operator with accurate and meaningful status/error reports and allow him to enter or receive instructions. Recent application software can make full use of the computers advanced features, such as smooth high resolution graphics to display, in pictorial form, the status of the manufacturing process. People relate far more to vivid and imaginative computer graphics than to endless rows of status bits and numbers. In particular, alarm or critical situations attract attention more quickly if they are displayed as flashing red symbols. While the operator is being presented with information in this way, the real work is still being performed in high speed behind the scenes.

Operator input devices can range from a full 86 key industrial specification keyboard to just a small heavy duty switch pad depending on requirements. Configuration and modification of program code has never been easier, with one simple menu choice invoking enormous amounts of pre-written code. Configuring the system for a specific application is also far easier to achieve where the operator or programer is guided and protected by means of "intelligent", interactive software.

Computer Workstation:

Industrial computers can be used as intelligent computer workstations, allowing the operator to communicate with the factory host or line control computer. This mode provides access to programmes and data which might include the Production Information and Control System and a distributed Engineering Database.

APPLICATION SOFTWARE (Fig 11 and 12)

* DOCUMENTATION AND LADDER LOGIC PROGRAMMING FOR PLC's
* PROCESS MONITOR/CONTROL
* JOB SHOP OPERATION CONTROL
* INVENTORY LEVEL TRACKING
* PART-PROGRAM GENERATION
* MAINTENANCE PROCEDURE SCHEDULING
* PLC DEVICE SUPPORT
* PLANT FLOOR GRAPHICS
* BAR-CODE GENERATION
* STATISTIC QUALITY CONTROL

INDUSTRIAL INTERFACING (Fig 13)

Data acquisition and control

Data acquisition and control subsystems are employed where the Industrial Computer is required to interface directly with plant sensors or transducers. These subsystems fundamentally provide signal conditioning to permit the digital computer to interface with external analogue signals and voltages with options to perform a certain degree of data manipulation. While doing so, the subsystem ensures a good deal of system isolation. Most general function adapters provide analog outputs, analog inputs, timer/counters and a varying number of digital in/digital out points. For more specific applications there are specialised products: included here would be - super high speed channel scan rates, higher resolution of analog signals (the standard tends to be 12 bit resolution.. or 4096 steps) and programmable range changing.

There are many Data Acquisition attachments available on the market. They can be used for monitoring the process through complete instrumentation sub-systems or through individual transducers and detectors. Information received in this way enables the computer to optionally modify or redirect the process and correct disturbances.

General purpose interface bus (IEEE 488)

One of the most cost-effective solutions for providing complete and powerful measurement systems using a range of instrumentation, yet still keeping flexibility, is to use the IEEE-488 General Purpose Interface Bus - GPIB.

This bus was originally developed as a simple arrangement for connecting up to 15 instruments to a controller in order to take a set of readings and store or print out results. The controller was originally hard-wired, often with the ability to modify the procedure manually via switches or a plug board.

It met a growing need for compatibility between various measuring instruments and data capturing devices, particularly in the field of automatic test equipment, and was widely accepted. Accordingly the IEEE decided that it formed the basis for a US national standard, and it was then designated the IEEE-488 bus in place of the earlier title of GPIB. It was also submitted for international recognition and a similar bus is now defined as the IEC 625 bus. This is electrically similar to the IEEE-488 bus but uses different connectors. The IEEE specified the original 24-pin stackable connectors, but the IEC 626 standard specifies the same 25-way subminature connectors as used for modems and other data-handling apparatus (V24 standard).

This is the most popular bus system for the interconnection of individual instruments into a complete test system. The acquisition, analysis and control aspects of GPIB systems have been addressed for some time by specialised instrument controllers and scientific computers fitted with a GPIB interface, but the recent acceptance of the PC "open architecture" as a standard for general purpose micro-computers has meant the development of many new combinations of hardware and software which utilise the features of the Industrial Computer.

Asynchronous communications: (20mA Loop,V24, RS 232, RS 422, RS 423)
Although parallel data transfer is simple and fast, it inevitably calls for many
lines between the computer and the data device. Unless the two are fairly close,
the cable cost becomes prohibitive, and serial transmission along a single pair
of wires is preferred. An early standard for the electrical signals was devised
to suit the teleprinters almost invariably attached to earlier microcomputers.
This was called the 20ma current loop interface. The computer provided a current
source to energise the teleprinter contacts and a voltage-sensing circuit to
detect whether the contacts were open or closed. This arrangement was convenient
in that the teleprinter was passive and needed no power for the interface
signals, but it was awkward in that the two halves were asymmetrical. Thus two
teleprinters could not be connected together to check one another, and similarly
for the two computer interfaces.
A widely used standard for similar purposes originated from the International
Telecommunications Union, whose telegraph and telephone committee(CCITT) proposed
the V24 and the V28 standards for connecting data-handling equipment to modems.
These standards define both a set of signal levels and line impedances, and a
set of signalling lines and their functional meaning. The V24 standard has been
adopted widely for connecting teleprinters, remote display units and data
terminals to computers. Almost all microprocessors with a serial data interface
will meet the V24 specification.
The standard was intended for short cable runs of 50 feet or less, since the line
cannot be correctly terminated, but at slow data rates up to 600 or 1200 bauds it
can be used over much longer distances of 1000 feet of more. For short runs the
maximum data rate specified is 20,000 bauds.
A virtually identical standard is known in the USA as RS-232-C. Like the V24
interface, it specifies the use of a 25-way subminature D-type connector, and
allocates particular pins for the various signals involved.
Although the V24 standard can handle any data rate which can be modulated onto a
telephone circuit (typical bandwidth 300-3400), it is unable to cope with the
much greater data rates of computer to computer, or computer to terminal links.
Primarily for this purpose two other standards were developed, RS-423 and RS-422.
These operate with lower termination impedances, reducing the effects of ringing
and signal reflections. A further difficulty with V24 circuits is that an
unbalanced line with earth return is used, and the earth return must be connected
to the local earth at each end. Consequently the circuit can suffer from
common-mode interference due to the potential difference between the two earths.
By allowing the transmission line to be terminated correctly, RS-423 enabled data
rates to be increased over distances of 4000 feet, still using unbalanced lines.
By changing to balanced line with differential drivers and receivers, RS422
enables the data rate to be increased to 10M bauds with the same cable length.
Whereas the V24 interface permits only one driver and one receiver, the RS-422
and RS-423 allow one driver and up to ten receivers to be connected to the line.
A future standard based on the RS-422 will allow up to 32 driver/receiver pairs
to be connected to the line, which is correctly terminated at each end. The line
then becomes a serial data bus.

Performance considerations:
Direct asynchronous communications requires the Central Processing Unit of the
Industrial computer to be exclusively involved in the transfer and formatting of
communications data to an external device. If the available processing power is
divided between the operating system, the communications program and other
concurrent tasks, which may well be accessing the CPU on higher interrupt levels,
then the direct communications attachment may not prove to be very responsive.
Multiplexors may be used to increase the physical number of communications ports
for each attachment but unless on-baord I/O processors are employed for data
packaging or line arbitration, they do not improve the Industrial computers
communications throughput.

Independent communications subsystem

A Communications subsystem expands the capacity of the Industrial Computer to create an integrated application environment without the installation of a larger computer.

The IBM communications subsystem product RIC (Real-time Interface Co-processor) is designed as a single-slot, multiple device interface subsystem for use in Industrial Computers. It can act as an independent processor, complete with it's own real-time, multi-tasking operating system, separate RAM for application programs and ROM for "boot-up" and diagnostic programs. The RIC provides facilities for off-loading applications and device drivers from the Industrial Computer into subsystem storage, and incorporates the following features:

a. A Co-Processor designed to attach a variety of peripheral equipment

b. A Realtime Control Program to supports user applications running on the Co-Processor
   * 253 concurrent user tasks
   * 255 interrupt levels

c. A Communications Subsystem to support a range of communications protocols

d. A range of pluggable interface boards to provide a variety of physical interfaces

Hardware:
The IBM RIC is based on a high-performance, Intel 80186 microprocessor with up to 256 Kilobytes (Kb) of user memory.   Up to three RICs can be added to the IBM Industrial Computer, giving six high speed serial ports and significantly increasing their processing capacity.

a. Data rate per port:
   64,000 bits per second with external clocking
   19,000 bits per second with internal clocking

b. Half and full duplex operation

c. Common interfaces for the Co-processor are RS-232c, RS-422a, V35 and 20mA current loop.

Applications using a communications subsystem:
Fig 14 Reveals the advantages of using a communications subsystem to remove the substantial work-load that direct involvement has on the main processor.

A multi-drop RS-422 communications port connected to a line of PLC's may be supported by separate send/receive tasks operating solely within the communications subsystem. These tasks may communicate with other tasks residing within the subsystem since all share the same RAM, and are controlled by a common task supervisor. The data retrieved from a PLC may easily be routed out to a plant host or line controller for logging to disk, an operation which may require the second port to use of a different communications protocol. Throughout this operation the industrial computer may have no involvement at all.

Alternatively the Industrial computer might easily read the data during it's transfer through the subsystem and use it to modify or update the operator's visual display unit. The operator may well be viewing the current production line status in graphical form, while the real-time work is being performed out of sight.

MARKETING CONSIDERATIONS
Fig 15 shows the usage of Ruggedised Micro-computers in six principle areas. (Engineering Industries only) Four areas are grouped together under the heading of "Controllers" and the remainder under the heading "Workstation".

INDUSTRIAL COMMUNICATIONS

The Industrial computer represents the "missing link" in the chain of industrial communications. Rather than the corporate host merely extending spurs into the manufacturing area, Industrial computers can penetrate much further, feeding up information from the closest possible contact with real events.
The industrial computer "bristles" with connectivity. It is capable of redirecting information from a variety of sources to any number of diverse destinations. An information exchange for the factory floor.
This section is divided into three parts:
*   COMMUNICATIONS OVERVIEW
*   NETWORKING
*   COMPUTER INTEGRATED MANUFACTURING

COMMUNICATIONS OVERVIEW
The Industrial Computer is capable of operating in three distinct communication areas. (Fig 16) Firstly it can attach to mainframe computers using conventional modems and public telephone or leased lines. Secondly it can attach to a number of Local Area Networks, where it can act as a ruggedised computer workstation or a manufacturing cell controller.
Thirdly, through the use of Real-time Multi-tasking communications subsystems, it can talk down to subordinate "shop-floor" devices such as PLC's or dedicated machine tool controllers.

NETWORKING
What is a local area network ?
Features:
*   Limited distance
*   High speed
*   Sharing of intelligent devices
Examples:
*   Telephones
*   Fire alarms
*   Energy management
*   Word processing
*   Closed circuit TV
*   Computers (relative newcomer)

Transmission techniques
Affect:
*   Function
*   Experience level to design, install and maintain
*   Distance
*   Cost

Baseband (ie twisted pair):
Single channel, digital, serial communications. The transmission is usually limited to less than 2.5 Km. The advantages of this medium is that it can be installed very easily, is less difficult to maintain and consequently is less expensive. The concerns are that it restricts the transmission to data only and has less noise immunity than broadband transmission.

Broadband (ie Coaxial cable, CATV):
Multi-channel, Analog, parallel transmissions. Can operate on networks over 2.5Km and supports data, voice and video signals simultaneously by the use of frequency division multiplexing.
Although the use of standard CATV components is widespread, there are concerns about cost, both to install and to maintain a system of this type.

Access protocols

Polling:
Polling is a simple method of attaching computing devices together. The network topology usually takes the form of a star configuration with a dedicated controller in the center. It has several disadvantages, chiefly relating to speed and efficiency. Firstly, each device on the network is polled in turn regardless of whether it has anything to say or not. Secondly, the computer assigned the task of controller, is dedicated to that task alone, and is effectively lost from the system.

Carrier Sense Multiple Access:
This protocol permits each node in a network to have equal access to the transmission line at any one particular time (Multiple Access). The only task a computer must perform prior to "speaking" onto the network, is to listen to the transmission line and ensure that other devices are not already using it (Carrier Sense). On receipt of a message or data file, the receiving device simply returns an acknowledgment to the sender to ensure network integrity. If the network is small and the amount of data moving between nodes is spasmodic then little contention will arise to degrade network performance.
Adopting this type of line access may prove to be satisfactory on very small networks and be relatively inexpensive.
Problems will arise when more computers are attached to the network or the conversation between existing computers intensifies. The number of instances where several computers may simultaneously sense the line, and transmit data onto it, will tend to increase. Colliding data will produce an abundance of negative acknowledgments from listening devices and the intensity of conversation will increase even more.

CSMA/Collision Detect:
The collision detection facility was developed to reduce the time wasting which results when data collisions occur on the line. The transmitting device simply listens to the line both before and during the transmission. If any collision occurs it immediately stops transmission, waits a predetermined length of time and retries.
A further time saving advantage of this system is that the receiving device is not required to send an acknowledgment of correct reception to ensure data integrity.

CSMA/Collision Avoidance:
This facility attempts to address the last remaining flaw in the "Collision Detection" system. Following a collision, when the computers in conflict wait a predetermined time before retransmitting, there is nothing to prevent yet another device from accessing the line also and confounding the situation still further. With "Collision Avoidance", all devices on the network, upon hearing a collision, drop into a delay and time slice sequence, the length of which is unique to each computer. The result being that conversations are restarted in an orderly way and the network can recover more quickly.

Token Passing:

Token passing on a network is analogous with baton passing in a relay race. In each case only the person holding the token is allowed to run, or in the case of the computer network, allowed to send information. A specific device on the network is charged with the task of monitoring the condition of the token and if necessary issuing a new one.

Token management may differ slightly, depending on whether the tokens are being passed around a ring or across a bus network. Speed is also a variable factor. 5mega-bits is regarded as quite slow while 10 or 20 mega-bits might be specified for the main backbone of factory communications, a token passing bus, MAP.

There are safeguards in using this protocol for Industrial applications.

a. The Token Passing principle is "deterministic":

For any particular system configuration it is possible to calculate the response time one device might expect when in conversation with another. This would not be possible in the case of CSMA for instance.

b. Token Passing supports device priority:

It is possible to permit more token use by one device compared to another. This priority system is also deterministic

Topology

Star:

Star wired networks involve the use of a central controlling device being directly linked to each individual computer on the network by a dedicated wire, conceptually arranged in a star shape around the center point.

Ring:

It's name suggests that this topology is simply a loop of cable connecting every node of the network together in a physical ring, but this is not always the case. The electrical circuit may well remain in effect, a ring, but the cabling could be placed in the star arrangement to provide extra network flexibility. The center of the star, instead of being a controlling computer, could simply be a switching box able to sense the availability of any device on the network and if necessary exclude it from the ring. This facility allows for the addition or removal of computers from the network without causing disruption to other devices. A failing computer would be dealt with in the same manor.

Bus:

The bus topology is arguably the most flexible system of all. Providing the bus has previous been equipped with connection points, a new device can be easily plugged into the network.

The broadband bus is usually driven, from one end, by a frequency translation unit or head end amplifier. This device is a multi-channel Radio Frequency turner which can detect the transmission frequency of computers attached to the network and translate the data into a common receive frequency for dynamic retransmission along the same cable. If the translator is capable of handling several transmit/receive frequency pairs then one bus structure may be used by different proprietary networks simultaneously.

Proprietary networks

Listed are examples of networks and access protocols/transmission medium they employ:

*	Ethernet	Baseband/CSMA/CD	802.3
*	PC network	Broadband/CSMA/CD/Bus	
*	Token ring	Baseband/Token Passing/Ring	802.5
*	MAP	Broadband/Token Passing/Bus	802.4
*	MAP(carrierband)	Baseband/Token Passing/Bus	

MAP/OSI

Until recently, vendors of mainframe computer systems, mini-computer systems and programmable controllers each developed their own solutions for solving communications problems specific to their needs. Much of this isolation was advantageous to the vendor but not to the customer. Although many de facto standards have taken hold in office systems and DP environments, the most positive action taken to solve the factory dilemma has been an effort initiated by General Motors called Manufacturing Automation Protocol or MAP.

MAP is a standard set of communications protocols which provide end-to-end connectivity for intelligent computing and programmable control devices operating over Local Area Networks. The intent of this standard is to allow equipment from competing vendors to share a common language and allow information to flow from top to bottom of the plant/corporation. The foundation for the MAP LAN is a seven-layer reference model promulgated by the International Standards Organisation (ISO) (Fig 17) called the Open Systems Interconnect (OSI) model. This LAN model defines seven protocol function areas needed for inter as well as intra-network communications. These capabilities are essential to the total integration of computing devices within a manufacturing organisation. (FIG 18) The OSI model with expanded lower section (Fig 19) shows the involvement of the IEEE in defining the standards for physical connect.

The MAP specification (802.4) combines the advantages of using broadband transmission technique, offering multi-channel flexibility and good noise immunity, with the advantages of a Token Passing communications protocol which is prioritised and deterministic.

MAP(carrierband), MINI-MAP and MAP/EPA

In the light of practical experience the full MAP specification is open to some criticism. Firstly the cost of using broadband technology at OSI layer 1 is proving to be prohibitive, with the result that MAP(carrierband) has been developed. With this version, the multi-channel broadband transmission technique has been replaced with the cheaper and easier to maintain, single-channel carrierband. Carrierband, like the full implemantation of MAP, uses frequency modulation to transmit analoge signals over the coaxial cable backbone. This retains the valuable noise immunity charicteristics of the broadband system. The difference is that the Carrierband system will only allow one channel of data to flow through the cable at a time, similar to a baseband transmission. Secondly the seven-layer route makes data transfer slow for time-critical operations. To address this problem two other versions of MAP have emerged: MINI-MAP which employs only layers 1,2 and 7 of the OSI model (The result is faster data transfer but at the expense of reduced formatting and session services) and MAP/EPA or Enhanced Performance Architecture. MAP/EPA provides two modes of operation: one corresponds to the full MAP specification and the other relates to the collapsed architecture of MINI-MAP. The mode can be switched and this might allow a computer operating such a protocol to act as a bridge between MINI-MAP and the full MAP spine.

Internetwork strategy

As previously stated, the Industrial environment is very much "Multi-Vendor". The intention of the MAP initiative is that devices from many different manufactures should be able to coexist within the same manufacturing establishment. Fig 20 reveals both the Industrial computers positioning, with respects to MAP and connectivity to shop floor devices, and the interrelationship of proprietary sub-networks, implementations of MAP(carrierband), MAP gateways, Host computer links and outwards paths to other communications networks such as SNA or X25.

COMPUTER INTEGRATED MANUFACTURING

Although this subject is being included in the communications section, it must be stressed that CIM is not a communications strategy. CIM is very clearly a business strategy and the mixture of computer hardware and software products which represent CIM in one company may be very different to another company. One factor of CIM howerer which has overriding importance is "connectivity". Without "connectivity the Islands of automation we already have, simply become more expensive Islands of automation as time progresses. In order for mainframe resident management software to become effective and thereby vastly improve a companies manufacturing productivity, it needs to tie in with all other sub-sections of the company. From the technical sales dept round to the final engineering design and production depts.

The Industrial Computer has a definite and distinct role to play in any such organisation. It can solve the "connectivity" problem and introduces a new measure of reliability at ground level, a factor on which the concept of CIM depends.

CONCLUSION

Although the concept of the Industrial computer isn't new, a very low cost, high powered, ruggedised micro-computer which offers total flexibility and adapt-ability, is new. In fact it sets new standards for computing and communications on the factory floor.

An Industrial computer of the type described in this paper is not simply another computing device looking for a marketplace. It is based on currently available and proven technology which doesn't require the whole of manufacturing industry to "catch up" before it's true value can be realised. The Industrial computer can solve today's problems.

In just the same way that the Personal Computer has revolutionised the office, so the Industrial Computer will begin to appear in more and more of our manufacturing plants.

It will make small manufacturing operations more cost effective and on a larger scale will represent the "missing link" in the chain of computer control from the factory floor to the corporate mainframe.

IBM 7532
INDUSTRIAL
COMPUTER

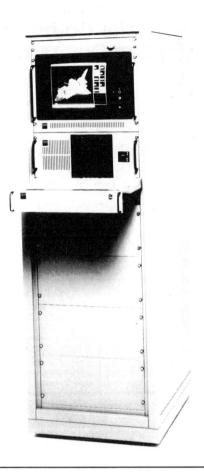

Fig 1

IBM 7552
INDUSTRIAL
COMPUTER

Fig 2

IBM Industrial Computers
Function Diagram

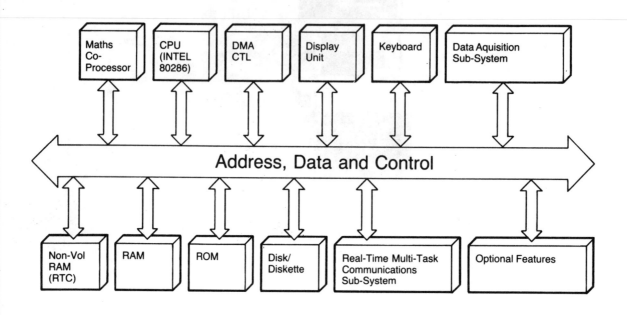

Fig 3

IBM Industrial Computers
System Description

- **INTEL 80286 Microprocessor**
- **Clock Speeds 6, 8 & 10 MHz**
- **24 Bit Addressing (16 Mb RAM)**
- **16 Bit Data Path**
- **7 – Channel DMA**
- **16 – Level Interupt**
- **64 – 128 Kb ROM**
- **Real Time Clock & CMOS Configuration Table**
- **7 I/O Slots**

Fig 4

Designed for the Industrial Environment

- **Design Criteria**
  - Extended Temperature
  - Vibration and Shock
  - Power and Voltage Fluctuations
  - Contaminants and Particulates
  - Operational Security

- **Design Features**
  - Filtration System
  - Cooling System
  - Designed Temperature Resistance
  - Industrial Power Supply
  - Industrial Specification Frame Construction
  - Ruggedised End User Interface
  - Operational Security
  - Data and Control Integrity
  - NEMA Compatible

Fig 5

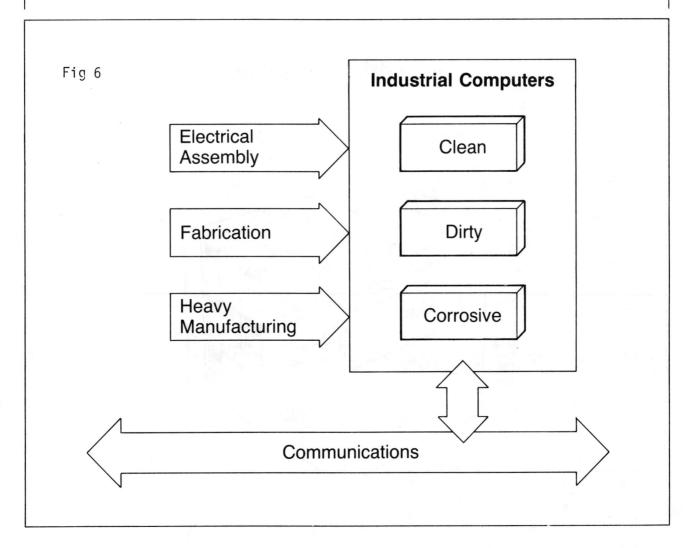

Fig 6

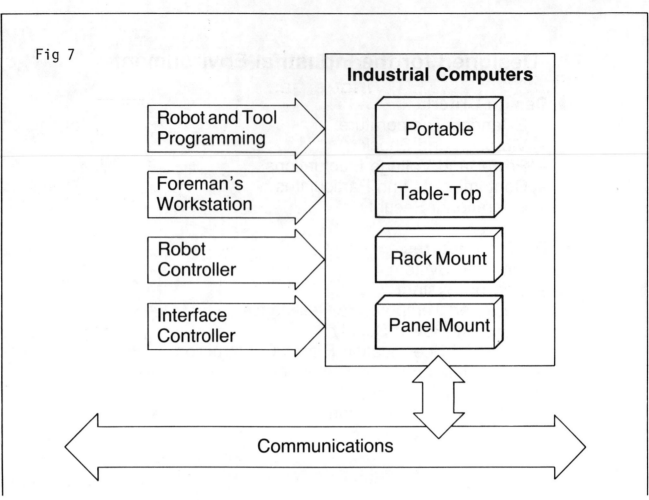

Fig 7

Industrial Computers

Robot and Tool Programming →
Foreman's Workstation →
Robot Controller →
Interface Controller →

Portable
Table-Top
Rack Mount
Panel Mount

Communications

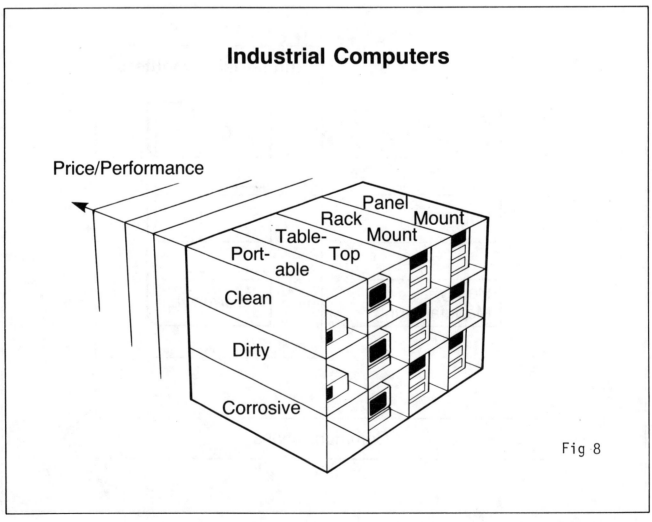

Industrial Computers

Price/Performance

Portable | Table-Top | Rack Mount | Panel Mount

Clean
Dirty
Corrosive

Fig 8

158

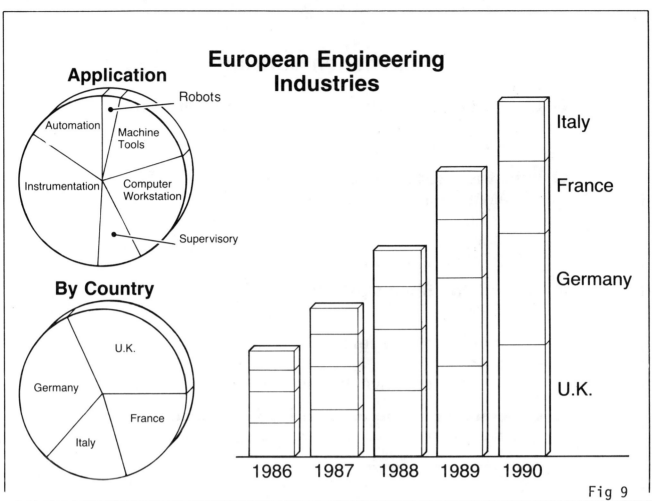

European Engineering Industries

Application

Robots
Automation
Machine Tools
Instrumentation
Computer Workstation
Supervisory

By Country

U.K.
Germany
France
Italy

Italy
France
Germany
U.K.

1986   1987   1988   1989   1990

Fig 9

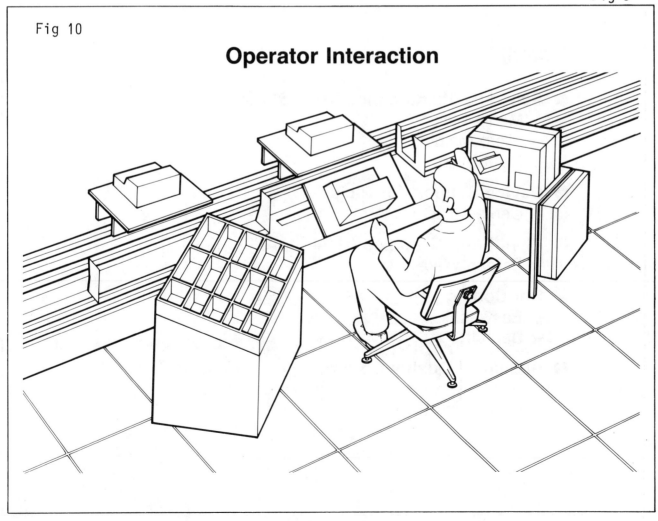

Fig 10

Operator Interaction

Application Software

- **Ladder Logic Documentation and Programming**
  - UP/DOC
  - Taylor Industries Software

- **Industrial Process – Monitor and Control**
  - CAMM
  - The Fix
  - Loopworks
  - PC Tables and Taxi

- **Control Job Shop Operations**
  - Job Boss

- **Track Inventory Levels**
  - Cribware
  - Manufacturer's Inventry System

- **Generate Part Programs for NC/CNC Machines**
  - Minute-Man

Fig 11

(contd)

- **Schedule Maintenance Procedures**
  - Media-Flex
  - Micro-Maint
  - Fleet-Maint

- **Device Support for Plc's**
  - Centec (RIC Drivers)

- **Plant Floor Graphics (Design, Animation)**
  - Screen Ware

- **Bar Coding**
  - Easylabel
  - Barsoft

- **Statistical Quality Control**
  - SQC Pack
  - Quality Alert

Fig 12

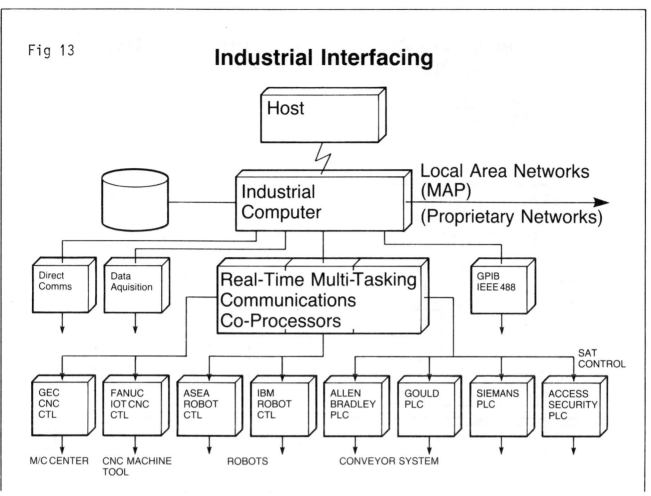

Fig 13

Industrial Interfacing

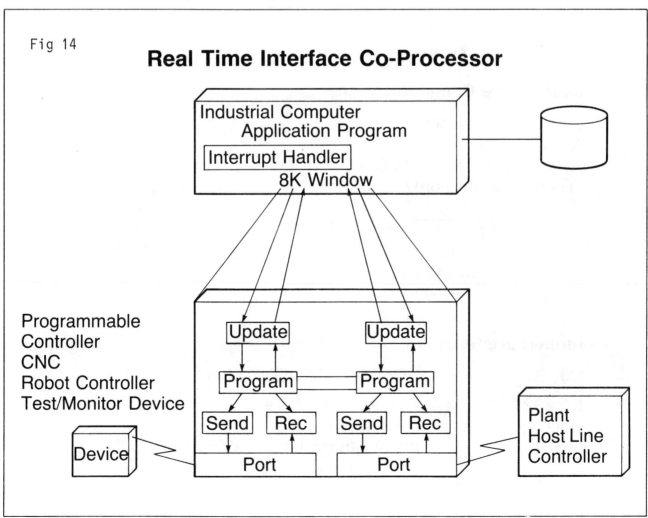

Fig 14

Real Time Interface Co-Processor

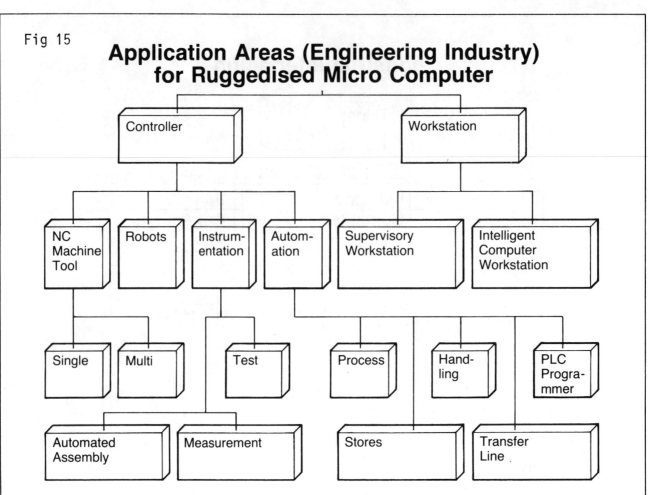

Fig 15

Application Areas (Engineering Industry) for Ruggedised Micro Computer

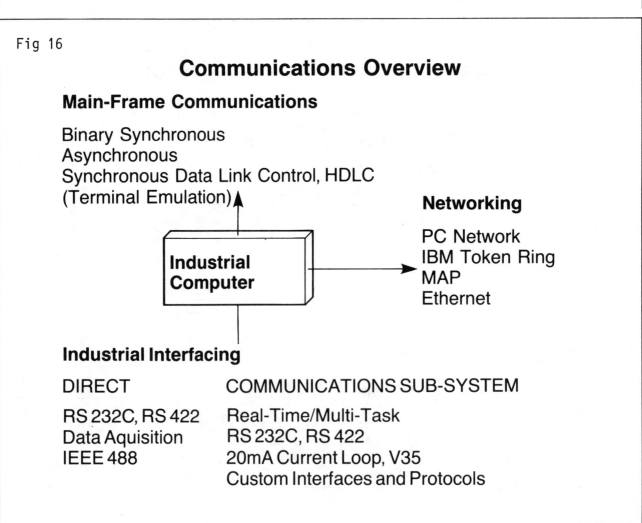

Fig 16

Communications Overview

Main-Frame Communications

Binary Synchronous
Asynchronous
Synchronous Data Link Control, HDLC
(Terminal Emulation)

Industrial Computer

Networking

PC Network
IBM Token Ring
MAP
Ethernet

Industrial Interfacing

DIRECT	COMMUNICATIONS SUB-SYSTEM
RS 232C, RS 422	Real-Time/Multi-Task
Data Aquisition	RS 232C, RS 422
IEEE 488	20mA Current Loop, V35
	Custom Interfaces and Protocols

ISO OSI Model

- A standard for designing networks in a series of protocol layers
- Upper layer – virtual communications
- Lower layer – physical communications
- Helps to reduce complexity in design and reduce redundancy of effort

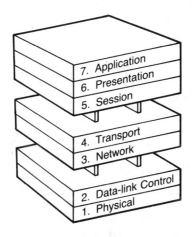

7. Application
6. Presentation
5. Session
4. Transport
3. Network
2. Data-link Control
1. Physical

Fig 17

OSI Model Interconnectivity

Common Communications Within the Seven Layers Will Free Resources to Increase End User Productivity

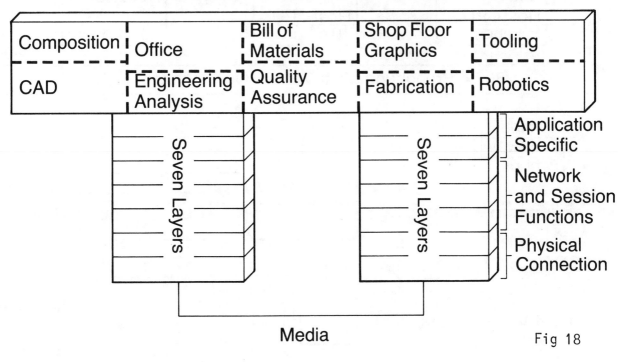

| Composition | Office | Bill of Materials | Shop Floor Graphics | Tooling |
| CAD | Engineering Analysis | Quality Assurance | Fabrication | Robotics |

Seven Layers

Seven Layers

Application Specific

Network and Session Functions

Physical Connection

Media

Fig 18

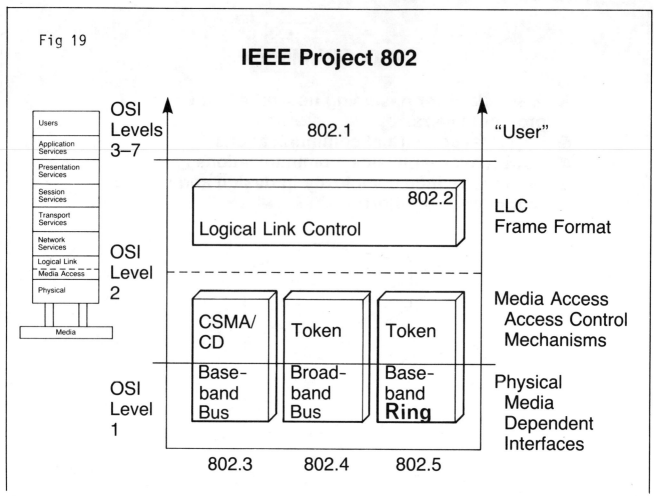

Fig 19

IEEE Project 802

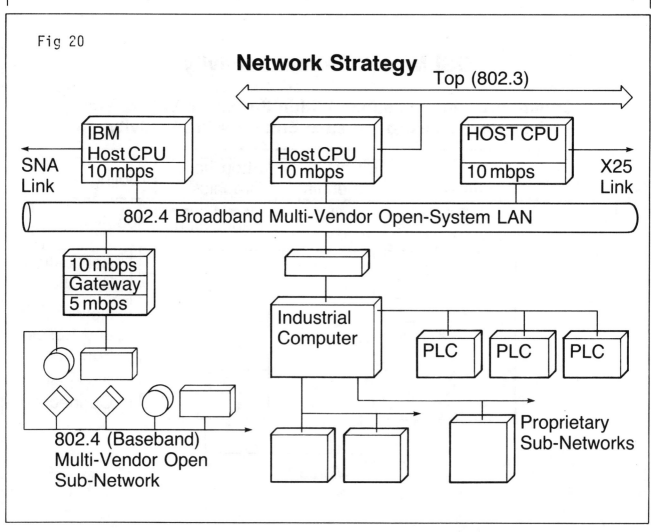

Fig 20

Network Strategy

Proc. 2nd Int. Conf. Machine Control Systems, 165-174
May 1987, © IFS (Conferences) Ltd and authors, ISBN 0-948507-52-7

A flexible assembly system controller

M Ashton, D A Harding and M I Micklefield
Thorn EMI Central Research Laboratories, UK

Abstract

The benefits of flexible robotic assembly systems are well known, but until now these systems have only been able to cope with minor variations in the product and a truly general purpose solution has been too difficult or uneconomic to produce. The *THORN EMI Central Research Laboratories* have developed a completely new intelligent integrated manufacturing cell. The cell contains a manipulator which has the ability to reconfigure the system such that product changeover can be achieved without operator intervention. This paper describes the development of a manipulator controller based upon *transputer technology* that provides the high performance specification required of today's robots at a much lower cost. It also discusses the *task oriented programmer*, the knowledge based assembly and error recovery system and the other software packages that have been produced for the control of the intelligent manufacturing cell.

1. Introduction

The need for flexibility in manufacturing assembly systems has been well established for some time. The attempts that have been made to produce a standardised robotic assembly system have often seen the solution to flexibility laying in a multi robot configuration or by incorporating sophisticated vision sytems. These are often rejected by industry as being economically unjustifiable.

The approach taken at *THORN EMI Central Research Laboratories* has been to produce a general purpose assembly cell capable of reconfiguring itself for rapid product change over within a realistic budget [1].

We have defined the specific requirements for an integrated flexible manufacturing system as being :-

(a) reconfigurable hardware and software enabling easy and rapid product changeover;

(b) the ability to operate with the minimum of human intervention;

(c) a range of assembly aid devices such as tools and sensors;

(d) compatibility with other industrial manufacturing systems;

(e) low cost;

The configuration of the cell that we have designed has evolved from knowledge acquired through developing several experimental assembly cells and assembling many different products.

2. Overall System Configuration

The specification for the cell control system was determined from the mechanical hardware elements required to perform flexible assembly; these were:-

(a) a manipulator with four degrees of freedom [2];

(b) an assembly fixture or vice incorporating a further two degrees of freedom needed for true flexibility;

(c) adaptable parts feeders that enable a diverse range of components to be introduced into the cell;

(d) a reconfigurable sensor station utilising low cost tactile probes;

(e) an array of different and adaptable tools;

(f) an end effector with lockable compliance, three turret mounted grippers with interchangeable fingers, and a retractable tactile sensor;

A fully detailed description of the cell hardware configuration and its justification is presented elsewhere [3].

Throughout the cell it was necessary to incorporate a number of simple sensors to provide feedback during an assembly, for instance the end effector required sensors to register activation of the compliance on impact, z-axis compliant travel, the presence of fingers etc. A programmable logic controller was used to control most of the supplementary hardware in the cell so relieving the burden on the cell controller's CPU time. The logistics of providing greater intelligence and the complexity of controlling the diverse range of hardware incorporated in the cell necessitated the use of a high level language. The choice of computer was a *Televideo AT (an IBM PC/AT clone)*, this provided low cost processing power coupled with industrial system compatibility.

The control architecture that resulted from these decisions represents a significant departure from conventional industrial robot control systems, see Fig 1.

This configuration has evolved from the development of several assembly cells over the last five years [4]. Initially the manipulator controller was used, not only to control the arm, but also a collection of peripheral hardware by utilising the simple I/O facilities provided, see Fig 1b. This is, typically, the manner in which most stand alone robot systems are controlled.

This first cell was built around a *Unimation PUMA* and soon it was found that the I/O capability provided was insufficient to control the increasing amount of hardware being added to the cell. The provision of a serial port on the PUMA enabled communication with an external computer, which could then control the supplementary hardware required for assembly. A *BBC microcomputer* was purchased and it was soon discovered that for general purpose control the 8 bit micro outperformed the 16 bit robot controller. The shifting of the cell control from the PUMA controller to the BBC was therefore a logical step to take. This established the BBC as a task scheduler and executor of those operations not performed by the robot, see Fig 1c, it also provided the power required to develop some simple error recovery strategies.

A decision was made to build a new flexible assembly cell in order to develop the control strategy much further and to make it more adaptable and user friendly. This system was shown at Automan '85. In the previous system it had been found that too much of the cell controller's CPU time was being taken up controlling the supplementary hardware and so a PLC with communications abilities was purchased to relieve some of the processing load. In order to develop more sophisticated software the cell controller had to be upgraded to provide greater power and more compatibility with industrial standards; an *IBM PC/XT* was purchased to fulfill these requirements. The new cell was built with a *THORN EMI TEAM-MATE* as the manipulator.

Two software packages were written; a cell programmer and a run-time system, that improved the flexibility of the cell and made it easier to use.

The cell programmer enabled the user to readily schedule all of the operations required to produce an assembly with little knowledge of the control system.

The run-time system incorporated some hard-coded knowledge of assembly and defined it in terms of three operations :-

(a) pickup (b) measure and (c) assemble

Not all of these operations were necessarily required for each component. The definition of assembly in these terms enabled the run-time system to determine the operations required to perform each task and provided an ideal structure in which to develop more standardised error recovery routines.

The success of this cell proved that a flexible control system could be produced with a standard computer, PLC and manipulator provided that each had sufficient communication facilities.

Further improvement in the control of the cell was necessary if it was to be able to assemble a diverse range of products reliably and with easy product changeover, and so a decision was made to upgrade the PUMA cell using the same hardware configuration as the TEAM-MATE cell, but with a completely new software suite.

Analysis of the task oriented structure of the previous cell's software led to the understanding that these fundamental assembly tasks could be broken down into a set of primitive actions. Building the control structure of the run-time system on this basis would enable a strict definition of assembly operations as an ordered sequence of tasks, and each task as an ordered sequence of primitive actions, see Fig. 2.

To reduce downtime and improve the reliability of an assembly cell error recovery strategies must be defined and used in a structured manner [5]. Analysis of typical faults that occurred during an assembly indicated that most problems could be solved by implementing recovery paths at various levels. Four distinctive levels were identified and can be described as :-

(a) assembly level - errors detected at this level would require repeating or aborting the assembly;
(b) object or component level;
(c) task level - where pick up, measure and assemble are defined as tasks;
(d) action level - the basic primitives;

Standard error recovery routines were developed for each of these levels. If the routine at one level does not have the capability of recovering the error is passed up to the next level where it would be dealt with.

The establishment of this error recovery structure led to the development of the run-time program as a hierarchical control system based on strictly defined levels.

The implementation of this control strategy in the new software suite was successful and at this stage it was decided to begin the design of a completely new flexible assembly cell.

3. The Cell Controller

The hardware configuration incorporates a *Televideo AT* running the cell control software suite, a manipulator controller based on *transputer* technology and a Z80 based PLC, see Fig 1a.

The development of modern robotic systems has produced a second generation of dedicated robot languages (*VAL 2, AML* etc.) that provide some of the facilities of general purpose structured programming techniques. These languages, however, do not have the power or adaptability to create a system flexible enough to enable easy assembly of different products or for product changeover to be implemented quickly. The system we have designed uses a high level language (*Pascal*) and has achieved the desired result of task oriented programming by using the natural generic qualities of assembly to produce a simple and well defined control structure.

The strict definition of the data structure involved the compilation of a comprehensive set of primitive actions that the cell had to perform. This set then provided the source of operations from which the primary tasks involved in assembly could be constructed.

As previously defined these primary tasks are pick up, measure and assemble. Picking up and assembling are closely related and involve similar actions. Both are performed at a predetermined location or at a slight offset from such a location. For example in the case of picking up this occurs if the method of delivery of the component is by pallet, the position of which may have to be initially measured. The assembly process often requires an offset as some components need to be measured in order to determine their alignment in the gripper or to calculate the individuality of the part introduced by manufacturing tolerances.

Simple low cost touch probes are used to perform these measurements. They are designed to give a binary signal and a transition is registered the moment that they are touched, this coupled with the manipulator's ability to latch it's location on such transitions facilitates very accurate measurement of components.

The requirements for measuring a particular component are determined by the method of delivery, the inherent characteristics of the part itself and the way in which it is grasped. The most complicated measuring process that may be needed is if the component is delivered with possible positioning errors in x, y and angular coordinates (the z coordinate is always accurately known), this can be performed most efficiently with just three simple probes. Several standard measuring methods were developed to cater for all the different measurement requirements that we had discovered. The modularity of these tasks being made up of a sequential list of primitive actions enables easy development and integration of new routines to cater for new measurement methods.

Supplementary to the primary tasks are other operations required for assembly. We have determined for this cell that the following operations should be incorporated in the software at the task level:-

(a) feed a pallet;

(b) measure position of a pallet;

(c) change tool;

(d) change fingers;

All these occur prior to the primary tasks. Other supplementary tasks may be easily included to satisfy a user's specific requirements. In the cell part delivery can be performed by a variety of methods, for instance using hopper based feeders or by pallet on a conveyor. In the case of the former the component is often delivered automatically and its positioning is known to within sufficient accuracy that no supplementary tasks are required to pick it up, however the latter case involves the cell controller scheduling the delivery and measurement of pallets and so requires further tasks.

Parts may be assembled using tools such as screwdrivers, nutdrivers etc. and so the ability to change tools between components is necessary. Similarly the ability to change fingers between components is also required.

At this level these are all the programmable tasks, however there is also a task described as discard that is automatically performed by the run time system if a component cannot be assembled due to some error occurance.

As previously described the data structure evolved from analysis of the most reliable methods of implementing error recovery. Separate standard recovery routines were written for each level of the hierarchical structure. Within each routine logical paths are hard coded and the selection of which paths to take are determined by the actuation of various sensors. The basic implementation of the recovery is to 'retry' the previous section of the assembly sequence. Success of the retry enables the assembly to continue, failure forces a decision on whether further recovery action at this level would be successful. If the error is considered to be too serious to be dealt with it is passed to the next level up and a similar sequence is performed. This is a simplification of the process but the data structure lends itself to the establishment of effective recovery in these terms.

The software suite comprises of four packages :-

(a) PROGRAM - an offline assembly sequence programmer;
(b) SIMULATE - a graphic simulation package;
(c) TEACH - a user guide to position teaching;
(d) ASSEMBLE - the run time system;

A diagrammatic interpretation of the software suite is given in Fig. 3.

PROGRAM is a task oriented system programmer that enables the user to create the assembly sequence data offline. It is specifically designed to be programmed by a user whose skills lay in production engineering and assembly techniques rather than robotics. It prompts the user to input all the necessary information required for a product's assembly and enables him to edit this data as he requires. The user is required to input data down to task level, eg. by specifying the type of measurement required to assemble a component, and to only input position labels at the primitive action level. In this way the more complicated usage of the primitive actions is invisible to the user. The task and action data are thus analogous to high level language and machine code in this respect. The output of the programmer is a disk file containing the assembly record (*.ass).

A drawback of modern robot systems is their inability to reveal logical programming errors without running the software online. The graphic simulation package SIMULATE allows the user to visually analyse the sequence of tasks he has created using PROGRAM without having to resort to expensive CAD based robotic simulation packages. In this way all such logical errors can be spotted and PROGRAM used to edit the assembly file and correct them.

The online software package TEACH guides the user through the assembly file and prompts him to move the manipulator to the positions required to perform the sequence. The taught positions are stored in a disk file (*.pos). At present this is performed using a conventional robot teach pendant. Future work will involve the automatic generation of these positions by modelling the cell and product on a CAD system and downloading them directly into the position store.

The run time system ASSEMBLE reads in the assembly data files and schedules the cell operations by communicating with the manipulator controller and the supplementary hardware via the PLC.

Fig. 4 shows the overall structure of the run time system software.

4. Robot Controller

Experience gained from using various robotic systems enabled the development team to specify the exact requirements for a robot controller in the flexible assembly cell. Supplementary to the standard robot control functions were other features that we required, these were :-

(a) to implement robot commands from an external computer;

(b) to interrupt moves in response to sensory inputs;

(c) to latch manipulator positions in response to sensory inputs;

(d) the position of the manipulator to be interrogated by an external computer;

(e) an external computer to alter the path of the manipulator in real time;

The above features were available in some robots but because of their unsuitability in other areas (mainly cost) their use was precluded. Investigations into the hardware options available that would meet the specification were undertaken. Typical modern robot controllers opt for a multiprocessor solution. In the extreme this consists of one processor per axis and a supervisory processor, this option was examined and determined to be too expensive. Finally a single *transputer* was chosen as controller. There were some risks involved in using such industrially unproven technology, but these were offset by the fact that the production costs of a single *transputer* system would be approximately a third of the multiprocessor option.

The trend over the past decade has been for the user interface of robots to become more intelligent , utilising higher level languages with structured programming such as VAL2 and AML. By determining the cell usage as being specific to assembly we were able to take the level of control higher and use task oriented programming. This removed the requirement for an intelligent language at the robot controller level and in it's place a simple instruction set was implemented. The primary commands in the instruction set activate manipulator movement and positioning of the assembly fixture.

The cell controller calls these instructions and always initiates the communication, the robot controller replying with a status message informing the system of the present state of the manipulator, and any other requested information.

The structure of the *transputer* with four serial communication links to the outside world enabled us to use two for communication with the interface hardware and one for communication with the cell controller. The remaining link being left free for further expansion if it was required. Of the two hardware links one is used as a control line and one is used as a data line. The interface hardware consists of:-

(a) digital to analogue converters driving the DC motor amplifiers;

(b) stepper motor control circuits;

(c) counter circuitry that receive the outputs from the motor encoders;

(d) circuitry to enable the latching of counter values on encoder marker pulses or on sensor transitions;

(e) interface circuitry for sensory data received from the manipulator;

The full hardware configuration is shown in Fig. 5.

The use of the *transputer* system involved writing the complete robot control software in *Occam*. The provision of concurrent processing in *Occam* was a favourable feature. The transputer implements multitasking in hardware and so switching between parallel processes occurs very rapidly.

Various configurations and levels of parallelism were experimented with before the most efficient structure was found. The two extremes were to either implement the control as one large sequential process or to execute all the procedures in parallel. The main advantage of using parallel processes in Occam is that the program can be ported with ease onto a system using several transputers. The main disadvantage is that communication between processes must be via channels which is slower than using variables in a sequential system. The compromise adopted was to split the code into two parallel processes where there was a natural break. This enabled the determination of a high priority and a low priority set of routines. Using a high priority process for the servo loops ensures an accurately controlled sample rate. Communication between high and low priority processes is initiated at low priority to avoid upsetting the timing of the servo control. Thus high priority generally only replies to requests for information. Certain instances do require the initiation of communication at high level, in these cases buffering is used.

The *T414 transputer* has 2k bytes of internal RAM. This is significantly faster than the RAM supplied on the development board. The servo loops themselves are the routines that are called most often and, by keeping their code size below 2k (enabling internal storage), fast execution is ensured.

In retrospect the use of the *transputer* for the robot controller has enabled fast development. The main aspects that have helped in this are:-

(a) *Occam's* ability to implement multi tasking operations;

(b) the use of only one language for the entire code - the need to resort to assembler was not necessary;

(c) the use of a single processor and single board system;

(d) *Occam's* operating system enabling a very fast edit, compile and run cycle;

5. Acknowledgements

Our thanks are due to the Director of Research of THORN EMI plc for permission to publish this paper.

6. Conclusions

This paper has described the design and development of a cost effective control system for an integrated flexible assembly cell. The knowledge of assembly acquired prior to the cell's construction has enabled the design of a task oriented programming system. The use of transputer technology as a basis of the robot control resulted in the fast development of a unique controller configuration. The overall system is now commercially available and has already generated interest from production engineers in industry.

Further work on the system will be undertaken to develop a method of generating the positions required for an assembly offline. This will be done by modelling the cell and product on a CAD system. The use of a Televideo PC/AT as cell controller has already enabled the cell to be incorporated on a network and future work in this area is anticipated to involve making it easy to integrate into the industrial environment.

7. References

[1] *Redford, A.H.* "General Purpose Assembly - The Way Ahead". **Proc. 6th ICAA, Birmingham, UK, (May 1985).**

[2] *Nevins, J.L. and Whitney, D.E.* "Computer Controlled Assembly". **Scientific American, (February 1978).**

[3] *Williams, A.M. and Lill, B.H.* "A Commercially Available Flexible Assembly Cell" Proc. **BRA-10, Birmingham, UK, (May 1987).**

[4] *Williams, A.M. et al.* "A Flexible Assembly Cell". **Proc. 6th ICAA, Birmingham, UK, (May 1985).**

[5] *Lee, M.H. et al.* "Research Into Automatic Error Recovery". **Proc. UK Robotics Research, London, UK, (December 1984).**

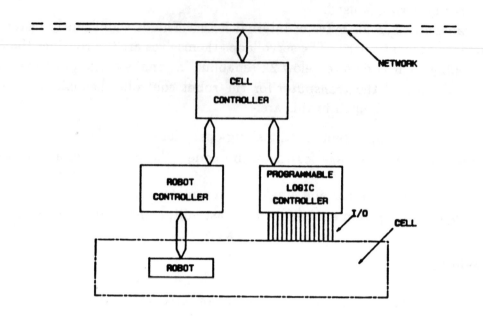

Figure 1a **The System Control Configuration**

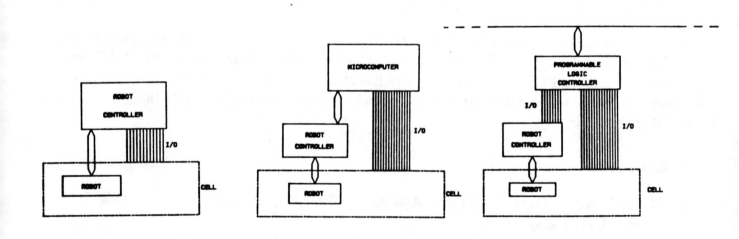

Figures 1b - 1d : **Conventional Robot System Configurations**

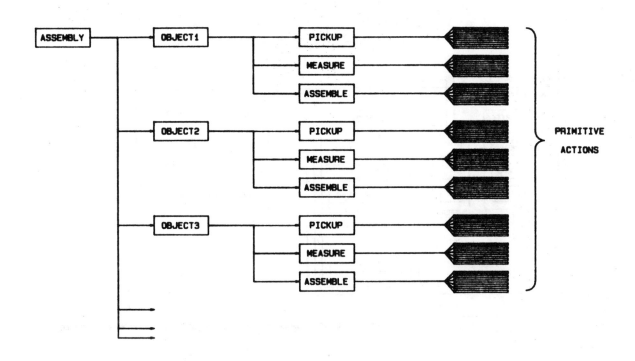

Figure 2 Data Structure for Run-Time System Control

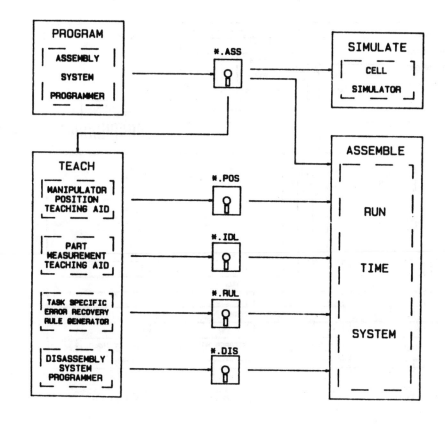

Figure 3 Cell Control Software Suite

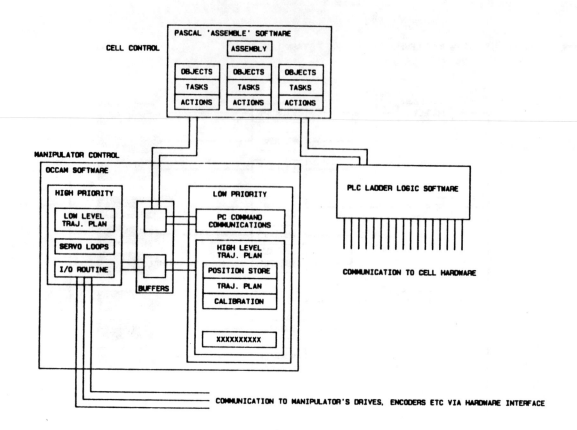

Figure 4 **Run-Time System Software Structure**

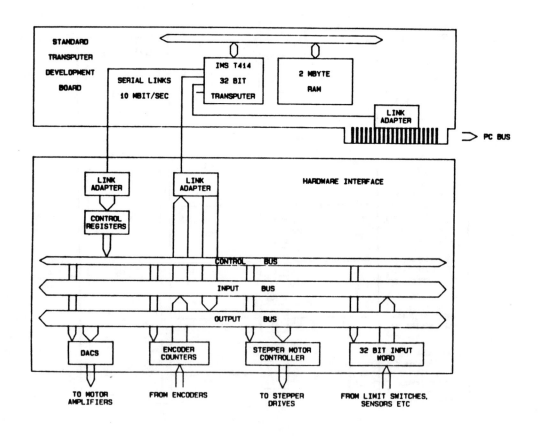

Figure 5 **Hardware Interface Structure**

Proc. 2nd Int. Conf. Machine Control Systems, 175-186
May 1987, © IFS (Conferences) Ltd and authors, ISBN 0-948507-52-7

A flexible automation controller

W Forsyth
Gould Electronics Ltd Industrial Automation Systems, UK

An overview of a Flexible Automation Controller describing
the architecture, programmability and versatility of a unit
suitable for a wide range of motion applications.

Flexible or versatile, words used to describe a controller which would be suitable for application in a wide range of motion environments.

The Gould 3220 Controller is such a unit. It is an amalgamation of computer, programmable controller, and servo amplifier in one assembly.

THE SYSTEM ARCHITECTURE

The 3220 divides into three distinct sections.

(a) The control section
(b) The axis section
(c) The communication bus.

The Control Section

This resides on the left hand side of the chassis and consists of two main circuit modules.

CPU - I/O Module

The module is based around the Z80A microprocessor, running at 4 MHZ. The microprocessor performs many functions, a summary of which best describes the capability of the module.

- Inputs are monitored
- Outputs are turned on or off
- Commands are passed to servo axis modules
- Axis modules are interrogated for information relative to position, status and diagnostics
- Data held in memory is read
- Real time calculations are performed
- The clock timer is read
- Fault conditions are monitored

If a terminal is attached then the CPU module will

- Print information to the terminal
- Prompt for infomation.

RAM - ROM Module

This module provides memory for the CPU module. It is divided into RAM, random access memory for the working program; and ROM, read only memory, in which the 'cyber basic' commands are stored. This latter executive memory is in eprom which is downloaded into the working or system RAM. The system RAM is protected from loss of information by battery backup. The battery backup will provide for up to 2000 hours of power interruption.

The Axis Section

This provides for up to eight axis of motion and fills slots on the right hand side of the chassis. Included in this section is one additional module, the reference/timer unit.

DNP II Axis Card

Each axis card has its own microprocessor, a 16 bit 8088 device running at 8MHZ. Each card processes motion information provided from a brushless resolver for control of brushless servo, conventional DC servo, or hydraulic drive units.

In the case of brushless servo control the axis card calculates commutation information, motor speed and position error. The results of these calculations cause three phase current reference or torque commands to be sent to servo power amplifiers for control of torque and speed and position.

All servo gains are adjusted in software and provide for the setting of velocity loop gain and velocity loop break frequency. Position loop gain, resolution, torque limits, in position bands, as well as independant control of acceleration or deceleration can all be set.

These settings are downloaded from the working or system RAM and allow for axis card replacement without further adjustment or set up.

The axis cards update information every one millisecond relative to motion requirements and in addition provide for diagnostics and information reporting.

The diagnostics capability of the axis card cover

- Loss of feedback from the resolver
- Movement on to hardwired end of travel limits
- Amplifier failure
- Excessive following error
- High RMS current versus time
- Software limits.

The information reporting provides for
- Actual position, speed, torque
- Status of the axis, done or in position
- Axis personality settings.

The Reference/Timer Module

This module provides a common clock signal to all axis cards and also sine and cosine reference signal to each motor resolver.

The feedback signal from the resolver is divided into 16,384 parts per revolution on the axis card (14 bit resolution) and updated every one millisecond. This provides for very high immunity to noise. Position information is held in 32 bit registers to provide for in excess of $\pm$ 120,000 revolutions of travel.

The common clock provides for synchronised and co-ordinated motion between all axis with zero drift between axis.

Battery back up condition is monitored on the reference module with battery charging circuitry maintaining the battery in a good condition.

The Communication Bus

The internal structure of the 3220 uses a common backplane or mother board onto which are plugged the various modules described.

THE PROGRAMMING LANGUAGE

Cyber-Basic - a high level language which combines the capabilities of 'Basic' with motion and machine control functions.

Cyber-Basic will support variable types, arrays, loops, conditional statements, subroutines and error handling routines.

Cyber-Basic is an interpretive language meaning that each line of the program is executed and interpreted as the program runs. This clearly is a potential disadvantage in that the speed of operation may be slow. It can also be an advantage in allowing the program to be altered as development takes place. The speed of operation once a program is written and debugged can be improved by compiling the program. This will speed up program execution by between 10 and 20 times the interpreted times.

To give an idea of execution times:-
A 'move command' may take 9 msec interpreted or 1.1 msec compiled.
A 'halt command' 4 msec interpreted or 0.5 msec compiled.
Mathematical calculations are speeded up but still remain relatively slow. The function 'x = sin (xxx.xxx)' 13 msec. interpreted or 11 msec. compiled.

All this does not detract from the ability of each servo card to maintain and control its own servo operation. Remember the axis card updates velocity - position - torque every millisecond. Once set in motion the DNP II axis card looks after itself within the parameters set and the motion commands downloaded.

CONSTRUCTION OF A 'CYBER-BASIC' PROGRAM

The following elements or sections will require to be considered during program construction.

(a) Initialisation of the system:
    This requires that variables are defined and initial values are set;
    That input and output variables are defined;
    That axis resolution, motor information, servo gains, average and peak torques and trip levels are set;
    That fault handling routines are set up.

(b) Terminal operation:
    When used as an interface between operator and/or progammer a menu printed to the CRT will help in execution.
    Prompts to the screen will invite keyboard input or information.

(c) The Program:
   This will require that input conditions are looked for and
   acted on;
   That any calculations required to describe motion are done;
   That motion commands are generated for execution by the axis
   cards;
   That the status of each axis is checked for proper
   operation.

(d) Error handling:
   It will be necessary to respond to fault conditions or
   interrupts such as an 'E' stop.

If the error occurs in the program then a print of error type by
code or description to a terminal would be useful.
To assist the process of program writing, a version of Ram-Rom
module exists, which contains a 'shell and start up' program,
resident in Rom.
The shell program contains important information which must be
part of and remain in every Cyber Basic program.

The application program is easily 'merged' with the shell
program with a command
X=20: call X
Part of the shell program allows use of a subroutine to
interrogate each DNPII axis card for axis personality details.
This subroutine will form an array of information relative to
any axis.

The 'start up' program, resident in ROM, allows the user without
further programming to check out the functionality of the
system. The start up program contains sufficient subroutines to
allow for rapid development of a usable application program.

To give some idea of the nature of start up the following
subroutines are installed. Any one of these can be incorporated
into the user's program.

Configuration

This module allows different terminal types to be set up to
communicate with 3220.

Diagnostics

This module enables the user to check on the status of any axis.
If used then information will automatically be printed to a
terminal.

Axis Set Up

This module sets up the 'personality constants' of each DNP
axis.

Machine Set Up

This module will allow the user to incorporate other information
from keyboard to change personality constants. This option if
used could provide a useful tool for 'optimisation'.

ADDITIONAL HARDWARE REQUIRED AND AVAILABLE

Outside the main 3220 chassis it will be apparent that additional components are required.

Input/Output Expansion

The standard CPU I/O module allows for 16 inputs and 16 outputs capable of interfacing with optically isolated devices. These are available for DC or AC operation with a wide voltage operating range.
This I/O count can be further expanded with additional modules up to a maximum of 64 I/P and 64 O/P.
An alternative option allowed for working with low voltage DC applications is to use isolated DC input and output cards. Each card supports 32 inputs or 32 outputs. The outputs can drive 24DVC 150MA devices.

Analogue to Digital/D to A Module

This Module allows for interfacing to analogue devices for example 'dancer' devices for control of web tension.

The A to D characteristics are, 12 bit resolution with conversion time of 12 microseconds. There are a maximum of 8 inputs if used as single ended inputs or 4 if used as a differential input. The inputs are limited and protected at $\pm$10VDC. Internal gain steps are programmable in the range of 0.5 to x 32.

The D to A outputs are again limited to 8 channels with 12 bit resolution. This can be configured for voltage or unipolar current outputs.

The voltage output range capability:- $\pm$ 10DVC; $\pm$ 5DVC; $\pm$ 2.5VDC. The current output range capability is:- 0-10MA; 0-20MA; 0-40MA; 0-80MA.

Serial Communication Module

There are four versions of serial communication cards to support defined modes of operation. If we consider general usage then the following examples will define where the module could be used.
Downloading of new part program data from a host computer to the automation controller, receiving status information from the controller relative to diagnostics information or program status.

Communication to a PLC where both the automation controller and the PLC require access to the same I/O information.

Communication to another 3220 controller . Because the SCC module has its own microprocessor and dynamic memory on board data can be stored in registers and flagged to the 3220.These registers will contain information concerning length and type of message. This allows the 3220 to continue operation of the part program without interruption. Similarly information can be collected.

Power Supplies

The 3220 requires its own low voltage supplies. A unit is provided which will run on 110 VAC or 220 VAC and are available for 50HZ or 60HZ operation. Actual voltage range 90VAC to 260 VAC. The units use constant voltage transformers.

Servo Drive Power Amplifiers

The 3220 is designed to operate with brushless servo technology and a range of power amplifiers are available from 5 to 60 amp continuous 10 to 120 amp peak rating.

These operate from a D C Busvoltage and interface with the DNP II modules. PWM techniques are used to support sinusoidal current and voltage operation for brushless motors.

The drive units are protected for short circuits, over and undervoltage operation and excessive temperature. The drive units also provide a visual indication of drive status.

SOFTWARE PACKAGES

Cyber Basic Compiler Software and Offline Development System

This software allows conversion from interpreted format to compiled format which allows the CPU module to run the program directly in machine language. This removes the requirement for on board conversion and speeds up program execution time. The compiled program can be written to ROM for dedicated machine operation.The on-line development system will allow programs to be written away from the 3220 on a IBM PC XT or AT. A minimum of 256K of memory will be required with PC-DOS or MS-DOS version 2.1 or greater operating system.

Cyber-CNC Software

This software can support up to four axis of movement, two spindle outputs and tool changer control. Part program download and upload with part program editor functions are included. The software will allow operational modes that include single step, automatic mode, MDI, and jog functions, linear, point to point, and circular interpolation with gauging, constant surface speed and threading functions.

G and M codes are used for part program construction.
The software uses a subset of EIA-RS 274 programming.

C.ROS Software

This software provides for rapid programming and operation of up to 8 axis of movement. It is menu driven and caters for point learning by direct input from a terminal or by jog of each axis to a point or by manual manipulation if possible to a point.

The software is available to support absolute or non absolute, point to point or circular interpolation.

Full diagnostics of drives, inputs and output status are
maintained and can be accessed via a terminal or hand held
pendant. Operating modes include 'set up' and execution or run.

Programs can be single stepped through their operation.

VERSATILITY OF THE FLEXIBLE AUTMATION CONTROLLER

The controller, by virtue of its ability to be programmed by the
user, and configured with a wide variety of optional modules
makes it a very useful device.

This is further enhanced by giving the user additional options
for application.

Conventional servo drive and motors can be used either by
configuring the DNPII axis card for a single torque command
output or by use of addditional position feedback devices such
as the encoder. The servo drive can then be set up as a current
amplifier or velocity amplifer. The encoder card will output a
bi-directional voltage output to the servo drive.

A servo motor axis card can be supplied to interface with a
stepper drive and motor.

Hydraulic actuators can be driven and the ability to interface
with linear tempsonic position feedback units is provided for.

CONCLUSION

The 3220 is truly an adaptable and flexible system and lends
itself to applications which would include

    Machine loading and unloading
    Robotic systems
    Continuous process lines. Web control.
    Automated assembly.
    Machines or systems which require synchronised motion
    Welding operations
    Cutting
    Milling.

FUTURE DEVELOPMENTS

A flexible automation controller capable of running a maximum of
32 axis with ability to run multiple prorams and/or machines.

Greater input and output capability, up to 1024 points with
serial link to vision systems and interfacing to analogue
devices.

A programmable languauge based on 'C' WHICH WILL ALLOW FOR
'English statement' and 'Ladder' program writing.

Communications via serial ports, modbus and in time map.

APPENDIX

Cyber-Basic Commands

Cyber-Basic provides a large library of commands for automation control. Here are some of the most powerful Cyber-Basic commands:

Motion Control Commands

ACTIVE: Tells Cyber-Basic which axes are used in the program
SETDRV: Enables and disables the motor drive
HOME: Causes an axis to seek the 'home' position
MOVETO: Moves an axis to a specified position
INDEX: Moves an axis a specified distance
EXECUTE: Causes statements to execute in the Deferred Mode
HALT: Terminates a motion statement
SETPOS: Redefines the current position of an axis
START: Starts a continuous move

Axis Personality Commands

MOTORSET: Lets the user configure the 3220 system for various
            types of brushless motors
SETRES: Sets position resolution
SETRIG: Sets the rate loop break frequency
SETPRG: Sets the rate loop proportional gain
SETAC: Sets the acceleration time constant
SETAVG: Sets the average torque fault trip level
SETEOT: Sets programmable end-of-travel limits
SETTORQ: Sets the torque limit

Input/Output Control:

GETIN: Updates the image array that stores status of the
            control inputs
SETOUT: Updates the control outputs

Fault and Error Handling Commands

SETCTL: Enables or disables the control interrupts
SETFLT: Enables or disables the axis fault interrupts

Axis Status Commands

GETDIAG: Gets the diagnostic status of an axis
GETPARAM: Reports the personality constants of any given axis
GETPOS: Obtains the value of the current axis position
TESTSTAT: Tests the status of the axis or axes specified
GETABS: Returns the absolute position of the resolver

Other Commands

GETTIME: Returns the time elapsed since the last timer reset
             (in hundredths of a second)
IOSYSTEM: Permits use of up to four serial ports and allows the
             terminal and auxiliary serial devices to be redefined
             in Cyber-Basic
LOCK: Locks out or unlocks the keyboard on the operator's
             terminal, to permit user input only under program
             control
RESETTIME: Resets the internal clock timer to zero
COS: Computes the cosine of a numeric expression
INKEYS$:   Returns a character from the keyboard
INPUT: Inputs data to the program
PRINT: Prints one or more items on the CRT display

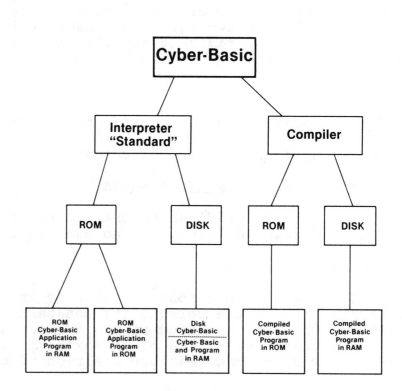

Cyber-Basic Configurations

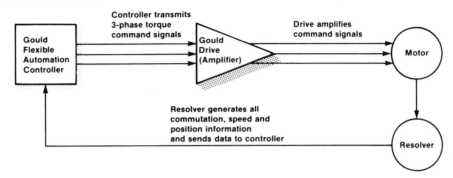

DNP Servo Control Systems

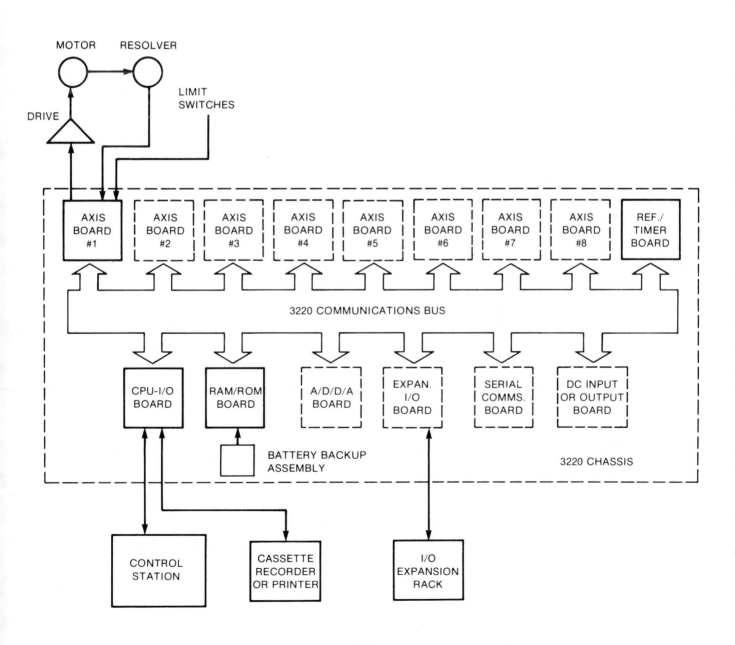

Proc. 2nd Int. Conf. Machine Control Systems, 187-194
May 1987, © IFS (Conferences) Ltd and authors, ISBN 0-948507-52-7

Off-the-shelf manufacturing systems software

P J Cornwell
Renishaw Controls Ltd, UK

ABSTRACT

Two principal factors govern the improvement of the productivity of machine tool systems. These are the technology that can be applied to setting up and proving part programs and the rate of production of 'good' parts. This paper addresses the second case of improving throughput of the machine shop reviewing the contribution that can be made by computer integration techniques.

Introduction

Advanced Manufacturing Technology, Computer Integrated Manufacturing and many other terms and philosophies have been discussed widely as matters of some urgency during the last four years. CIM certainly employs computer communications quite heavily, even though real installations are often frustrated by the different data connections supported by vendors of all the equipment that goes to make up a factory.

The MAP initiative in industrial communications has led to almost as much publicity, discussion and urgent committee work as the whole of the CIM movement recently, but commercial MAP tools and solutions are still few and far between. Many reasons can be identified for this slow rate of uptake, including high connection cost and rate of consolidation of standards. Shifting requirements arising from a growing awareness of the need for local real-time communication performance have also clouded the issue.

However there is one important goal of the MAP initiative in supporting CIM which should not be forgotten; that is the potential to develop MAP-based software systems for the control of manufacturing plants, which are independent of the equipment selected for the site. If this could be achieved, then manufacturing software systems can be made portable,and re-used in different plants with a considerable reduction in the amount of custom software for 'system integration' which has to be written.

Transportable Control Software using MAPs MMS Protocol

MAP's Manufacturing Message Services (MMS) Protocol is powerful enough to allow truly 'off-the-shelf' manufacturing control software systems to be designed. It represents a significant contribution to the fundamental tools available to build CIM systems, because it constitutes a Universal Command Language able to describe manufacturing operations in a way which transcends vendor-specific differences in equipment. The challenge that now faces us is to implement software systems which use MMS effectively.

The real barrier to such work has been that no existing equipment supports the level of rich communication facilities that MMS requires. This extends beyond the communication protocol interface, to the actual facilities supported by equipment to a remote computer program. Sadly, many of the MAP interfaces now available provide little more than the facilities traditionally available over RS232 and similar connections.

Consequently, an equally or possibly more demanding challenge is to implement portable MMS production control software for existing equipment, either already installed or being designed or commissioned now. Given the lifetime of machinery, especially in the metal-cutting industries, this will remain a challenge for many years.

One notable exception which has succeeded in implementing a complex machining cell using MMS is ESPRIT's CNMA project. The Computer Network for Manufacturing Applications (CNMA) programme uses production control software running on a collection of 'host' computers supplied by several vendors, connected by common communication networks to a machine tool, robots and an automated guided vehicle.

CNMA uses a faithfull implementation of the MMS specification (which they have published) and the contractors of the project have built new MMS interfaces into the various CNC, robot and programmable logic controllers. The system was demonstrated successfully at the Hannover exhibition recently.

Requirements of a MAP-based Machining Control System.

The goal of the work reported here was not to control quite so sophisticated a flexible manufacturing system. Instead, the ability to use existing unmodified machinery was more important, and we concentrated on developing generic, portable software packages in contrast to a specific cell controller. This allowed us to explore the feasibility of using MMS technology to improve the throughput of an existing facility.

In particular it was hoped that a MAP communications system could be used to improve the efficiency and security of part program transfer between machine controls and host computers and reduce the machine memory limitation on large programs: particularly those using additional in-cycle-gauging instructions. As important a goal was the addition of 'health monitoring' and access to inspection information gathered on machines, to lengthen periods of confident unmanned operation. This has the effect of acquiring feedback information to apply in Statistical Process Control of the manufacturing cycle as a whole. Such a control software package can then be used for quantitative evaluation of the payback expected from investment in computer integration. Because of the independence from machine specific communication interfaces, there are no hidden costs in system integration. The resulting package provides a truely generic off-the-shelf MAP solution to improve throughput in this particular class of machine shop problems.

The Manufacturing Message Service (MMS)

A key to being able to implement transportable communications software for manufacturing control then, lies in a Universal Command Language appropriate to the communication needs of manufacturing systems, and backed by International standardisation. Such a standard is now maturing in the form of the Manufacturing Message Service developed by the IEEE and which is under review in ISO. MMS will be completely specified by the MAP 3.0 specification during the next year. However, its definition has been formalised using a computing language grammar called Abstract Syntax Notation (ASN1.) and so the sections that are stable now can easily be expanded as the other features near completion.

Agreement between vendors for a protocol standard at the application level (MMS is a layer 7 protocol) of the OSI seven layer model is far more important than adoption of common lower protocols, since inter-network relays (bridges, routers or gateways) can always be used to resolve incompatibility problems in the lower layers. Such relays are becoming readily available and will play a vital part in glueing together the industrial communications systems of the future.

MMS is, and needs to be, a sophisticated and versatile language, so that it can control the many kinds of operations needed in different installations and manufacturing tasks. Individual machine controls do not need to implement all of the MMS commands though, nor must they support all the functions of particular commands. The MMS protocol provides for such variations in complexity to allow the integration of older machines. Higher functionality equipment interfaces will need the flexibility to adapt to the needs of less sophisticated ones.

All this implies that the communication interface to equipment supporting MAP/MMS-compatible host software systems needs to be significantly more intelligent than is available at the current time. In fact the structure of machine control systems would have to be substantially revised to make available facilities previously inaccessible from a communication interface. This has been borne out by the CNMA implementation. However, the network connection cost had to be commensurate with retro-fit to existing capital-depreciated equipment, in the context of our goals in this programme, while providing the local real-time performance for Statistical Process Control.

A MAP/MMS Communication Adapter Approach to CIM

Consequently, a Communication Adapter approach was adopted, such that 'black box' interfaces were programmed to provide a MMS connection for each of the different equipment types employed. In this way, the goal of providing uniform

MMS network connections was achieved without custom work on the machine controls. Features such as health monitoring can be added using sensors attached directly to the communication adapter, while their data is made available using the MMS interface to the machine as if that facility were implemented directly by the machine control. Simple part program transfer is accomplished using the machine RS232, or similar, interface from the communication adapter, to provide an MMS DNC facility which can support the streaming of large part programs as discussed earlier.

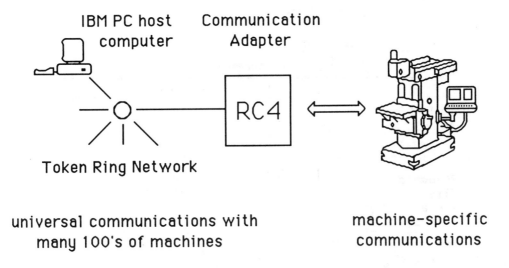

IBM PC host computer   Communication Adapter

RC4

Token Ring Network

universal communications with
many 100's of machines

machine-specific
communications

RC4 translates between universal MMS network
commands and individual machine tools, robots,
instruments and sensors

The network physical media chosen was IBM Token Ring (IS8802.5) because of its high performance and reliability in the face of failure of cabling and individual machine connections. A fibre optic media option is also available for significantly increased channel reliability in harsh environments. In addition Token Ring is supported by a large body of software for network file management and direct connections with large site mainframe computers. This choice also had significant impact on the cost per connection of the 'RC4' communication adapter, because of the 802.5 chip set solution now available in high volumes for the IBM-LAN™ connection to Personal Computers. An INMOS Transputer™ was used on the RC4 in order to provide sufficient processing power to execute the MMS protocol interface and the translation function between MMS and the particular attached equipment.

While the implementation of each of these MMS communication adapters represents significant engineering investment, most if not all of the work goes to form a generic MMS adapter for the machine in question, which can be re-used whenever that machine is encountered again. In this way the effort is non-recurring and a library of standard interface products can be built up.

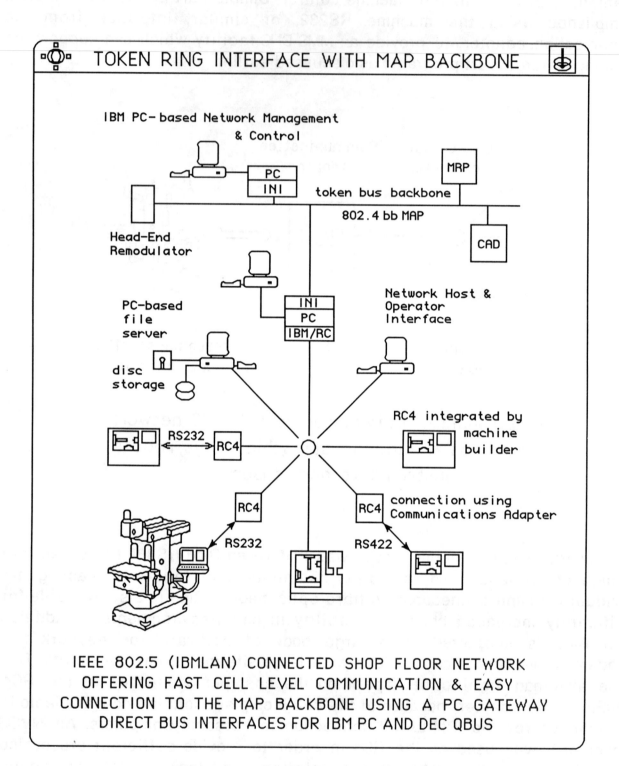

TOKEN RING INTERFACE WITH MAP BACKBONE

IBM PC-based Network Management & Control

PC
INI

token bus backbone

802.4 bb MAP

MRP

CAD

Head-End Remodulator

INI
PC
IBM/RC

Network Host & Operator Interface

PC-based file server

disc storage

RS232 — RC4

RC4 integrated by machine builder

RC4 RS232

RC4 RS422

connection using Communications Adapter

IEEE 802.5 (IBMLAN) CONNECTED SHOP FLOOR NETWORK
OFFERING FAST CELL LEVEL COMMUNICATION & EASY
CONNECTION TO THE MAP BACKBONE USING A PC GATEWAY
DIRECT BUS INTERFACES FOR IBM PC AND DEC QBUS

With these basic building blocks in place, the design of truely portable production management software systems becomes very structured. Initially Personal Computer-based packages have been developed to evaluate the principles of MMS system design. These have been particularly convenient because of the support available from vendors such as IBM and Industrial Networks Inc. for both Token Ring and (IS8802.4) Token Bus media connections for the PC. An internal installation at Renishaw Metrology Ltd. has used such a PC-based system in full-time CNC manufacturing operations since September-October 1986. It is notable that an identical PC-based software package has subsequently been installed and used successfully with industrial robots at Austin Rover Group.

More recently, multiple local RC4 networks using the Token Ring have been successfully connected using the Token Bus MAP backbone. The extension of DNC and Statistical Process Control facilities across the backbone, while still using the same MMS production management software systems is an encouraging indication of the portability of this approach, while addressing representative plant-level control problems. It is hoped that an accurate assessment of the rate of return on investment will be possible in the near future as the cost of a complete installation becomes available. Probably the most important lesson that we have learned from the exercise is that it does indeed appear to be possible to design truely generic systems solutions for this class of problem, for installation and commissioning off-the-shelf.

ACKNOWLEDGEMENTS

I should like to acknowledge the direct support of the Renishaw Controls Group.

REFERENCES

MAP USER GROUP   The Society of Manufacturing Engineers, Manufacturing Automation Protocol (MAP) Reference Specification

EIA/IE-31/1393   Electrical Industries Association, Manufacturing Message Service for Bi-directional Transfer of Digitally Encoded Information

CNMA Consortium, Commission of the European Communities.   CNMA Implementation Guide

APPLICATIONS

Proc. 2nd Int. Conf. Machine Control Systems, 195-206
May 1987, © IFS (Conferences) Ltd and authors, ISBN 0-948507-52-7

How to improve a pressline efficiency through modern control strategy

D Hellström
SattControl AB, Sweden

INTRODUCTION

The content of this paper is based on several pressline installations at
the VOLVO and SAAB-SCANIA manufacturing plants in Sweden. The degree of
control sophistification differs from small PLC controller tasks up to the
highest level of what is possible with today's advanced PLC controllers.
This, the most modern control technology with LAN communication and cell
controller configuration is used in a complete new pressline installation
at SAAB-SCANIA in Trollhättan. The pressline consists of seven eccentric
presses of the latest model and is disigned to operate with a minimum of
human control.

Quality increases by the fact that the die setting paramethers may be be fine-tuned and stored as a recipe for any sheet-metal used. Also the overall control of the pressline, statistical data handling and trend curve display will positively affect the quality.

Number of stops decreases as the overall control of the line is co-ordinated and more accurate. The possibilities for preventing maintinance and display facilities given by the cell controller also contributes to lower number of stops.

Motivation of the production staff may be increased through training courses in PLC technic. As a result of this and the user-friendly control systems many of the stops which earlier required involvement of the maintinance staff now can be handled by the production staff itself. This in turn gives lower stop time ratio, higher quality and a more competent personel.

Traditional control of a pressline

A pressline consists of a number of presses (Illustration No.1). In an automized pressline each press has in- and output loaders and some kind of mechanized feeding system between them. Traditionally each of these parts has its own control system. In addition to this many of the internal press functions have had separate control systems, because of the very different control demands as fast analog control loops, exact positioning and digital interlock functions (Illustration No. 2 and 3).

Because of the many different control systems in a pressline with this old concept, all new settings caused of a change of dies required very well trained personnel and proportionately long time.

Modern technology sets new standards for control

Many of today's PLC systems have the ability of controlling both analog and digital signals. Some of them also have the additional option for advanced positioning control. The requirements on a press control system are very unic. SattControl therefore have developed certain hardware and software modules for the standard PLC systems in order to fulfill all control demands. As a result of this one press with all its feeding systems is to be controlled by one single PLC (Illustration No.4 and 5). In a modern press there might be up to 1000 in - and output signals connected to the control system.

All necessary settings for different dies are stored in each PLC. A die change and start-up is therefore made very quickly. Programming of new settings, supervision and maintenance will also be made more efficient.

Dan Hellström

Higher productivity in a pressline with sophisticated control systems?

There are in a pressline several items which can be affected in a positive way by using advanced control systems. Some of the most important ones may be found below:

Stop times duration caused by electrical malfunctions will decrease because of the integration of all control tasks to one single system (PLC controller) with built in error tracing facilities. These facilities also will be very helpful by examination of mechanical defects or faults in the external electrical wiring. - Especially the stop intervalls caused by the

Die change time will drastically decrease using PLC controller solution for the press control. One of the most time consuming tasks by die change is all the different adjustments of the die, press and balance forces as well as, positioning of loaders/unloaders and conveyors. In a PLC controller all necessary paramethers for different dies may be stored. A simple operators command will give the complete settings for a whole pressline. By older control technics all subsystem at each press had to be separately adjusted sometimes causing hours of time obtaining a perfect stamping result for a pressline.

The number of rejected plates will decrease as a direct result of the fast and exact readjustment of the pressline by die change.

Maintinance will be much more efficient by using the error tracing facilities of the PLC systems. Additional power for main-tinance will be added by also installing a cell controller super-vising the complete pressline. By studying trend curves and historical data collected from different parts of the line, many faults will be traced down before they would occur.

The flexibility of a pressline controlled by the PLC and cell controller solution will increase in a high degree by the fact that the die change time is shorten to only minutes for a com-plete line. This gives the possibility of shorter production rates for each die setting and more frequent die changes. The storing of all the die settings in the cell controller also gives the oppotunity of changing the settings between the presses. This may for instance be used in the case of one press breakdown. The die in this press together with all setting paramethers, may be moved to another press if the plate in production not has to be stamped by every press in the line. In a case like this the faulty press will simply be bypassed.

Dan Hellström

Cell Controller and Local Area Network give a new dimension to the control strategy

For exchange of necessary control signals between the PLC systems no LAN architecture is needed.

The need, however, grows up when specifying flexibility in Man-Machine communication. And this is the matter of course when introducing a Cell Controller. A Cell Controller drastically increases the over-all control of the pressline. For instance:

- All die changes may be programmed and stored in the Cell Controller.

- Advanced colour graphics may be used for supervision and programming.

- All functions in the pressline are supervised and monitored in one system.

- Historical data with trend curves may be stored and calculated.

- Sheet-metal measuring gives data for registration of different sheet-metal batches.

- Easy connection to the factory computer central with for instance MAP.

- Automatic stop time registration.

- Simplified maintenance.

- Production planning.

- Basic data for wages and bonus.

Simplified Man-Machine communication

By introducing the concept "one press, one PLC" automatically the Man-Machine communication is more uniform. One CRT terminal is connected to each PLC giving all control and supervision possibilities for one press. Through the LAN and Cell Controller there will be possibilities for reaching data also in other press control systems. With one terminal in each press and one connected to the Cell Controller, the operators and maintenance technicians have all possibilities for efficient control of the total pressline with dynamic operator tools in each part of the line.

Conclusion

Old presslines can be updated and new lines should be equipped with modern PLC systems, LAN and Cell Controllers. The investment will rapidly pay off by considerable increased productivity, in some cases up to 20 percent or even more. (Illustration no. 8).

Dan Hellström

PRESSLINE

PRESS CONTROL AND SUPERVISION

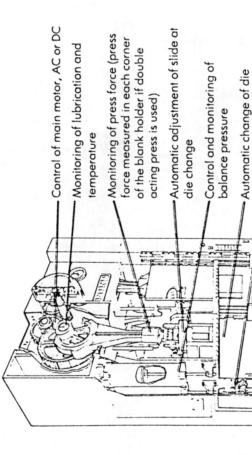

- Control of main motor, AC or DC
- Monitoring of lubrication and temperature
- Monitoring of press force (press force measured in each corner of the blank holder if double acting press is used)
- Automatic adjustment of slide at die change
- Control and monitoring of balance pressure
- Automatic change of die
- Hydraulic control
- Monitoring of oil pressure and temperature

- Control of press loader and unloader
- Automatic control of loader/unloader settings at die changes
- Control of transfer units between presses
- Control of destackers
- Production control
- Alarm monitoring
- Operating reports

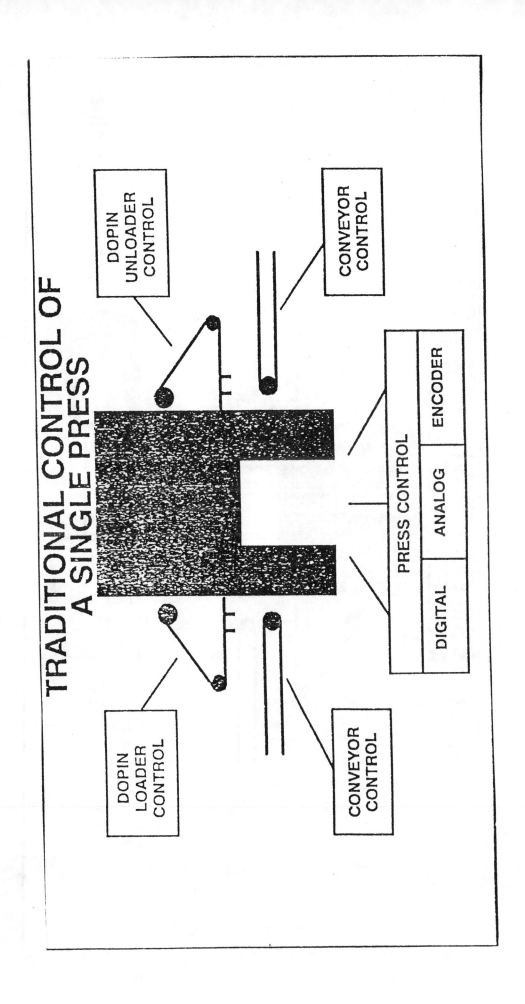

TRADITIONAL CONTROL OF A SINGLE PRESS

DOPIN UNLOADER CONTROL

CONVEYOR CONTROL

PRESS CONTROL

DIGITAL | ANALOG | ENCODER

DOPIN LOADER CONTROL

CONVEYOR CONTROL

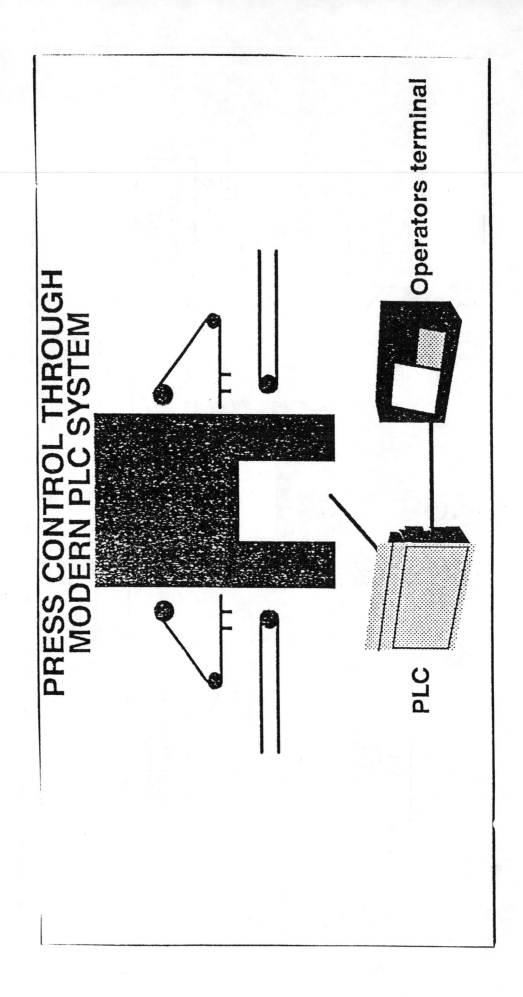

PRESS CONTROL THROUGH MODERN PLC SYSTEM

Operators terminal

PLC

PRESSLINE CONTROL

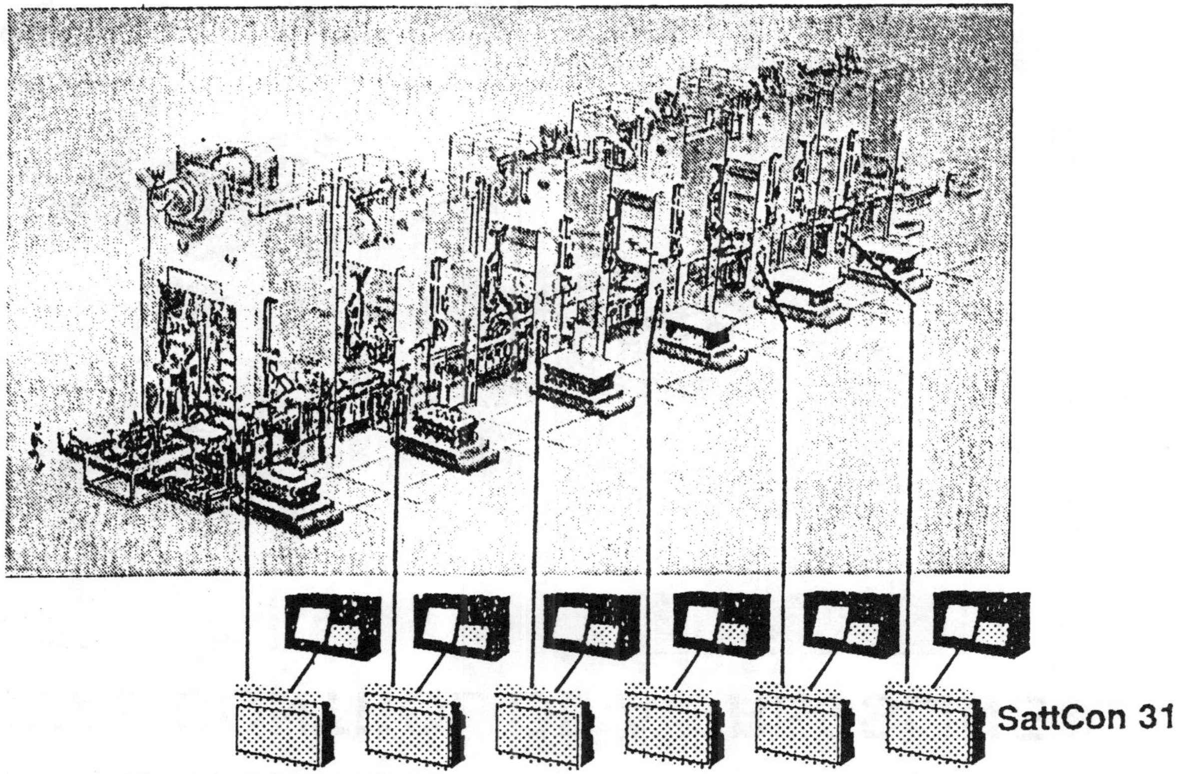

SattCon 31

203

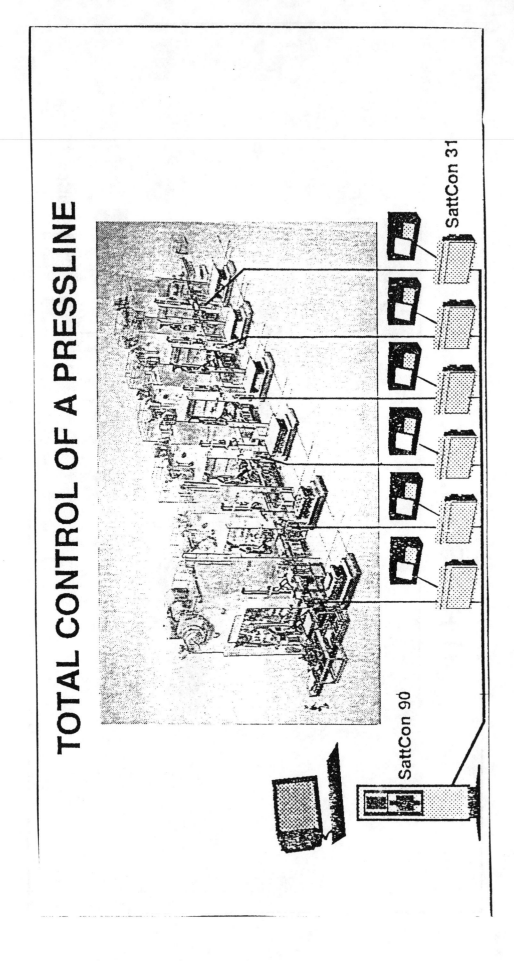

TOTAL CONTROL OF A PRESSLINE

SattCon 31

SattCon 90

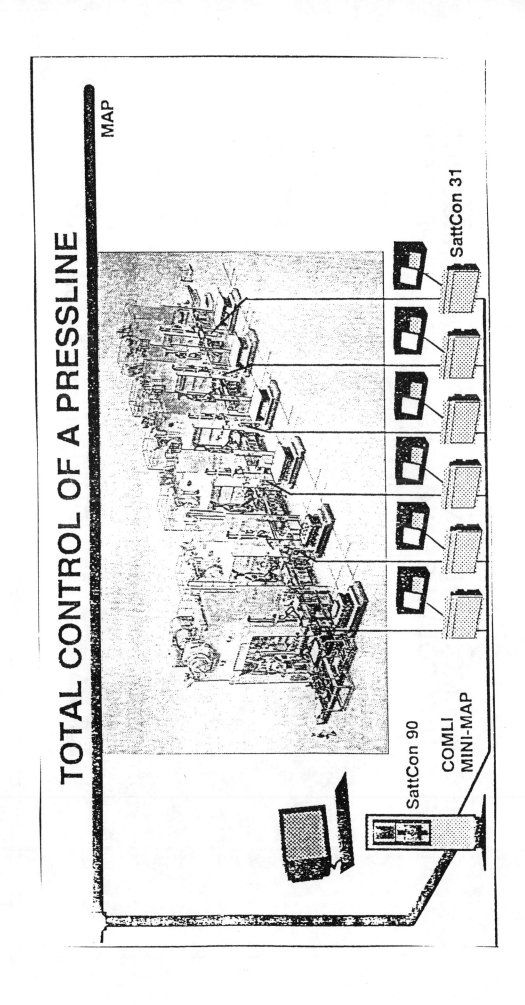

TOTAL CONTROL OF A PRESSLINE

MAP

SattCon 31

SattCon 90

COMLI
MINI-MAP

THROUGH MODERN CONTROL SYSTEM A PRESSLINE EFFICIENCY COULD BE INCREASED WITH 20 PERCENT ...OR MORE

- Shorter stop times
- Higher flexibility
- Minimized die change times
- Simplified maintinance
- Higher quality
- Lower number of stops
- Minimum of rejected plates
- Increased motivation

20%

Proc. 2nd Int. Conf. Machine Control Systems, 207-218
May 1987, © IFS (Conferences) Ltd and authors, ISBN 0-948507-52-7

The control of a programmable three roll bender in the flexible production of colliery arches

S J Williams
Cambridge Control Ltd
and
B Mason
Caledonian Mining Company Ltd, UK

ABSTRACT

A flexible manufacturing system incorporating off-line programming has been developed for colliery roadway supports. A new bending machine and control system lies at the heart of the system. The controller was developed using the latest computer-aided design techniques to embody robotic control design principles. This paper describes the principle of operation, the development of the control system, highlighting the role of CAD software tools and the hardware system implementation.

INTRODUCTION

The Caledonian Mining Company is a major supplier of colliery arches to British Coal. The arches are steel I sections (typically 152x127 or 127x114mm) and up to 15m in length. Two typical arches are shown in figure 1. Arches are currently bent using fixed forming machines capable of bending one arch profile only. These machines can supply the needs of British Coal for standard arches; however there is a growing requirement for non-standard arches with up to 100 different profiles needed to suit different tunnel requirements.

Even in the economically difficult period of the coal strike, Caledonian, a well-established civil engineering contractor in the coal industry, maintained a policy of diversification into manufacture and invested heavily in automation. The fixed forming lines were completely automated and controlled using PLC's. On these production lines beams are cut to length, punched, and fed into the forming machines under PLC control. Once a beam is bent it is cut by two PLC-controlled saws and finally stacked in sections using a hydraulic crane.

In order to produce non-standard arches a flexible manufacturing system was required. It was decided to base the system on a three roll bending machine.

THE IMPACT OF TECHNOLOGY : A NEW MACHINE

Figure 2 shows a schematic of the machine. Each roll is approximately 0.65m across. The third roll is driven by a hydraulic ram causing it to rotate about a pivot. The rotation about the pivot determines the instantaneous curvature imparted to the beam at roller 2. The rollers themselves are driven in rotation by hydraulic motors through 4:1 reduction gearboxes. By cooordinating the position control of the ram and the speed of the beam through the machine any beam profile may be produced.

THE IMPACT OF NEW TECHNOLOGY : A NEW CONTROL SYSTEM

Caledonian had developed the mechanical design of the bending machine prior to March 1986 when Cambridge Control Ltd. were invited to design and implement a control system for it.

The Objective : An Off-Line Programmed System

A key requirement was the need to program the mechanical system using a computer-aided beam design program. Beam profiles had to be achieved within a tight geometric tolerance. An advanced control system was designed based on robot control system design principles whereby geometric and servo control are closely coupled. The controller required advanced algorithms and advanced hardware to be developed.

The role of CACSD tools in design

The increase in available computing power is impacting not only the applications control engineer making him capable of implementing very sophisticated hardware control systems, but also the control system _designer_. Interactive computer-aided design software is revolutionising modelling and control design. Complex dynamic systems in the process, aerospace and automotive fields may now be simulated on a computer. Automatic control systems may now be designed to guarantee stability and performance even for systems with many inputs and outputs. The key is that CAD software makes the designer highly flexible and efficient. The burden of complex mathematical manipulation and computation is shifted to the computer leaving the designer free to exercise his engineering insight. Cambridge Control Ltd. is a company committed to the application and marketing of CACSD software and advanced control techniques.

FLEXIBILITY : THE KEY TO THE NEW BEAM MANUFACTURING PROCESS

Essentially, the bending machine lies at the heart of a flexible manufacturing system for colliery arches. As with the fixed forming lines beams arriving from British Steel are cut to length and punched under PLC control. The punched holes define the positions of sawcuts which are made later in the process. Typically an arch is cut into three sections during bending so that it can be assembled conveniently underground. The infeed to the bending machine is under PLC control. Once the beam is datumed in the machine, control is passed to the new system developed by Cambridge Control which controls the bending process. The PLC supervisor monitors the process and handles the coordination of a computer-controlled saw which tracks the beam in-process and makes cuts when appropriate. On exiting the machine, beams are transported using a conveyor table and are stacked with a crane in preparation for fishplate welding before transport to the colliery.

THE NEW CONTROL SYSTEM : HIGH-LEVEL DESCRIPTION

New beam profiles are defined in a CAD system in terms of height, leg splay distance etc. The CAD system converts this data into a desired beam curvature profile (see figure 3). Curvature is defined as a function of the chord length (s).

The new control system then converts this desired profile into torque and velocity setpoints for the servo system. We will now describe the design of the new control system bringing out the role of CACSD tools.

DYNAMIC SIMULATION OF THE BENDING MACHINE AND SERVO CONTROL SYSTEM DESIGN

Identification

Dynamic modelling of systems can be based on the physical derivation of the governing dynamic equations or on the 'identification' of models using experimental data acquired from the system under investigation. Occasionally a combination of both techniques may be used. Identification software _automatically_ generates dynamic models for use in system modelling and for control design by analysing process input and output data (see figure 4).

Identification is a completely general technique and is being used increasingly in a number of applications. Cambridge Control Ltd. use the 'Identification Toolbox' developed by the Mathworks Inc. in the USA for identification of models. This is a comprehensive set of identification algorithms which Cambridge Control market and support in the UK and Europe.

Identification experiments were performed on each of the three rollers and the hydraulic ram. Data was collected using an acquisition system devloped in-house and available commercially. Velocity and differential pressure measurements were logged for each roller and position for the ram. The open-loop (uncontrolled) responses of the system were characterised by two resonances. One was the hydraulic resonance, which is shown as a damped oscillation in the pressure responses (see figure 5); the other is a high frequency gearbox resonance which dominates the velocity response (see figure 6). The latter, if excited, would cause poor controlled performance and machine wear. It was essential for the control system to overcome this problem.

Dynamic Simulation

The linear dynamic parameters yielded by the Identification software were used to assist the development of a dynamic simulation for the bending machine in the TSIM simulation language. TSIM is a gneral-purpose nonlinear dynamic simulator widely used in the aerospace industry which is now finding application in other industries such as process control, automotive and hydraulic systems applications. It is marketed and supported by Cambridge Control Ltd. Nonlinear dynamic models of the hydraulic system were developed incorporating the dynamics of the servo-valves, hydraulic motors, gearboxes and ram. This enabled a full assessment of the capabilities of the hydraulic system to be made. The next stage of simulator development was to incorporate the complex geometry of the machine.

In order to evaluate the third roll pivot rotation (and thus ram extension) we adopted the following conceptual approach. Instead of considering processing the beam through a fixed machine we imagined moving the roll set around the finished profile, while making an allowance for springback (see figure 7). The geometric configuration was evaluated for every 4mm of chord length and the reference frame then transformed back to the base coordinate system fixed to the real machine.

A consideration of geometric configuration and the maximum plastic bending moment of a particular section yields the necessary torques that must be applied to the rolls. Desired torques were calculated so as to minimise the risk of slip occuring. Torque demands for rolls 1 and 2 were calculated for every 4mm of chord length. TSIM enabled the simulation and rapid evaluation of the algorithms calculating the torques and geometric configuration (see figure 8). As is described later these same algorithms were eventually encoded in the system controller.

Dynamic simulation also enabled the servo controllers to be evaluated. These controllers were designed in the control design package CLADP.

Control Design

CLADP, the Cambridge Linear Analysis and Design Program, was initially developed at the University of Cambridge under Professor A.G.J. MacFarlane : it is now being marketed and supported by Cambridge Control Ltd. CLADP can be used to design controllers for systems with many inputs and many outputs, i.e. it is a **multivariable** control design package. It has a wide user-base and has been applied in the process, aerospace, automotive, power and robotics industries. CLADP makes use of graphics to assist the designer. Figure 9 shows the Bode plot generated by CLADP for the open loop transfer function of the hydraulic motor driving the third roller (the transfer function was obtained from the model produced by the identification software). Figure 10 shows the open loop transfer function for the motor and designed controller. Note that integral action has been incorporated, the hydraulic resonance has been suppressed and increased 'roll-off' introduced at high frequencies to minimise the effect of the gearbox resonance. A sample period of 3ms was used for the discrete controller design. CLADP is equally at home in the continuous or discrete time domains.

Two torque controllers were designed for rolls 1 and 2 and a velocity controller for roll 3. The controllers were tested and proven in the TSIM machine simulation and then implemented in hardware. The performance of the velocity control tracking a desired trajectory during the bending of an actual beam profile is shown in figure 11. Note that the tracking performance is very good and the resonant gearbox oscillations have been heavily suppressed. It should be emphasised that the controllers which were designed are more sophisticated than standard PID controllers and thus require more sophisticated hardware for implementation.

SUMMARY OF CACSD DESIGN

1) Identification of dynamic models for dynamic simulation and control design.
2) System simulation to test dynamic performance.
3) Servo control system design.
4) Test of controller in simulation.
5) Implementation of the control system in hardware.

Figure 12 shows a diagram of the CACSD environment used in the control design for the bending machine. This environment is supported by software products from Cambridge Control Ltd. The CACSD environment assisted in the efficient design of a sophisticated control system which is comprised of high-level geometric and low-level servo control. Cambridge Control Ltd. then implemented this design in hardware.

STRUCTURE OF THE BENDING MACHINE CONTROLLER

Geometric Control

This is handled by a dedicated microprocessor (Motorola 68000). It interfaces to the profile definition CAD system and converts a desired curvature profile to setpoints for torques on rolls 1 and 2, angular velocity of roll 3, and desired chord speed for each 4mm of chord length. It thus generates a setpoint table and for a beam of length 15m this table has almost 4000 rows. The table generation is done off-line.

An incremental encoder measures chord length in-process and this measurement is used to interpolate the setpoint table on-line and generate demands for the servo system which runs on another 68000.

Servo Control

Every 12ms demands are passed to the four servo control loops running in the low-level 68000. The servo controllers have a sample time of 3ms and interpolate their demands appropriately. A diagram of the overall system is shown in figure 13.

Sawcuts

At selected points along the profile the bending machine stops for sawcuts. A stop is achieved by detecting optically a hole in the beam webb and using this to trigger a ramp down for a sawcut. The ramp-down is automatically incorporated into the setpoint demand table. The saw is controlled by the supervisory PLC and was constructed by Mr. J. Vince (an associate of the Company).

Results

The bending machine has now been in production for 4 months. It has been demonstrated that it can bend successfully all the beam profiles demanded of it within the specification required. It represents a breakthrough in the flexible manufacture of colliery arches and a triumph of CACSD in the development of control systems.

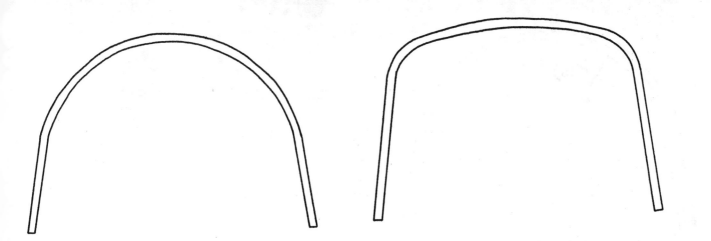

Figure 1   Typical Profiles

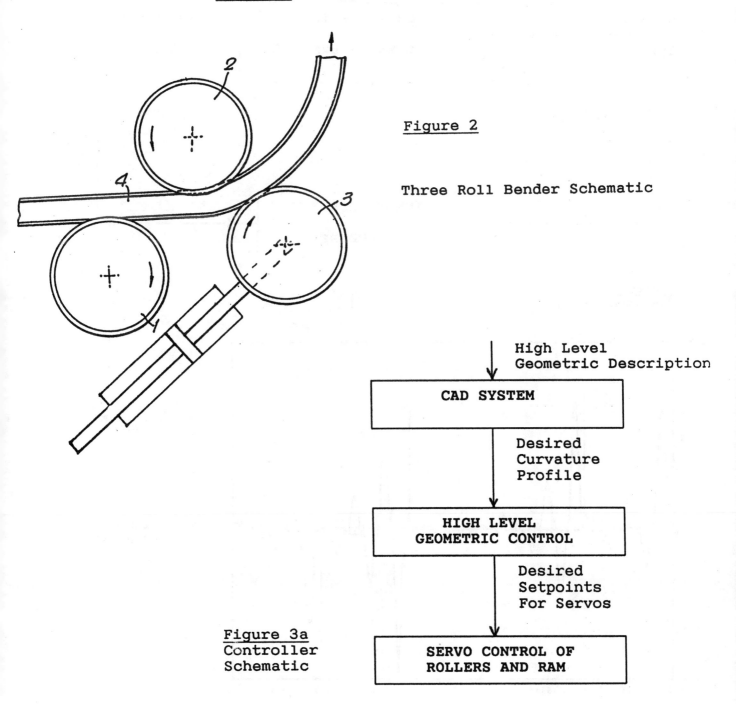

Figure 2

Three Roll Bender Schematic

High Level
Geometric Description

CAD SYSTEM

Desired
Curvature
Profile

HIGH LEVEL
GEOMETRIC CONTROL

Desired
Setpoints
For Servos

Figure 3a
Controller
Schematic

SERVO CONTROL OF
ROLLERS AND RAM

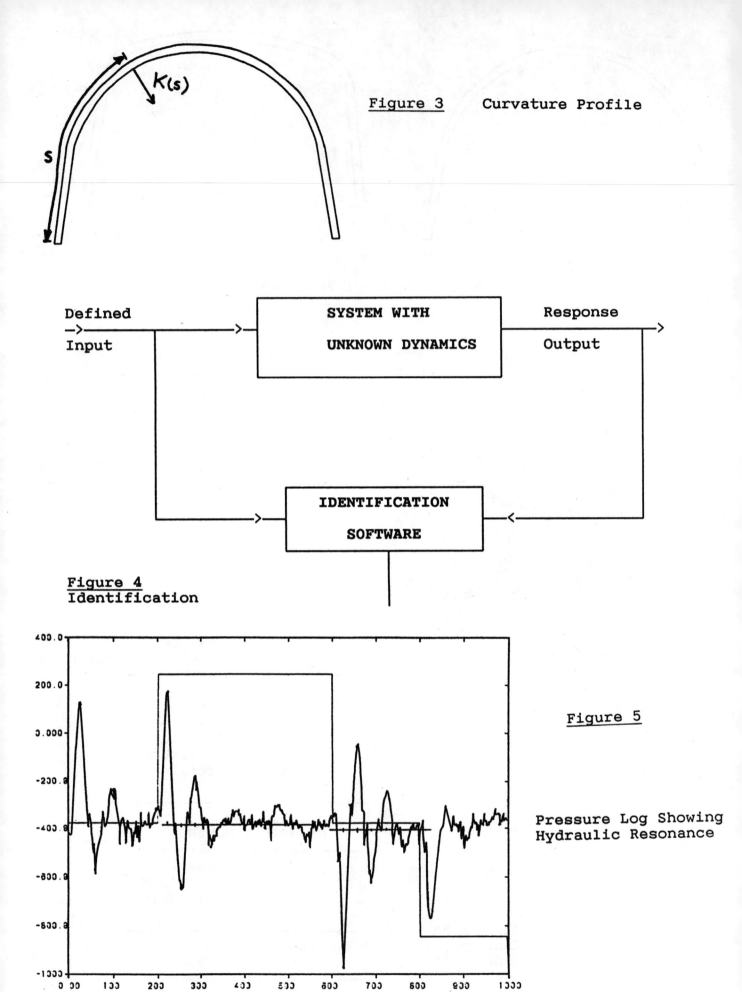

Figure 3   Curvature Profile

Figure 4
Identification

Figure 5

Pressure Log Showing
Hydraulic Resonance

Time ms

214

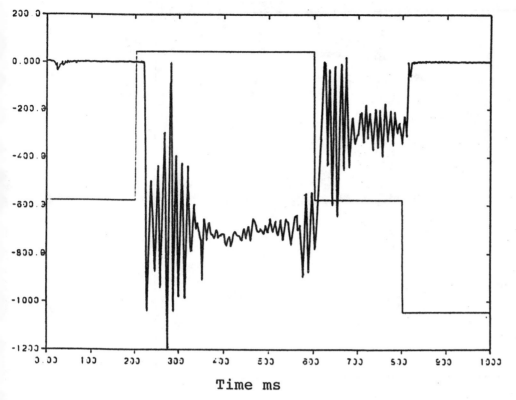

Figure 6

Velocity Log Showing
Gearbox Resonance

Figure 7   Movement of the Roll
            Set around the Beam

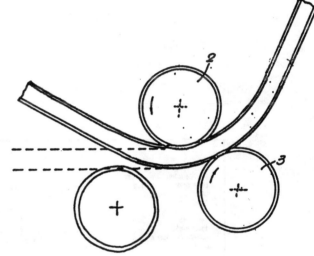

Figure 8

TSIM graphics of
Inverse Kinematics

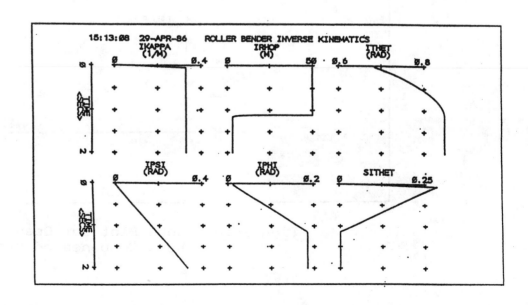

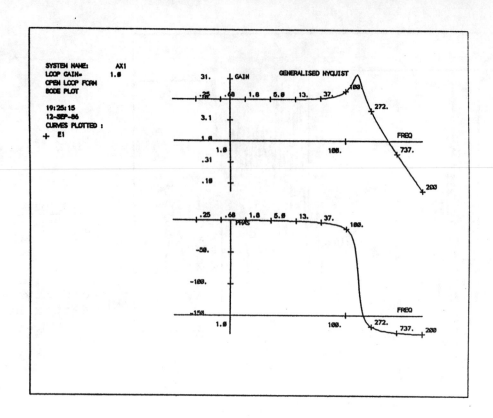

Figure 9   Bode Plot for Open
            Loop System

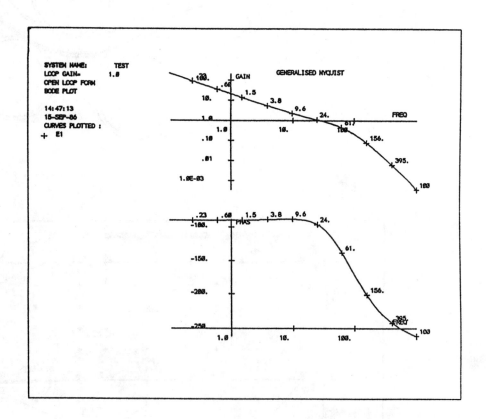

Figure 10   Bode Plot for Open
             Loop Compensated System

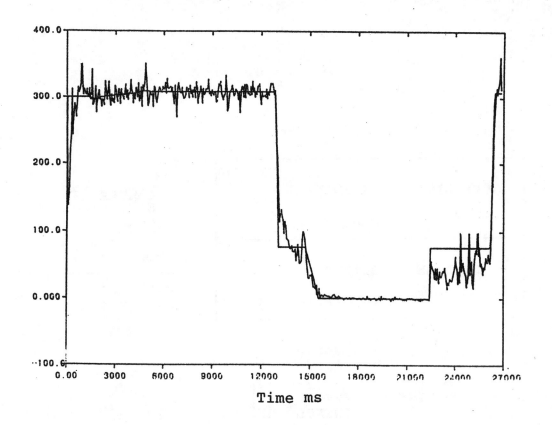

Figure 11   Actual Beam Velocity Tracking

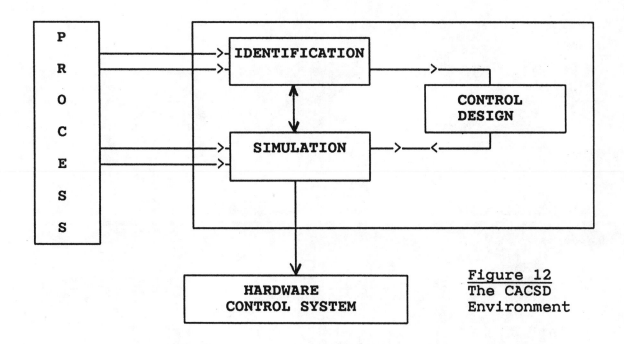

Figure 12
The CACSD
Environment

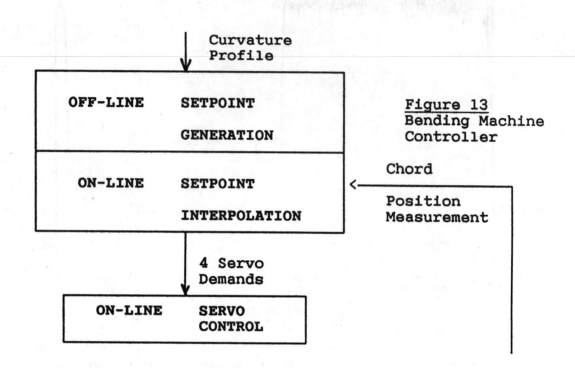

Curvature
Profile

OFF-LINE   SETPOINT

GENERATION

ON-LINE   SETPOINT

INTERPOLATION

4 Servo
Demands

ON-LINE   SERVO
CONTROL

Figure 13
Bending Machine
Controller

Chord

Position
Measurement

Proc. 2nd Int. Conf. Machine Control Systems, 219-230
May 1987, © IFS (Conferences) Ltd and authors, ISBN 0-948507-52-7

An FMS user's design and application of a computer control system

P G Hudson and S Webb
AMECAS, UK

The paper describes an FMS end-user's design and application of
an FMS computer control system. A distributed computer control
system was designed, installed and commissioned in-house to meet
the end-user's exact requirements of controlling, co-ordinating
and monitoring advanced manufacturing equipment used in a £4.2
million FMS. Seven autonomous manufacturing cells, utilising
gantry robot loaders and automated guided vehicles are used to
manufacture a turbocharger shaft and turbine wheel component.

1.0 INTRODUCTION

An FMS computer system enables the designers to fully automate and optimise the operation of the production system. However, the majority of the cost reduction achieved during the automation of traditional manufacturing facilities is usually due to the re-organisation of inefficient workflows, to improvements made to manufacturing processes and to the automatic loading of machine tools. These factors result in a significant increase of machine utilisation.

Computers can be used to automate the transport and identification of components, supervise automatic machine set-ups, monitor safety systems and generally improve the availability of information essential to the efficient running of the FMS. At a higher level of control they make it possible to integrate the production scheduling and engineering systems.

An FMS project team, now known as AMECAS, have designed, developed, installed and commissioned a £4.2 million manufacturing system at Holset Engineering. The implementation of the FMS computer system was strictly "bottom-up" with regular assessments of the total system design as it developed. In this way the computer hierarchy was clear before the software design was started, and made it possible to assess the advantages offered by computer suppliers before reaching the installation stage of the higher system levels. The aim was to build a successful, cost effective system, that produced quality parts, efficiently, rather than one that justified the label of FMS but was less effective.

2.0 THE COMPANY

Holset Engineering is one of the world's leading turbocharger manufacturers, supplying to nearly every major diesel truck manufacturer in the world. Holset, a wholly owned subsidiary of Cummins Engine Company, employs a total of 1600 people with approximately 1000 of those engaged in turbocharger manufacture. There are two manufacturing plants, one at Huddersfield, West Yorkshire, the other at Madison, Indiana in the USA.

During 1983 a study of Holset's world-wide turbocharger business concluded that, to achieve maximum cost reduction the manufacture of the shaft and wheel component should be centralised at one plant given the possible constraint of transportation costs.

Additionally, the projected business volumes for the following year exceeded the existing capacity. The shaft and wheel component had the longest lead time of all turbocharger components. It's manufacture was very complex consisting of many processes and requiring considerable labour. The work was performed on old machines and their output essentially scheduled the turbocharger assembly.

At the time of the study there were 5 different frame sizes of turbocharger, an active demand for over 50 different shaft and wheel designs and nearly 300 different turbocharger assemblies. A more aggressive rationalisation of components couldn't be performed without seriously affecting customer relations. This variety of part numbers made it difficult to achieve the company objective of supplying the customers with the exact design of turbocharger required. It also restricted the designer's freedom to design for optimum performance.

To be able to offer the customers their exact requirements and increase the company's productivity it was apparent that flexible manufacturing was required to produce shaft and wheel assemblies in small batches at the same cost as if they were produced in high volume on dedicated plant.

Co-inciding with the Holset study, the Department of Trade and Industry (DTI) was inviting applications for financial assistance towards FMS consultancies, development costs and capital expenditure. The possibility of a financial grant accelerated the interest to go for the ambitious option of a full FMS.

Consequently, in December 1983 a technical FMS specification was submitted for the computer controlled batch production of every manufacturing process required to produce a turbocharger shaft and wheel sub-assembly. In March 1984 the DTI's offer of a £1M grant towards the total £4.2 million cost was accepted with a projected completion date of March 1987.

An FMS project team, later to become AMECAS the Advanced Manufacturing Equipment and Automation Division of Holset, was formed and given the total responsibility for the design, the development, the installation and the commissioning of the flexible manufacturing system.

3.0 THE COMPONENT

The shaft and turbine wheel is the most significant element in a turbocharger both in terms of cost and difficulty to manufacture. It is a two piece welded sub-assembly comprising a high precision investment casting made from Inconel 713C and a forged shaft of 8740 steel.

The shaft diameters are ground to close tolerances on size and roundness, require a good quality surface finish and are dynamically balanced to fine tolerances. The high quality level must be attained due to the high operating speeds of approximately 120,000 rpm. Fig. 1. illustrates a typical Holset shaft and wheel.

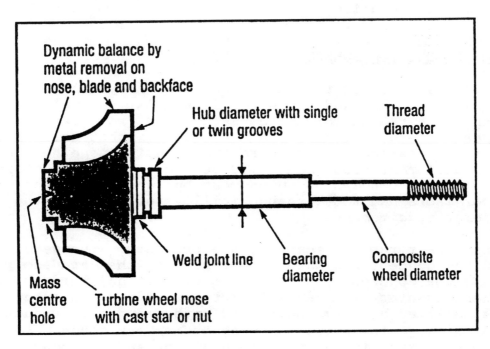

FIG. 1. TYPICAL HOLSET SHAFT AND TURBINE WHEEL.

4.0 AN OVERVIEW OF THE FMS.

The installed FMS is designed to produce 50 different types of components at the rate of 800 per day. It involves 17 different sizes of investment cast turbine wheels ranging in size from 60 to 125mm, and eight sizes of forged shaft.

The nature and sequence of the machining processes required in the manufacture of the shaft and wheel dictates an overall workflow, from raw material to finished parts stores, in a similar manner to that of a transfer line. Alternative routings need only be considered when there are machine breakdowns, preventative maintenance is being carried out or perhaps a machine or cell is being used to produce prototypes.

The system includes 32 successive operations which take place in seven autonomous flexible manufacturing cells. Scissor-lift Automated Guided Vehicles (AGVs) are used to transport components on pallets between each cell. Work is transferred between the pallets and the machines by 5-axis area gantry robot loaders. Fig. 2. illustrates a typical gantry robot cell and fig. 3. the total FMS layout with AGV routes.

At each cell an AMECAS local area controller is used to co-ordinate the equipment and execute the functions expected of an autonomous business, receiving customer orders, calculating and monitoring capacity and issuing purchase orders.

The local area controllers contain two Heckler & Koch controls. The lower level programmable controller is used to monitor the safety systems, guard interlocks, the AGVs travelling through the cell and the status of the machines. It also displays diagnostic information and is used as a digital interface between the higher level control and those machines where serial communication is not cost effective.

The higher level 16 bit microcomputer is used for the cell production control, AGV cell traffic control, the machine and gantry robot programme selection, the identification of pallets and the inter cell communication via a local area network. Fig. 4. shows a typical cell control configuration.

5.0 THE FMS PRODUCTION SCHEDULING CONCEPT.

The manufacture of the shaft and wheel component dictates that the layout of the plant and processes is similar to that of a transfer line, each process performed consecutively from raw material to finished part. The evolution of 8m x 4m gantry robot cells established separate manufacturing units where the grouping together of either similar or different processes could be made. This structure was the foundation for the concept of autonomous business cells for which the manual supervisors had total responsibility for ensuring that they met their customer requirements.

During the first two years of the project, the development of the scheduling concept was made with regard to the Japanese philosophy of JIT and the concept of pulling the production through the line rather than pushing it. An attempt was made to ensure that the components followed a fully controlled path along the production line, hence constraining the growth of unnecessary overheads, keeping WIP to a minimum, minimising the lead time and increasing machine utilisation.

FIG. 2. A TYPICAL GANTRY ROBOT CELL

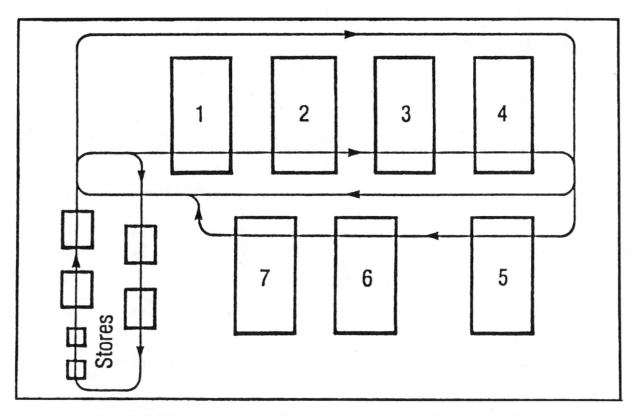

FIG. 3. THE LAYOUT OF THE SEVEN CELLS, STORES AREA AND AGV ROUTES.

223

It was recognised that the traditional method of controlling a factory from a central mainframe computer, with complex MRP production control software, was not suitable for the FMS. Usually the high degree of occurences and manual intervention within a manufacturing process render it impossible for a computer to follow and accurately control. Consequently to accurately schedule the FMS, with the large amount of automation planned, it was thought better to separate the FMS into small units.

Just-in-Time dictated that each process was placed as closely together as possible and storage space was not allowed between cells. This ensured that WIP was kept to a minimum, people such as progress chasers, storemen and inspectors were kept to a minimum, equipment had a high percentage utilisation, split batches were eliminated, excess supervision was eliminated, scrap and rework kept to an absolute minimum and paper work non existent.

Set-up times had to be drastically reduced to encourage the scheduling of batch sizes that met exactly the customer requirements. Manufacturing for stock was not allowed.

To schedule such a production line each cell controller was considered as a company business system. The business consisted of a maximum of four machines and the gantry robot. Nevertheless each had to satisfy customer orders and produce material requirements. Those software modules considered to be essential to each cell were specified as follows:-

1). Real time scheduler, capable of working with maximum batch quantities of 30 and component cycle times of approximately 90 seconds.

2). Capacity planner, calculating cycle times, set-up times, AGV delivery times and accurately predicting when manual tasks occur.

3). Receipt of Customer Orders.

4). Purchase order production.

5). Receipt of material delivery promises.

6). Production of delivery promises.

7). Real time AGV traffic control.

The main aspect of the philosophy was that the combination of the scheduler and the capacity planning module made it possible to accurately predict when components would be completed. Simulation of the whole production process by cascading schedule data between cells in both directions was only possible by virtue of the close, real time control of each LAC.

Upon receipt of a customer order, the cell control calculates the latest material delivery date in order to deliver on time to the customer. This calculation is performed by accessing performance data regarding production cycles and AGV delivery times. The calculated material required date is transmitted via the LAN to the supplier cell. This cell in turn performs the same task and eventually receives an accurate material delivery promise date to meet the order, from it's supplier. Upon calculating the necessary processing time to meet the order it can determine whether it can meet the requirement on time

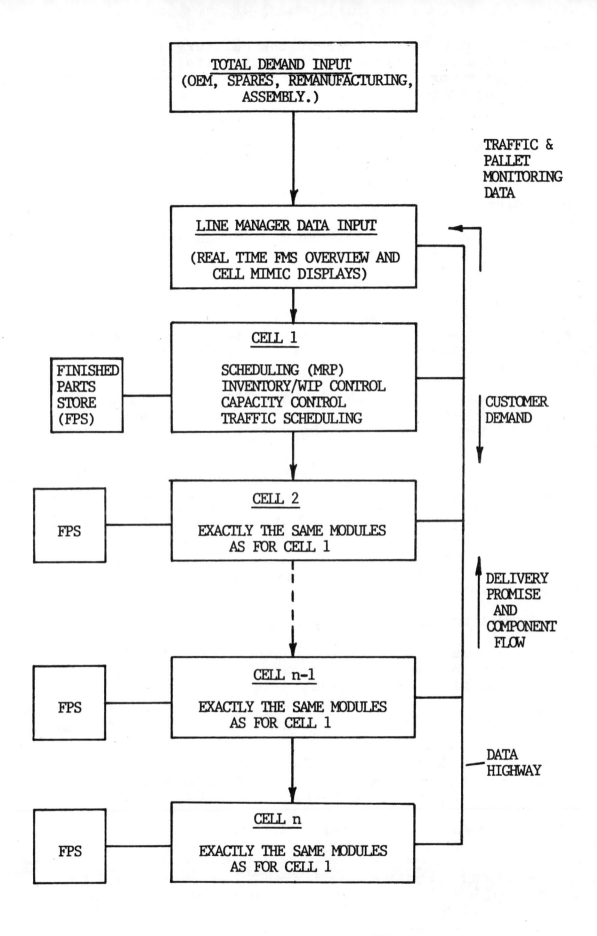

FIG 5.   THE SCHEDULING CONCEPT.

225

or whether it is going to be late. If the delivery is going to be late this will cascade down the line, through the finished part stores and be flagged to the supervisor for action to be taken or accepted. Fig. 5. illustrates the scheduling concept.

6.0 THE COMPUTER CONTROL SYSTEM

It was thought essential that production could continue if any of the automation or control equipment failed, consequently a hierarchy of distributed computers was chosen.

A distributed computer network of independent controls supports a degree of manual intervention when a section fails and is inherently more resilient. Machines can be manually loaded to continue production whilst other areas continue to produce automatically. More importantly, the independence of the sections is an advantage during commissioning and software development, allowing each section to be proven as a working unit before connection to the whole system. It is also possible when one computer fails for it's duties to be executed by another and hence not effect the total system.

The Local Area Controls (LACs), see fig. 4, had to be able to sequence control many digital signals, interface to several sophisticated devices and allow the user to easily reconfigure the system.

Many different cell control configurations were defined, each influencing the LAC specification. Because of the complexity and the number of different project modules it was difficult to determine the optimum cell control configuration until the design of each area was near completion. Consequently a flexible approach towards the design of the LAC was essential throughout the project. The project areas having the most significant effect upon the development of the LAC configuration included:-

1). The development of the machine - LAC interface.

2). The successful investigation and acceptance of the Heckler and Koch LNC 825 robot control ensuring that a separate control for the LAC was essential.

3). The development of the gantry robot to LAC interface.

4). The design of the gantry robot cell configuration, the monitoring of the safety and guarding systems and co-ordination of AGVs through the cells.

5). The specification of the gantry robot's capabilities and functions.

6). The LNC 825 robot controller's DNC capability with the Heckler & Koch MT - microcomputer offering greater design flexibility.

7). The distributed AGV transport system requiring a communication link to the on-board AGV microcomputers, allowing automatic AGV programme selection.

8). The design of the remote component identification system and it's interfacing requirements.

To satisfy these requirements and offer maximum flexibility for the future, it was decided that the LAC should consist of two independent controls, a high level control, programmed in a high level language and a low level programmable control (PC) capable of coping with the digital sequencing of the cell.

The HK-C50 programmable control was chosen for the low level cell control because:-

1). Each gantry robot LNC 825 had been specified with the integrated HK-C50 to interface to the enviroment.

2). Other machines also had the integrated HK-C50.

3). A considerable amount of programming expertise had already been developed in-house during the investigation of the controls.

4). All the cards for the machines, robots and programmable controls were interchangeable, consequently fewer spares were needed.

5). The peripherals required for programming the PCs were already available.

6). Infinite I/O expansion was available.

The possibility of using the HK-C50 to interface to the AGV and identification systems was investigated. Although possible, the programming of quite complicated routines in assembler was considered unnecessary when the routines were more suited to a higher level language. The sequencing and data handling capabilities required to perform these functions were more suited to a higher level control.

The possibility of using the higher level control to perform the production scheduling, traditionally considered to be the domain of a mainframe computer, was investigated. The presence of quite powerful microcomputers within each cell was in line with the philosophy of designing autonomous business units and could be directly applied to the JIT scheduling philosophy. The cell management and scheduling functions would have been impossible to run upon a programmable control and consequently the LAC design was altered to incorporate a real time production control microcomputer.

A thorough study of commercially available production scheduling and business management software for microcomputers was performed with the intention of using the most suitable. This study produced a clear specification of the requirements, however, the available commercial software was not found to be suitable for managing small business cells with lead times of minutes, running real time capacity planning and communicating data files between each other. It was recognised that the required expertise to develop this software had to be available in-house.

Consequently resources were allocated and based upon the good relations developed with Heckler & Koch it was agreed that technical assistance was available with interfacing and hardware related problems using their microcomputers.

To ensure that maximum design flexibility was available a 16 bit computer was selected, the HK MT-III. A 19" rack version of the MT-III

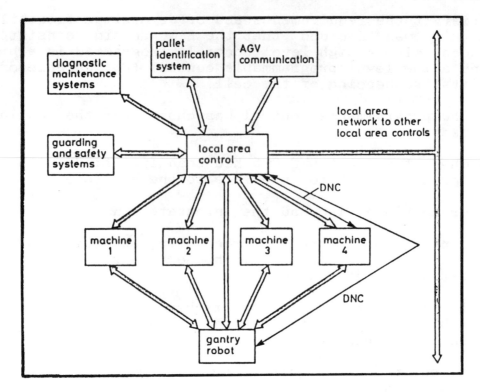

FIG. 4. TYPICAL CELL CONTROL CONFIGURATION.

FIG. 6.

AN AMECAS LOCAL
AREA CONTROL (LAC).

228

was selected for each of the seven cells and the stores area, because they were to be sited on the shop-floor. An equivalent desk top version, the MT-IV was specified as the line supervisor's control to enable the manual entry of customer requirements as produced upon the company's mainframe computer. If required other data could be entered. The MT-IV was identified as the area where relevant alarm conditions could be displayed and management reports produced. Additionally, the MT-IV being on the communication network with each of the LACs could display all monitored data required from the FMS. All MT controls were specified with graphic screens.

The interface configuration for each MT-III consisted of four interface cards, two with 4 x TTY channels, one with 2 x RS232 channels and the fourth, a 24V digital interface card with 16 inputs and 8 outputs.

Each of the eight MT-III microcomputers was specified with an MS-DOS operating system. The selected programming language for the control and scheduling software was "Turbo Pascal." This language was selected because of it's suitability for software development and it's relative ease to learn, mainly due to it's readable structure. In comparison with other languages the listings are very readable and consequently the documentation is inherently better. An AMECAS Local Area Control is illustrated in fig. 6.

7.0 THE LOCAL AREA NETWORK.

It was decided that the configuration and topology of the communication system between cells was not important providing it was simple for the programmers. The prefered system had to be transparent to the user in a similar manner to the drivers used for communicating to the AGVs, the identification system and between the HK-C50 and the higher level LAC microcomputer.

A study of propriety LANs suitable for the shop-floor determined that their range of costs and facilities was great. Again, as for all the other aspects of the system, a specification of requirements was produced and it was calculated that to communicate typical messages with estimated occurence rates, a LAN with a baud rate of 9600 would be transmitting a message for approximately 16% of it's total operation time.

The LAN requirements were discussed with Heckler & Koch. A standard Local Area Network did not exist but they agreed to develop one incorporating the guidelines produced and also commercially acceptable to other customers. Upon completion of the development a LAN licence was purchased for the nine controls required for the FMS. To enable the communication software to run apparently simultaneously and also offer greater flexibility for the future, licences were also purchased for a multitasking capability.

8.0 FUTURE DEVELOPMENTS.

The most significant developments for the future involve the integration of the FMS with the rest of the plant. The integration of the FMS with the rest of the Company would involve clearly defining and implementing interfaces to the CADCAM facilities and also to the existing central mainframe computer which is used to production schedule both the Huddersfield and Halifax factories.

The MRP system operating on the mainframe computer, produces weekly requirements for each component. It is planned, that at the start of each week the shaft and wheel requirements will be manually entered into the FMS schedule. It is possible to install a direct interface between the FMS and the IBM mainframe, by using an asynchronous serial port on the IBM and treating the interface as a batch reader-batch printer port, however the lead time of the shaft and wheel FMS, measured in hours, can not be sensibly incorporated into the company MRP system which works in weekly time buckets. In addition it is thought that there isn't any benefit in up-loading production information to the mainframe although it is technically possible.

The link to the CADCAM facility has been considered for some time, however at present it is too early to specify the exact requirements of both the FMS and the CAM system. It is thought that the only relevant information required from the CAM system at present is numerical dimension information. Pictures are not required, making a possible link much simpler. All NC programmes are too short to merit DNC from the CAM system although there is the possibility of the downloading of production engineering changes and relevant planning information.

9.0 CONCLUSION.

An FMS computer system enables the designers to fully automate and optimise the operation of the production system. However, the majority of the cost reduction achieved during the automation of traditional manufacturing facilities is usually due to the re-organisation of inefficient workflows, to improvements made to manufacturing processes and to the automatic loading of machine tools. These factors result in a significant increase of machine utilisation.

Machine tool selection is probably the most influential factor towards the success of a production facility. No matter how successful the automation, the FMS computer control and the supporting systems they can not compensate for the selection of the wrong machines.

The distributed computer control system, specifically designed to operate with a just-in-time manufacturing facility has clearly indicated how it is possible to make obsolete the large, centralised mainframe computers often regarded as the hub of a successful manufacturing company. They are not needed in their present form and only serve to increase a company's overheads and unnecessarily overcomplicate the scheduling process.

Proc. 2nd Int. Conf. Machine Control Systems, 231-240
May 1987, © IFS (Conferences) Ltd and authors, ISBN 0-948507-52-7

A management information system for automated assembly equipment

equipment

R L Tomlin

John Brown Automation Ltd, UK

ABSTRACT

To stay competitive in manufacturing today, it is not sufficient to merely automate the process; management control must be maintained. This can only be achieved by implementing supervisory and monitoring levels within operating the system. By this method of reporting, the information required to make decisions is available when it is needed i.e. "immediately". In automated assembly and other manufacturing system the term "Management Information System" has been adopted. It is the purpose of this paper to put forward the criteria for such a system, and to discuss the various attributes.

INTRODUCTION

Most modern industries are very competitive in world markets. To enable management to maintain their market share it is essential for them to have available the most up-to-date information. This information must be accurate and valid at the time when decisions are made and the data should relate to material costs, production costs and sales related costs.

Traditionally these figures would be manually compiled at routine intervals, but with the rapid changes that can occur in market prices of money, material costs and product demand the data would be of a regressive nature, and probably not accurate.

Since the rapid progress made in computer technology, progressive companies have started to introduce automatic means of collating and analysing data. In manufacturing industries this process can start at the lowest levels of production. Then by the use of hierarchical computers linked to one another, high level systems can produce reports of current production, stores levels and work in progress.

Such systems have been given names dependent on their use or industry. Process industries tend to use the acronym SCARA representing Supervisory Control and Reporting Acquisition. Manufacturing industries use MIS. representing Management Information Systems. It is this area that I shall cover in this paper.

OBJECTIVES

The objectives of a Management Information System are to collate production related data, generate management reports and act as a diagnostic tool. Management Information Systems can be configured in many formats. At John Brown Automation we have adopted the "remote control room" technique with additional shop floor displays. Alternatives include "local" small to medium sized systems, up to very large corporate main frame based systems. This is a decision based on the scope and scale of the requirement. Whatever the decision, it is possible to modify the installation to meet any new requirements. The John Brown Automation system is modular in design, and being of a hierarchical nature many combinations can be defined.

Remote monitor screens can be located in departmental offices relaying pertinent data to quality engineers, production engineers or maintenance personnel.

Shift patterns can be incorporated so that production schedules, batch build and machine performance monitoring can be analysed. Reporting can be automatic on the completion of shift, or on demand from management. Hard copy results can also be printed out at these times if selected. However, there is a limit to the amount of data that can be stored in the system memory. For longer term storage it is usual to archive to floppy or hard disc. In this way it is then possible to re-enter the data at a later date for further analysis.

Most Management Information Systems have a main VDU screen as the operator interface. Modern systems have colour monitors, so that ergonomic colour patterns are easily interpreted by the operator. At JBA we use a touch screen colour monitor with optional keyboard, for the operator. The philosophy for this was to make the system easily operated by non-computer personnel . If changes have to be made to the system, then the keyboard is available. For normal operation of the system the current screen incorporates coloured panels with a label for their use. Simply by touching the panel a print out, change of screen, or subsequent analysis is peformed. Other systems use this or similar techniques such as light pens, a 'mouse' or joystick. See Fig. 1 and Fig. 2

JUSTIFICATION OF THE MANAGEMENT INFORMATION SYSTEM

During the 1960's and early 1970's the emphasis was on direct labour costs. The emphasis today has moved to include indirect costs and cost of working capital. One way of increasing cash lock up in a company is to reduce materials stock and work in progress. The trend is towards production techniques that adopt a "materials requirement when needed" philosophy, known as Kan Ban or Just-In-Time techniques. Materials suppliers deliver goods on a pre-determined timed basis and the goods go straight to the production line.

These techniques are only possible now due to the low cost and availability of modern computers. To be able to control the timed requirements of a large volume of parts was virtually impossible by manual means. Automatic means are now possible by using standard system software packages. M.R.P (Materials Requirement Planning) and B.O.M. (Bill of Materials).

These programmes will runon the plant level computer where the master production schedule is determined. From this base automatically generated works orders are implemented, and the requirements of all departments established.

Clearly this manufacturing philosophy will not work unless companies monitor all levels of their operation, especially production. In order for them to achieve this effectively, they need to know at any time the current state of production. Accurate real time data acquisition is only possible by means of monitoring production automatically at the machine level. This is the function of the management information system and its constituent components. Work in progress is constantly known, performance of the production lines calculated and quality of components audited.

BENEFITS OF A MANAGEMENT INFORMATION SYSTEM

Having established some of the critical reasons for implementing a management information system it is worth explaining what benefits are available.

Increased productivity is possible due to close monitoring of the process, analysis of failures and adverse trend or pattern analysis. From data gathered regarding build or batch combinations, production may be re-scheduled so that awkward tool changes or component mixes can be avoided. Smooth operation of the machinery or process is ensured.

From the data gathered, various forms of output reports can be generated, using graphical representation, such as histograms, pie charts, bar charts, etc. Production engineers are able to decipher this information quickly and accurately and where necessary take the correct course of action.

Quality related data may also be collated and analysed, using techniques such as Statistical Process Control (SPC) and SQC (Statistical Quality Control). These techniques allow data to be used to bring a process into statistical control whereby trend patterns are used to forewarn operators of impending failures, so that remedial action can be taken. In this way the process will not produce scrap components and thus be more efficient. Not only can this be used in final assembly, but also where measurements are taken. These could involve faulty part supplies to the line either from sub contractors or machining facilities. In this way suppliers are automatically being monitored, and assessed, which in turn will increase quality to the line and hence productivity.

Varying levels of diagnostic sophistication can be incorporated at machine level. These can vary from simple fault identification to "in process" vibration analysis monitoring. Whatever the level used maintenance departments can be informed of problems. This can take the form of a remote VDU in the Maintenance Supervisor's office, displaying the problems on a machine. It could also indicate which of his engineers are required, i.e. electrician, fitter, millwright etc.

The system that JBA have developed displays a message for every fault, with the probable cause and remedial action required.

Routine maintenance schedules can also be printed out for maintenance personnel. These are generated by a real time clock and watchdog programme, that logs the times between services. From this report maintenance and production can establish the most convenient time to perform the services. Regular maintenance of machinery will inevitably reduce the number of breakdowns, and hence maintain the machines productivity.

RESTRICTING FACTORS TO IMPLEMENTING MANAGEMENT INFORMATION SYSTEMS

The installation of management information systems carries an initial additional cost to the capital equipment. However, the advantages over the life of the equipment far outweigh this cost. Extra overheads are incurred in the running and maintaining of the equipment, but again are minimal when compared to the benefits and savings that the system offers.

Communication systems have to be installed to enable the management information system to communicate to plant computers and remote stations. In modern factories these will have to be installed anyway, for office automation equipment, telephone lines, and local area networks.

The intellectual level of personnel required to maintain and run these systems has to be of a high level to utilise them to their full potential. Too often sophisiticated equipment is installed in a factory, only to be criticised through ignorance. It is often left switched off because it is not properly understood when all that is required is a little practice or training.

Good initial training in the equipment is essential, at JBA we offer full training on all our equipment, and offer fully supported maintenance contracts where applicable.

It is possible that suitable accommodation is not available on the shop floor if the management system is to be installed there. JBA and some other suppliers offer industrially ruggedised equipment that can withstand the shop floor environment. The alternative is to install the equipment in special cabinets or rooms that are electrically and environmentally "clean".

To retrospectively implement management systems to existing plant is usually possible, but each installation would have to be assessed on its practicallity. The limiting factors could be the processing power of the original plant control equipment, the modularity of the resident software, and the amount of spare memory available.

To reiterate the point; initial costs are easily compensated with the savings in material usage, scrap rates are reduced and production increased. The savings in these areas are ongoing for the life of the equipment, and analysis of MIS data might well show when that life is reached. The Management Information System on any equipment made obsolete, may well be suitable for those machines replacement. Software should be easily modified to suit the new requirements, and most computers are part of an upgradable family that can be compatible with new technology. The JBA management information system is based on industry standard products and falls into this category.

MANAGEMENT INFORMATION SYSTEMS IN AUTOMATIC ASSEMBLY

In manufacturing and many other industries rising costs of materials, overheads and labour is forcing companies to find more efficient production methods. Full automation of processes achieves these aims. By reducing scrap and work in progress, material costs are reduced. Overheads can be minimised if heating, lighting, and environment requirements are reduced. This can be achieved by automation and unmanned factories or areas of factories.

Management Information Systems are the first level of supervisory control and are essential for Computer Integrated Manufacture (CIM). As more equipment becomes computer controlled, the MIS will be used as the gateway for DNC programme up and downloading.

Flexibility in automated assembly manufacturing is achieved with the use of robots. The control systems on most robots are becoming more sophisticated. The DEA Pragma robot for instance can run programmes downloaded from a host computer over a local area network or direct serial link. JBA are exclusive UK agents for this robot and systems integrators for IBM and Bosch robots. The Management Information Systems that we recommend and build include interfacing with these and other robots.

Common protocols in communication networks such as MAP, (Manufacturing Automation Protocol) enable equipment of different manufacturers to communicate. With this facility management information systems can be built using a multitude of different equipment suppliers. This will help tointegrate islands of automation into a cohesive structure, that will ultimately increase production efficiency.

Most suppliers of PLC (Programmable Logic Controllers) and CNC (Computer Numerical Control) equipment are now incorporating communication channels into even their smallest ranges. Larger systems are capable of communicating direct with Local Area Networks.

TECHNOLOGY AND MANAGEMENT INFORMATION SYSTEMS

Interactive and stand along operations are already available using artificial intelligence techniques. Vision systems integrated to robot control are making Flexible Automated Systems (FAS) more viable. Using these techniques and MIS to host communications, processes are capable of taking self initiated remedial action or reprogramming for alternative production, automatically.

Material supply to the shop floor using MRP and automated handling devices such as AGV's are already operating. Order intake can be automated to generate material requests and production. Output of production to delivery points and automatic invoicing using Management Information Systems and the other tools described can be implemented.

The technology to achieve full CIM is already available and in operation. But it tends to be restricted at present to modern large installations where the overhead costs can be carried.

Several manufacturers of control equipment are now offering Management Information Systems hardware. Interactive colour monitors have been with us for a few years already. With the rapid changes in CAD/CAM workstations and graphics packages available, some manufacturers are using this technology for the basis of very powerful management systems. Some of the standard features offered include screen editors that allow the operator to construct icons of common forms. These may be adjustable in size and orientation with very simple commands. Tabular and graphical results, tables and screens are easily configured. Standard algorithms permit pie charts, histograms, or bar charts to be constructed. Trend analysis, statistical analysis are incorporated and called up using function calls. Direct communication with PC memory images are possible, so that sequential control is not affected.

These and other features are controlled and updated on a real time basis by the management system. Communicating with host computers is carried out using parallel processes so that the system integrity is not affected.

Local Area Networks and wide area networks are currently in use, with the forthcoming MAP specification offering universal conformity. The implementation of multi vendor management information systems and CIM systems for reasonable costs are achievable.

CONCEPTION AND IMPLEMENTATION OF A MANAGEMENT INFORMATION SYSTEM

As automated assembly machine manufacturers John Brown Automation realised at the very early stage of evolvement of PLC systems, the need for diagnostics. This is a twofold requirement, one to minimise machine downtime, the other to enable shop floor personnel to quickly diagnose where a fault is. This was achieved by designing a PLC system with accurate and simple to understand diagnostics.

The JBA PLC has been designed using a distributed intelligence approach, utilising a modular basis. Each module contains its own microprocessor, which monitors only 16 input and controls 8 outputs. These rack mounted modules can be programmed so that each input used can have two fault states i.e. 'ON' or 'OFF'. This information is first passed via a bus system to a simple fault display unit. Operators would read the display, and refer to the mimic diagrams to establish the fault. Fig. 3.

It soon became apparent that higher level processing was possible, and a VDU has been added to the system. This VDU can communicate to 16 fault display modules. The memory of the VDU can store messages for the operators for each of the fault codes generated by the controllers. Other codes have been added at a later stage to give analogue value recording facilities, and non fault code messages for production data gathering. History files of these codes were then introduced and the facility for print outs added. Fig. 4.

From this intelligent VDU evolved a hierarchical structure of computers, that terminated in a Management Information System. The communications protocols for this system have been developed with the JBA system in mind. The next step is to introduce other communications to enable the Management Information System to communicate with other PLCS. Communications to upper level computers is already available, and data is formatted so that it is available on request from the host. Fig. 5.

Having developed this Management Information Systems JBA have the experience to develop and integrate other systems to customers' needs. Whilst still maintaining development of our MIS, we recognise that large customers with preferred PLC equipment need to rationalise on these systems.

OTHER CONSIDERATIONS FOR AUTOMATED ASSEMBLY

Design for automation is a critical feature in all future manufacturing systems. At JBA we offer design studies to our customers, so that functional specifications may be drafted prior to "invitations to tender" being initiated. Without some prior thought to the "assembly by automation" it is improbable that a fully automatic system can be successfully implemented.

Factory or plan layouts must also be addressed and carefully planned with automation in mind. Being part of the Trafalgar House Group of Companies JBA also have architectural design and construction expertise within our group of companies.

Some considerations in plan layout are material flow paths and storage areas, carefully laid out for ease of access and automatic retrieval. Line balancing from one process or operation to the next should be considered. Critical paths in the process should be identified and highlighted so that special arrangements can be made. Flexibility is the keyword of modern manufacturing techniques, and this should be catered for in the plant layout as well as the assembly machines. By arranging the manufacturing environment in this manner, the full advantage of new technologies can be incorporated.

CONCLUSIONS

Computer control of the environment and factory facilities is vital to successful manufacturing in the future. Linking the corporate computer or main frame, with Management Information System and operation system will create a whole manufacturing environment that is fully integrated.

In this full computerised world of automated manufacturing it can be seen that the Management Information System plays a vital role. Gathering, collating, and analysing the raw data from the production environment. All areas of production and support can benefit from its installation. Management can monitor and control, and through this make the decisions that are necessary to the efficient and profitable running of their business.

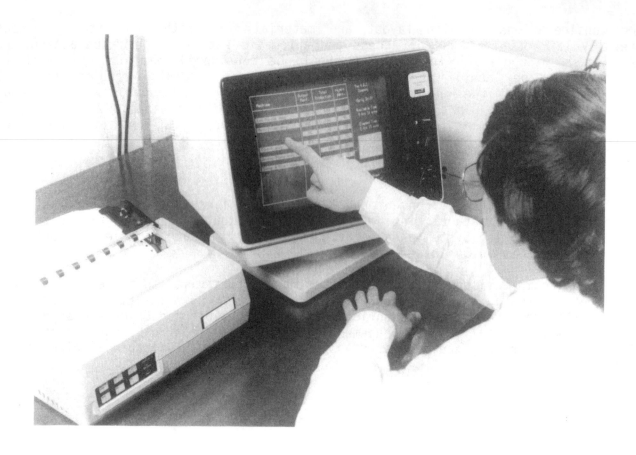

FIG. 1 THE JBA MANAGEMENT INFORMATION SYSTEM OPERATOR TERMINAL

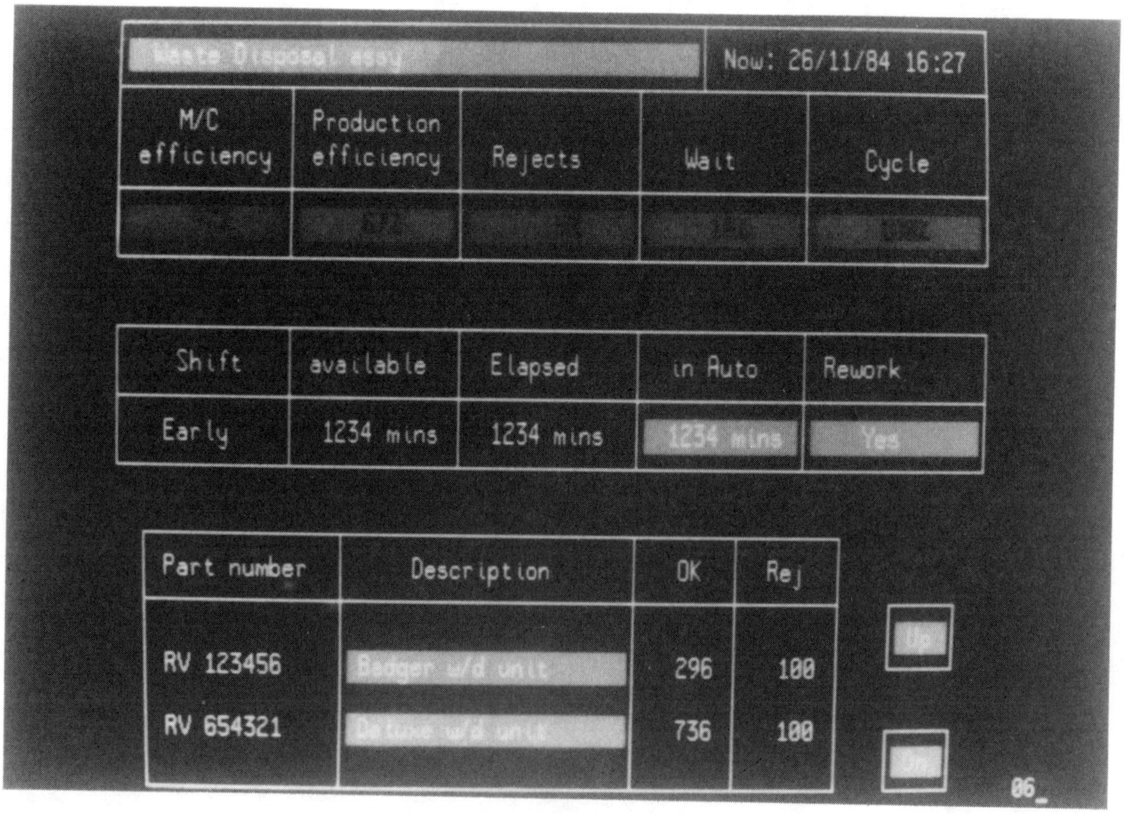

FIG. 2 TYPICAL PAGE DISPLAY ON OPERATOR TERMINAL

FIG. 3 TYPICAL SELECTION OF JBA CONTROL MODULES

FIG. 4 THE MACHINE BASED OPERATORS DIAGNOSTIC VDU.

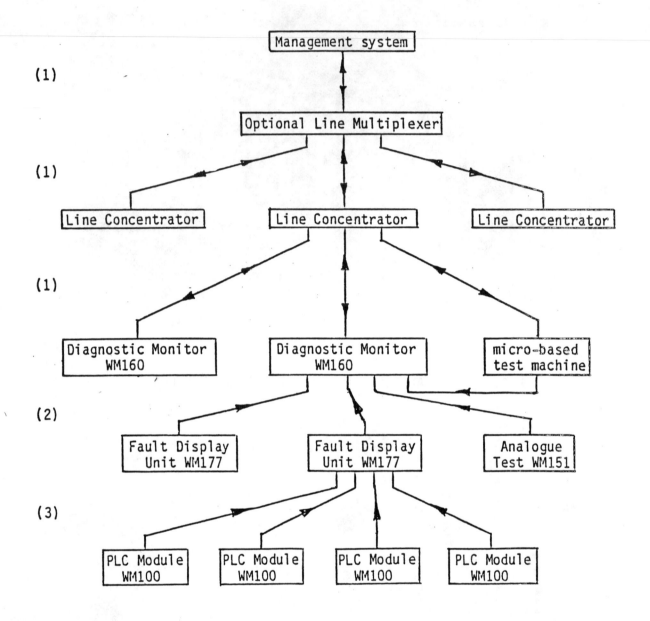

(1)

(1)

(1)

(2)

(3)

Key to data protocols:

(1)   Bi-directional long-distance serial protocol, with dual duplex
        operation.

(2)   Unidirectional multiplexed current-loop serial polled.

(3)   Unidirectional multiplexed parallel, polled operation.

FIG. 5

Proc. 2nd Int. Conf. Machine Control Systems, 241-248
May 1987, © IFS (Conferences) Ltd and authors, ISBN 0-948507-52-7

Software disasters and how to avoid them
I A Gilchrist
IPL Information Processing Ltd, UK

The main causes of software projects going disasterously wrong are
discussed. An "architecture" for successful projects is described based
on the "three pillars" : good specifications, good design and good
testing.

A software disaster should not be considered solely in terms of loss of life or vast sums of money. For a small company even a small project going wrong can be a disaster. In loose terms a software disaster occurs when a project runs drastically (say more than twice) over the cost/time allowed for it. Figure 1.

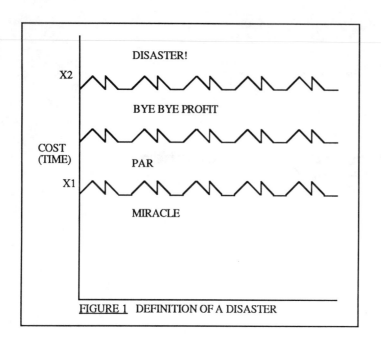

FIGURE 1 DEFINITION OF A DISASTER

My favourite example is the 6 month job which is still going after 6 years!

There are two possible general causes for a disaster:

a) It was <u>underestimated</u> in the first place.
b) Although correctly estimated, it was <u>poorly run</u>.

The purpose of this paper is to look at the main aspects of running a software project so as to ensure success. But first the question of estimating must be looked at briefly.

A. <u>Estimating</u>

The main ingredient for a disastrous estimate is a specification with holes in it. This is discussed in greater detail later, but it is obvious that an estimate based on an incomplete and/or ambiguous specification is bound to understate the time and effort required.

However, not all specifications are bad, in which case failure to produce a proper estimate is due to not spending enough time on the task of estimating. For larger jobs, estimating and proposal writing should be treated as small projects in themselves and not be regarded as a filler activity for an individual otherwise unoccupied. The aim here should be to produce an outline design and hence estimate the number of software modules needed to meet the specification. Then, using an in-house formula for time per module, produce a total cost. Allow extra for specification writing, if required, integration, and a 10% contingency. IPL's guideline is 4 man days to design, code and test a single high-level language module of ca. 60 executable language statements.

The headings and sections at the heart of a reasonable estimate are shown in Figure 2.

	Man Days / Weeks	@ Rate	Cost
Software Spec (if rqd.)			
Detailed Design and Program Spec's			
Module Design, Test and Code			
System Test			
On-site Integration and Testing			
10% Contingency			
Total			

FIGURE 2   HEART OF A SOFTWARE ESTIMATE

In summary, to avoid disasters at the estimating stage follow the golden rules:

1.   Issue/demand a reasonable specification.
2.   Devote appropriate resources to the estimating task.

B.   Running a Software Project

Even when a project has been estimated correctly there are many areas where a disaster can start. In my opinion there are "three pillars" of software success once a project is under way:

1.   Specification
2.   Design
3.   Testing

I will deal with these in some detail, and then three further matters in less detail.

B.1   Specification

The need for a good specification has already been mentioned in the section on estimating. There I was referring to the User Requirements Specification (URS), which is produced by the User to indicate to potential suppliers what he wants. In its minimum form it will consist of an overview, a description of the system objectives in terms of functionality, and a description of the interfaces (I/O, comms, and human). An important proviso is that few restrictions are placed on how the implementation is to be carried out. For example, the hardware may not be specified, nor the language, etc.

However, the eventual basis for agreement between the User and the Supplier (when chosen) will be the Software Functional Specification (SFS). This will state how the User's requirements will be met in terms of the Supplier's chosen means, and what precisely will be delivered. It will hopefully demonstrate conformance to the USR and in addition outline the main design features, such as programs/tasks, database structure, etc. Lastly, it will describe the nature of the Acceptance Test procedure.

Production of the SFS is a joint matter between Supplier and User, and usually a little effort is required to satisfy both sides. Acceptance Testing is worth paying special attention to if legal wrangles are to be avoided. Once lawyers get involved a project becomes a disaster for all concerned! Ideally, agreement on the SFS should be the last point at which User and Supplier need to meet before Acceptance Tests start.

B.2 Design

The starting point for good design is a thorough understanding of the problem, thus enabling it to be broken down or modularised.

Top-down techniques must be employed and the designers must be willing to undergo frequent reviews of their work. The point of reviews is to make sure that all the requirements are being met and that nothing in the specification is being left out. The top level design document, the Detailed Design Specification (DDS) will list the programs (tasks) to be produced, their functions and interfaces, and also give details of all global data including files to be used. Data flow diagrams are also essential.

At the next level, the task designs should be such that every task conforms to the following general structure (Figure 3).

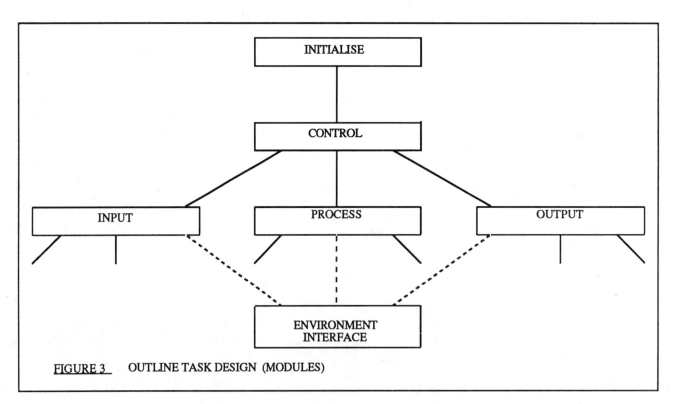

FIGURE 3   OUTLINE TASK DESIGN (MODULES)

Initialisation can be incorporated into the Control Module if required. However, the purpose of the Control Module is to get

244

data from the principal input data stream, cause it to be processed
and then output the results. The point of the Environment
Interface module is to make all the other modules in the task
testable by confining system dependency to the one module.

The difficult part is to choose the modules so that they are
economical in number and functions. Inter-module communications
should be kept to a minimum and be carried out preferably using
explicit parameters rather than reference to common data. Common
data itself should be kept to a minimum. The aim of these
precautions is to reduce scope for data corruption; extremes
however are to be avoided!

The task design stage will require much iteration and produce much
wastepaper, but it is here that the ultimate success probably most
heavily depends. To summarise the Task Design Specification there
should be the following sections.

1.   Task ID
2.   Function Description
3.   External References (Global Data, Files)
4.   Intertask Communications Details
5.   Module Functions
6.   Module Interfaces
7.   Task Common Data
8.   Task Test Plan

At the bottom level of design, the modules, the main features have
already been determined at the Task Specification level. Make sure
that the rules of structured programming can be observed and no
problems should occur. The main headings of each Module
Specification should be as follows:

1.   Module ID
2.   Function Description
3.   External References (Subroutines, Common Data)
4.   Logic (written)
5.   (Flowchart or PDL)
6.   Test Plan

B.3   Testing

There are two aims to testing;

1.   To ensure that the system will, as near as possible, be
      "right-first-time" when it goes on site. By thorough testing
      we should be able to eliminate extended embarrassing
      integration time getting the 'last' bugs out.

2.   To ensure that the system is maintainable throughout its life.
      Only by following a careful testing procedure is it possible
      to avoid introducing new errors when fixing old ones.

Testing should preferably be carried out in a 'Bottom Up' fashion.
That is modules are tested first, then tasks, then the system.
Module testing removes coding errors, task testing removes design
and module interface errors, and system testing removes task
interface and timing errors. Provided the tests were well thought-
out and thoroughly performed there is no reason why the whole
should not perform properly first time when taken to site.

So far I have avoided saying what I mean by 'testing' software. Traditional methods for module testing employ single-step debugging until the programmer feels that his module 'works'. This approach is emphatically no good at all! To be worthwhile testing must:

i) Be rigorous   - every path in every module must be exercised at least once.

ii) Be repeatable   - the same test must be capable of rerunning until the module is correct.

iii) Give hard-copy proof - of what has been tested and the result.

The same criteria apply for task and system testing but without the need to exercise every path.

The ideal set-up for testing will involve the use of a standard test harness which reads test data from an input file and returns the results in an output file.

Testing is not an inexpensive option and will typically double coding time, but if done properly the dividends over the system's life-cycle are immense. As mentioned before it is possible to reduce integration time to almost nothing, and give the product an indefinite life span.

C.   Other Important Factors

So much for the three pillars of software success - specification, design and testing. Three other factors which can determine whether a project is a disaster or a success are:

1.   Documentation
2.   Standards
3.   People

C.1. Documentation

This is in fact so important that I have assumed its existence whenever I have discussed the three previous topics. A Software Functional Specification is a document properly written and presented. The same goes for all Design Specifications, and hard-copy proof of successful testing should also form part of project documentation.

The final document in the set will be the User Documentation to enable the User to run the facility when the supplier hands over the keys. It should give all details of how to run the system, how to maintain it, and offer guidance on how to enhance it. The latter is only possible if the User has all the design documentation as well.

C.2 Standards

Standards are set out in a document that should have company wide circulation. They explain the formats to be used for all specification documents, and are applicable at all levels in a software project. At the most detailed level they will describe symbol-naming conventions to be used and most features connected with programming in a particular language. It is essential that all personnel on a particular project be familiar with the standards that apply to their particular roles. The importance of the use of standards is principally that they ensure project independence of people.

C.3 <u>People</u>

Last but not least are the human considerations. For software success the staff employed for a particular project need to be suitably experienced, appropriately trained and motivated.

To summarise all that has been said, Figure 4 offers a view of "an architecture for avoiding software disaster".

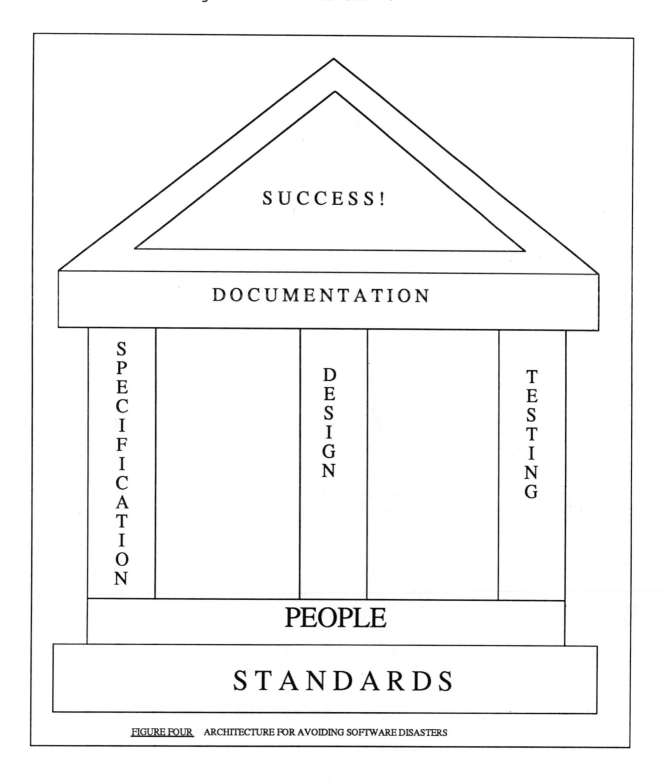

FIGURE FOUR   ARCHITECTURE FOR AVOIDING SOFTWARE DISASTERS

THE FUTURE

Proc. 2nd Int. Conf. Machine Control Systems, 249-256
May 1987, © IFS (Conferences) Ltd and authors, ISBN 0-948507-52-7

Increasing the applicability of programmable controllers through task sharing

E C May
Siemens Ltd, UK

The paper briely mentions the histrory of the programmable controller and discusses its prime requirements and features with a view to showing how the user may make better use of it and how it will develop in the near future.

Introduction.

Before we proceed to look at the future let us quickly review the past, why is there a generic class of computors called Programmable Controllers and why have they been so phenominally successful?

The programmable controller owes its origin to the large users of control systems becoming unhappy with the first introduction of programmable systems to the shop floor.   This was largely due to three aspects.   Firstly, few people were able to service and maintain the systems.   Secondly, the hardware was not always suited to the shop floor environment.   And last and most significantly since most of the people who programmed them were not experienced in the requirements of machine and process control the initial results were often not as desired either in performance or reliability under adverse conditions. The result was the birth of the computor with a 'hard hat' which spoke the language of the shop floor.

What does a 'hard hat' look like on a computor?

The industrialisation of the computor into the frame of the programmable controller includes the following features-

i)   Noise immunity to both supply borne interference,and also radiated pick up.
ii)   A robust physical and electrical structure to allow for a good survival rate with a minimum of precautions during system build and maintenance.
iii)   A wide range of input and output devices as   required by the diverse applications and with suitable protection ratings for industry.
iv)   Predictable   speed and performance comparable with that of the machine or process.
v)   Reliability, but failsafe if it should actually fail.
vi)   The progamming   should be easy to understand and quick to implement.
vii)   Diagnostic   aids should be available which allow easy fault location - both of the program and also of the hardware.

Making the most of the programmable controller.

Possibly the most important benefit of a   programmable controller is its ability to assist the user to locate faults quickly.   This is true both during the early stages of developement and commissioning and later during normal plant operation.   The basic package available depends upon the power of the programming unit and is available from the start.   The power of the computor hidden inside the controller may also be used via the applications program to provide automatic identification of the problems during operation.   This may be taken as far as the user likes, but it normally is most effective if the basic program is logically constructed so as to facilitate automatic diagnosis.   In todays environment any saving of time may easily be equated with money.

Another important feature is that, by allowing alternative control strategies to be stored in the same program, modern flexible production techniques may be more easily   realised.   The rapid responses necessary to different sets of conditions within the same plant as different parts or products are handled is achieved by simply changing values and sequences not by resetting equipment manually. This means that the use of measured analogue values and also position is more common and the corresponding types of the interface cards will be increased.

This leads onto the next area of interest, the ability to link the controllers to each other and also to production control computors where the necessary information about the manufactured items resides. This further enhances the flexibility of the production layout by allowing the control level to call on large stores of parameters and settings as required. Also data will be sent in the opposite direction, since the controllers can signal both production data when things are going well and also fault information when they are not! This not only allows the detailed production settings to be updated but also by logging faults over long periods new counter strategies can be planned and evaluated. Despite the fact that this is far from the initial concept of a simple relay replacement system these tasks are still required to be carried out by personnel who are not specialists in computing.

So how does task sharing relate to the usefullness of these controllers?

The result of all these requirements of course places conflicting restrictions on the design of the control system. For example trying to cope with data handling in a language originally designed for relay ladder logic is neither easy nor efficient. The idea of automatic diagnostics places considerable restrictions on the program writer unless powerful tools are available to help him write the programs, both in the basic structuring and also in the detail. If in the case of a flexible machine we require a servo position loop and if the loop performance is high either a very powerful central processor is required or restrictions will be placed upon the other programs if the loop is not to suffer. Also the loop would be subject to errors in the other parts of the program if only one processor is available. Whilst it is technically possible to design a single unit with sufficient power to do virtually everything it is not actually desirable since it would no longer be a simple unit to use nor would the result be as reliable in terms of program interaction not to mention the much greater cost of the unit.

The obvious answer lies in creating a range of basic controllers graded in performance with a common I/O structure and a range of subsytems capable of solving the special tasks with only a minimum of interaction with the basic controller to co-ordinate events. Further, they should support a language which supports both logic, data handling, arithmetic etc. and in a structured fashion such that each may easily be achieved and understood. This should be supported by tools to create the programs and integrate them into a working solution. Difficult tasks from say networking would be placed on a communication interface. The setting up of this interface would be easily done with interactive menus.

An example which may be seen today is the area of colour graphics on an operators VDU, it is currently possible to find systems programmed on the one hand in machine code or BASIC and on the other hand there are screen orienttaed systems which allow the picture to be drawn directly on the screen and then data points associated to relevant picture elements. This clearly demonstrates the way forward as opposed to the past, the future must lie in a subsystem for the VDU control closely coupled to the main controller for easy data location. This will plug directly into the rack not via a serial link and also provides a much more responsive screen displays to the operator.

The optimal solution for any particular application will, therefore, use a suitable basic controller and then such optional subsystems as required, if none are required then the basic cost of the controller has not been compromised.

The program will be divided up according to task not only within the basic controller but also across the various programmable elements. Thus providing a clear view of each element as it functions, hence facilitating testing as first the programs are written and then the complete application is built up and commissioned.

What are the requirements this view places on the controller?

The programming environment must support a structured program in which the language format may be freely changed according to the type of program being written. There must be an ability to handle subroutines which should be available ready written for common functions and also which may easily be written for specific application tasks. To make better use of smaller programmable controllers the commonest subroutines should be integrated into their own operating systems thus allowing more efficient operation.

As the control problems become more complicated the system must support increasing numbers of intelligent subsystems and also multiprocessing is a useful option for the main processors, thus further supporting the structured approach.
The increasing requirement for data handling will also mean more use of maths functions. For extended precision and the lesser used functions these may be present as subroutines provided that the execution time is not excessive when compared to the task. As the co-ordinating task becomes more apparent the need to convert data formats will also grow as will the need for data tables and the means to address them (both directly and indirectly). The increased amount of data on the move will also require the ability to handle strings of characters reasonably efficiently ready for the networks to transport them.

The logical consequence of this is that memory capacities will increase steadily and it would be a definate advantage if extra data memory can be added to existing controllers to cope with application growth in an orderly fashion.

This brings us to networking where the primary task is to move blocks of data easily and efficiently between controllers and also other computors found on and around the production area. The requirement defines industrial quality and not office or laboratory equipment. The installation and support must be possible using forseeable levels of trained staff and existing technologies. Using recognised standards for various elements of the systems will allow, for example in the case of 802.3 standard physical media, easy replacement of the co-axial cable with a fibre optic system thus catering for the exceptional case of say, high energy physics!

The use of recognised standards will also allow communication to equipment from other vendors, a classic example being the ubiquitous range of minicomputers. The use of ECMA72 standard implementation of the ISO model level 4 transport layer will further ensure the compatability of the network to this level.

Once the network is implemented it would be expected that programs and diagnostic information should also be available via the network to suport the maintainance of the system.

As time passes the introduction of new and more powerful CPUs must be able to be absorbed into the range, in both hard and software terms. Also it must be possible to upgrade existing systems to cope with the growth of the application without having to change the entire hardware of the existing system just to gain access to the extra power required.

What impact does this have on the development of the coming programmable controllers?

Clearly it dictates that a common family approach is required and that the user environment must be flexible and already fairly sophisticated. Ladder diagram on its own is already insufficient.   The language must allow for extension.

If the environment is to be more sophisticated then it must have a longer life to make understanding it worth while,so again the starting point is critical for success.

If the I/O sub-systems are to be shared then a common I/O bus is required with adequate capacity for forseable expansion, this will also ensure that the life of the sub-systems is enhanced by virtue of being compatible with more than one type or generation of controllers also it will then be possible to create a wider range of systems over an extended period of time.

The structure of the communications interfaces must allow for changes in overall strategy.   Initially by using recognised standards and later by ensuring the applications interfaces are closely controlled for future products.

What requirements does this place on the user, and how can the system help him.

The prime task placed on the user is that of planning and defining what his requirements are going to be within the realistic life of the application.

This starts with the production strategies to be used and proceeds to the main choice of control system family.
From here the more detailed planning of the direction and general time scales allows realistic definition of control system tasks and expected capacity margins.   This is the first of the big cost questions, does the scope of the initial project include all of the very desirable attributes of the total factory concept or must we concentrate on the initial stand-alone production unit?   How can the former not be compromised for the price of the later if it does not fit in the same hardware?   It may boil down to such simple solutions as, put in what is required today and leave the footprint of the larger controller in the cabinet for later, provided that the I/O structure and program can be easily configured into the larger controllers!   Such compromises depend totally on the integrity of the family and the cost effectiveness of the smaller machine which will be retired prematurely from this application, will it still be compatible with the then current range and so be deployable elsewhere?   Again the strength of the current controller system design concept directly affects the

future and the viability of this solution.

As the detail begins to crystalise the decisions become less enormous, how much empty space to leave in racks and memory? Which are the special locations with extra features to be reserved for later and so on through the hardware?

In large applications involving many controllers it is very productive to consider the software in the same way, reserving certain areas and addresses or structures for specific tasks thus easing the maintainance burden later and also identifying common areas which could be setup as common routines and thus only written once hence saving significant costs. Also a frequently overlooked task is drafting a standard for documentation and then including it in the order requirements so that when the duty of support passes to the user he has adequate, similarly laidout, informtion for all controllers and is not hampered with black boxes. It is also important to know that where a supplier tries to claim proprietry rights to his software he describes it so the user may still descriminate between bugs within it and an external fault's influences upon it. This should be found out before the order is placed not at 3 AM on breakdown!

Having placed an order the important phase of monitoring progress starts. This may be greatly assisted if the documentation standard has required the design specifications before the implementation thus allowing verification and simplifying progress monitoring. At this point the strengths of the programming tools will begin to be felt. If they readily support the documentation and relate it to, as yet non existant, code the task becomes efficient and no time is wasted creating separate documents which will become out of date all too soon. Such descriptions will also form the basis of the various tests along the way which culminate in the final witness test for hand over. They will also prove invaluable during commissioning as a guide to the press-ganged extra engineers who always seem to end up trying to solve the problems. Again the programming tools must support the documentation or the end user will not be able to track the ammendments! This may be vey important in terms of health and safety liability should anything unfortunate ever happen due to some alteration made at some undefined time in the project.

Then its a question of the service life of the equipment and both normal maintenance and probable enhancement, either due to plant expansion, phased integration or using the flexability of the controller to help learn more about the application and thus allow more efficient methods to be tried out. A controller is when all said and done still a form of computor capable of keeping tireless watch through the small hours of the night for anything you can define to it, no mater how infrequently it may occur. Any form of alteration is clearly going to require a structured environment to allow the monitoring software to run without affecting the original program.

The progress of the range so far:-

- Range of CPUs sharing common family
  characteristics
- Multiprocesssing option available.
- Tandem CPU option for redundant systems.
- Tandem CPU option for two out of two fail safe systems
- Supporting a choice of 3 styles of analogue and digital I/O all interconnectable.
- Also a wide range of intelligent peripherals.
  - Interface to position encoders of various types.

- Counting and rate measurement to 2MHz
- Fast analogue value capture/output/limit monitoring.
- Zone heating controller cards with directthermocouple input.
- Direct output to analogue hydraulic valves.
- Choice of servo position controller cards.
- Direct output to stepper motor drives.
- User configureable drive/loop controller card.
- Extra data memory card.
- Colour and monochrome VDU controller cards.
- Choice of communication strategies,
    - Point to point
    - Low cost low data rate network.
    - Competative high data rate network.
    - User interface to communication interfaces is standardised
- Use of existing ISO standard for H1
    - Using ECMA 72 Transport protocol ensures interface to MAP is easier to implement.
    - Use of IEEE 802.3 ensures availabilty of alternative physical media, eg. fibre optic.
- STEP 5 supports 3 freely selectable formats
- It is a structured language.
- It supports subroutining.
- It is an expandable language.
- Its programs are easily ported around the family.
- It supports Graph 5 to the draft standard.
    - Structured programming-aid to design.
    - Automatic diagnostics
    - Flowchart structured overview and documentation.

How will the programmable controller fare against the increasingly common personal computor?

In the field of control it is unlikely that therelatively low price of the central processor will actualy overcome its lack of suitable I/O, since in today's terms the cost of CPU power is decreasing much faster than that of reliable industrial quality I/O cards. In fact it is interesting to note that the current cost of a two port serial I/O subsystem with its own intelligence and memory is approximately the same from a leading personnal computor supplier and from ourselves.

In the case where the I/O is not present to affect the decision then this is just another example of task sharing splitting the duty on to a suitable system. There is little doubt about the occurance of such tasks increasing in the factory of the future in such areas as local management information systems acting in a stand-alone mode rather than global systems based on mini computors. In such cases is will be typical for the user to be using high level structuring techniques rather than programming as at present even on personal computors. However, it will normally be the case that they will gather their information from programmable controllers.

In some cases it may even be most effective if the personnal computor is interfaced to the I/O of the programmable controllers directly, where the nature of the task is most suited to the type of environment resulting. Typically this might be a research task involving suitably trained staff or at the other extreme where a standard spreadsheet type program can be used to devise a non critical control task with even less control knowledge than is required for a programmable controller.

Were there to appear a personal computor in the market with similar range of I/O and similar programing methods to a programmable controller then it would by definition be a controller itself and not a PC! The difference while small is still real, and must not be forgotten.

What then is the unique contribution that the programmable controller can make in the future?

This will be based on two things:

1) Its ability to provide economic off-the-shelf solutions to control problems of increasing complexity with an expanding number of interfacing options.

2) Despite this increase in complexity it will not require expert programming knowledge to successfully implement them, by virtue of the language which will continue to develop to encompass enhanced functions within the basic concept. The use of software tools to assist the user will also increase to further improve the user's efficiency.

Proc. 2nd Int. Conf. Machine Control Systems, 257-264
May 1987, © IFS (Conferences) Ltd and authors, ISBN 0-948507-52-7

The influence of sensors on control systems

D Braggins
Machine Vision Systems Consultancy, UK

ABSTRACT

The development of moderately intelligent sensing for robots, driverless vehicles and other automated equipment is bringing into prominence the concept of the semi-ordered state. There is always a cost in moving from a disordered to an ordered state, but there is also a cost in maintaining the ordered state. The effect of modern sensor systems in permitting some limited relaxation of conventional ordering requirements is considered with examples. Ordering may be considered in terms of both space and time, and machine-sensing has an especially important part to play where human influences can disrupt order in either of these dimensions, and in reducing the burden of centralised control of systems generally.

INTRODUCTION

This paper is based largely on observations made during research for two market studies carried out in 1985 and 1986, concerning factory scale automation in the semiconductor industry, and industrial vision systems [1,2]. Because the author specialises in vision, many of the examples involve this form of sensing, but it should be recognised that other techniques such as tactile and ultrasound sensing may be used in addition to, or instead of, vision, as the basis of 'intelligent' sensing. Machine vision is fairly generally accepted as being 'intelligent' while it is not so easy to define what forms the borderline of 'intelligence' with other forms of sensing; it is not intended to offer any formal definition except by example.

ORDERING IN TIME AND SPACE

In any discussion about robotic vision it is common to hear the claim that there should not be need for it, because 'the system' should always know what part is coming down the line at any given time, and the part should be in a known position in space, eliminating the need for either recognition or positioning by vision. It is useful to separate the two cases and consider them individually, though there are times when sensing will conveniently identify and locate a part in a single operation.

SEQUENTIAL ORDERING

Within the realms of industry, any recognition task is likely to be restricted to a choice between a relatively small number of possibilities. If a 'station' forming part of a complete system can recognise what is being presented to it, and that object or assembly is one of a known library of possibilities, the station can 'look-up' the action it should take with respect to that particular item from a pre-entered list; this can all be held on a local basis and the message passing from local station to central control can be reduced to a simple record of action or, possibly, even eliminated entirely.

One way of allowing the station to 'recognise' the object is to use a form of coding, such as a bar-code or pin-code on a pallet; this is perfectly valid and will remain the most attractive and reliable form of recognition in many cases for the forseeable future, but there are situations where the additional work and/or risk of mis-labelling involved in such coding is best avoided, and it is here that we see the more 'intelligent' sensing systems making a contribution.

One of the simplest examples of such recognition was installed on a number of Ford car lines around 1983, to provide recognition of car type prior to robotic application of paint. A relatively simple binary vision system uses the silhouette of the rear of the car body to determine whether it is saloon, estate, or hatchback type - the only relevant differentiation needed. [3]

In 1985 and 1986 more sophisticated vision systems were installed at Ford's new Transit van lines at Southampton and Genk, to check that the expected body variant (out of two dozen or so possibilities) is being presented to a robotic assembly station. In this case the recognition task is a check rather than a primary source of control information; its task is to ensure that human error has not

258

inserted an incorrect panel at some point in the assembly operation. Bar-coding or similar approaches would not detect such errors.

A vision system coping with a very large number of variants was installed in the Volvo truck factory at Torslanda, Gothenberg, Sweden, in 1984. This examines the pattern of holes in truck side members, immediately prior to a robotic plasma-arc cutting operation. It might be thought that, since the holes are drilled automatically, a simple signal from the drilling system to the cutting system would provide sufficient identification, but in fact the two stations are separated by a buffer which can affect the sequence of presentation, and there is also the possibility of manual re-work immediately after automatic drilling upsetting the sequence. The system copes with some 250 or so variants of side-member, each in a left and right hand version. As a bonus, the system also checks that all the holes have indeed been drilled to make the side-member a valid component.

Also in Sweden we find the example of a vision system being used at an ASEA contactor factory to recognise which of eight or so models of plastic housing is being presented on a conveyor belt to a de-burring robot. This system also provides positional information, so that the robot can grasp the box according to the attitude 'seen' by the system, then move 'blind' by dead reckoning to follow a path around the deburring tools which has been pre-programmed for the particular box type recognised. [4] A similar 'recognise and locate' approach is used in deburring toilet seats at the Presalit factory in Denmark - no less than five vision assisted robots are said to engaged on dealing with the various shapes of seat demanded by different national markets!

The common characteristics.

Although the technology of vision sensing is internally complex, the resulting action of the system is extremely simple in the cases outlined. The addition of 'intelligent' sensing to the system provides two distinct advantages. Firstly it allows for a degree of dis-order in the sequence of presentation of components, either through 'unprogrammed' human intervention (whether error, rework, or simply lack of synchronisation). Secondly, it eliminates the costs (both capital and revenue) of identifying the component through the use of some sort of secondary coding, often involving the provision of a carrying device, and it eliminates any source of error from mis-coding, because recognition is based on characteristics of the object itself.

Notice that while recognising the difference between saloon, hatchback, and estate may not appear to need much intelligence, recognising one of about 500 truck side members from its intrinsic pattern of holes is probably beyond the capabilities of most human operators.

Recognition in the semiconductor industry.

The semiconductor wafer fabrication industry is a rather special case of a flexible manufacturing system. On a gross mechanical scale, the wafers on a given line will look indistinguishable, but their properties are quite different according to the patterns exposed and etched into them, and to the chemical layers formed on them. Unlike most mechanical engineering production lines, where output can be almost directly calculated from throughput and input considerations, the process of making semiconductor wafers is affected by significant losses at many manufacturing stages, ranging from loss of a whole wafer due to breakage at an earlier stage, through downgrading of final specification due to process variation, down to rejection of individual 'chips' while still part of the whole wafer, again after dicing, and finally after packaging.

Equipment in the semiconductor industry is generally operating at or near the state of the art, and availability can be a long way from 100%, leading to the need for rescheduling at frequent intervals. Since the yield of each stage in the process can vary significantly the problem of control in a semiconductor plant is daunting, and it is essential to have up-to-the-minute information on the location of each batch of wafers. So far, this has mainly been based on the use of bar codes on, or transponders built into, the cassettes used to transport 25 or 50 wafers at a time. However, wafers are getting bigger and batch sizes are getting smaller, to the point that the industry is talking in terms of 'single wafer batch sizes'. This makes identification of the wafer itself important. The recognition technique must cope with the degradation of the identification as successive layers of silicon and insulating material are built up on the wafer, blurring any initial pattern. It is also highly desirable that the identification is readable by both people and machines. The problem is being tackled in two directions - vision system makers are coming up with lower cost systems which can read even badly degraded alpha-numeric characters, while some manufacturers are moving to identification with numeric-only characters formed by parallel lines whose angle to the horizontal also helps to identify the character. In both cases, notice that the identification is by a 'built-in' characteristic of the component rather than via coding of any secondary carrier.

Because of the particular characteristics of the semiconductor fabrication process, the sequence of output of finished wafers will bear very little resemblance to the input sequence; by identifying each wafer intrinsically, control can be maintained by a combination of manual and automatic identification at relevant points in the process.

SPATIAL ORDERING

The use of sensors to determine the attitude (position and orientation) of a component or assembly is obviously of particular relevance to robotic handling, but also has implications for less flexible automatic handling devices.

The great bin-picking debate.

The task of picking jumbled parts from a bin has long been held out as a kind of 'intelligence test' for robotic vision, just as playing chess was held out as challenge for 'Artificial Intelligence'. Technically, the bin-picking problem was solved as long ago as 1983, when developments at the University of Rhode Island were commercially licensed; a vision guided robot would quite competently pick bolts from a jumbled pile, and at the University, even mixed parts could be picked and identified after picking. [5,6] The development has not been a commercial success; there are two or even three schools of thought about this. One school holds that parts should never be in a jumble; it is fairly easy to point to specific examples where jumbling is necessary for mechanical reasons such as de-burring, or economic reasons where the cost of maintaining an ordered state during transportation would be prohibitive.

A second school holds that a vibratory bowl feeder costing a few thousand pounds is always going to beat a sensory-equipped robot costing several tens of thousands of pounds. The author has much sympathy with this school, but there are limits on the size and shape of what bowl feeders can handle and some components, notably electronic parts, would be damaged by the use of a bowl feeder. The tooling for bowl feeders also tends to be highly specific for each part, reducing the flexibility of systems using them, and the feed mechanisms are notoriously easily jammed, making unattended operation impractical for any any extended period.

The third school, which is perhaps no more than a variation of the second, says that current costs of sensory-equipped robots are far too high, and a radical re-think is necessary to make a machine which has the dexterity and flexibility of a manual bin-picker at a capital cost which can be readily justified as doing no more than replacing a single unskilled operator. In the long term, this may well be what happens, but there is little sign of it becoming reality in the near future.

The practical answer.

What is actually happening now is the adoption of partial ordering coupled with sensory equipped robotic handling, but only for a very limited range of applications.

What do we mean by 'partial ordering'? In general terms, this implies restricting the degree of freedom of the components to a single (usually horizontal) plane at any one time, so that the sensory problem is restricted to two dimensions only. This can mean items lying in a stable state of repose on a pallet or conveyor belt; sometimes a three dimensional arrangement with a separator (probably no more than a sheet of cardboard) restricting operations to a single plane with a step-function between planes.

Examples of this approach range from a vision equipped gantry robot which depalletises engine blocks at Saab-Scania's Sodertalje factory in Sweden, to a vision-equipped SCARA type robot at IBM's Boigny factory in France which takes typewriter ribbon-case mouldings from layers in a cardboard box, orienting and loading them onto an automated assembly line, and discarding each separating layer of cardboard. The contactor-box and toilet-seat de-burring tasks mentioned previously are also examples of this kind, in which the parts are fed on a conveyor belt rather than from pallets or multi-layer pallet-like arrangements.

The economic justifications for these installations are not entirely clear. The contactor-box installation is something of a showcase for ASEA's vision guided robots, though the lack of any need for jigs specific to each model of box provides both an immediate capital saving and a potential saving each time a new design is introduced, and ASEA claims that just one design change will be enough to justify this approach. The toilet-seat installation provides the same benefits and, because the items are relatively large, jigging would be even more costly and less convenient. The Saab installation was justified not so much on direct labour saving (it replaces only one operator) but on eliminating an unpleasant manual task (albeit mechanically assisted) which had a very high labour turnover.

Looking for a moment at the semiconductor field, we see vision being used as an adjunct to specialised automatic handling machines rather than fully flexible robots. It is now becoming common to stick the wafers to a mildly adhesive backing before they are diced; in this way the individual chips remain in position and can be picked up ready for bonding and packaging in an automated fashion. However, as individual chips get bigger it becomes important to precisely orient the positioning head so that the chip is placed squarely and correctly into the package, and here vision sensing is playing a part. There are also situations where chips must be transported individually in 'waffles' (miniature pallets with a depression for each chip), and here the vision sensor must completely orient the chip, using pattern information within it, rather than making a minor correction from the edge information only.

THE CONTROL ASPECT

Where does control come into all this? The message is that adding sensors to handling equipment provides a local positioning control which compensates for variations in position which arise from limited flexibility in presentation of the component. The use of sensory controls relaxes the positioning requirements of handling systems from the rigid, dead-reckoning requirements of a 'blind' robot to the kind of positioning which it would be reasonable to expect in a well ordered but manually operated line. Components are not presented in a totally random fashion; the sensory system is not expected to locate items unless they are on the pallet or conveyor, just as a manual operator should not be expected to search the floor and surrounding workbenches for components.

Positioning for assembly.

So far we have looked at sensory controls for positioning handling mechanisms for individual components; it could be argued that for these, there is always the alternative of jigging and using dead-reckoning instead of a sensory-controlled system. When we look at the use of robots and other devices for assembling additional components or materials onto existing assemblies, we see a further problem which jigging cannot always solve, namely the problem of build-up of tolerances.

Two examples from the automotive field illustrate this problem. One is the automated insertion of windscreens and rear windows in car bodies. The glass needs to be positioned within 1mm tolerance with respect to the aperture, but the aperture can be anywhere within about a 10mm tolerance with respect to the mounting-points without there being anything wrong with the body. (This arises both from build-up of tolerances as the sheet metal parts are assembled, and to distortion in the paint-curing ovens.) It is interesting that the first-ever vision guided auto-glazing system, developed in a very short time for Austin-Rover by VS Engineering in 1983/4, used a separate positioning mechanism mounted on the end of a robot arm because of the difficulty of controlling the robot position directly. Since then, several suppliers offer better integrated sensory control systems, and the one used on the Rover 800 line at Cowley was installed by Automatix.

The second example also comes from Automatix and can be seen on the Rover 800 line; seam sealing robots need to know fairly exactly where the seams are along which sealant must be applied. Tolerance build up, and inexactitude in the mounting of individual bodies, means that simple dead reckoning could lead to application of sealant alongside, rather than on, the seam line. One approach would be to use a true seam-following sensor, similar to the types which have been developed for weld seam following. Another, and the one adopted by Automatix, is to use stereoscopic vision sensing to determine the exact position of the underside of the body in three-dimensional space. Once the co-ordinate transformation from the nominal to the actual position has been determined, the vision system can then simultaneously inform all the robots of the transform so that each follows its own corrected path in space to put the sealant down the true position of the seam.

Yet a third approach would have been to use a combination of projected laser stripes and vision to calculate the position of the body; this is used for the glazing system and elsewhere for some welding applications, and is used for checking the body dimensions of the Rover 800, but the stereo vision proved cheaper for the less demanding sealant application task. (The width of the sealant bead means that tolerances need not be too strict.)

A different approach is to use ultrasound sensors to determine the position and attitude of the entire body in three-dimensional space; developments along these lines, aimed at precision control of painting robots, were reported in 1986 by the Peugot Citroen group. [7]

Driverless vehicles.

The automatically guided vehicle, following stripes on the floor or buried cables, is already a familiar figure in automated factories. If we look again at the semiconductor fabrication industry, we see driverless vehicles which require an even greater degree of control. The vehicle needs to be able to sense what batches it is picking up, carrying, and discharging, and since the objective of automating semiconductor fabrication is to eliminate the presence of people who are inevitably a source of yield-reducing contaminants, the vehicle must automatically interface with the workstations it serves. Some 'clean' AGV's carry their own robots, others depend on automated mechanical handling facilities at the workstations being served. In both cases, the spatial relationship between AGV and docking station is crucial for proper transfer of cassettes of wafers.

Rather than work on a precision mechanical docking arrangement, which would be likely to involve undesirable mechanical shock to the wafers, manufacturers of 'clean' AGV's have looked to sensing systems to provide information about the spatial relationship following an 'approximately correct' docking. One system uses a vision system carried by the AGV-mounted robot to 'look at' reference markings on the docking station; from this, a set of co-ordinate corrections can be made and used to modify loading and unloading paths. Another uses laser triangulation between the body of the AGV and reflectors on the side of the workstation to provide similar information.

IMPLICATIONS FOR THE FUTURE

So far, virtually all the examples quoted have been already installed in industrial situations, mostly during the last three years. What can we expect to see in the future?

Firstly, the cost of vision sensing systems is falling and can be expected to fall further. The original 'enabling factor' for vision was the reduction in the cost of memory; any form of image processing is very memory hungry. This has now fallen to a virtually insignificant level. What we are now seeing is the effect of lower cost cameras, the use of 'industry standard' control processors (typically VME bus and IBM PC bus based), cleverer image processors, and development software which is very much easier and quicker to use for the development of new applications.

The cost of other forms of sensing has not been such a barrier; what can be said is that developments in vision are likely to have a 'knock on' effect on utilisation of other, complementary, sensors.

Secondly, we are beginning to see some self-evidently successful applications of vision sensing which will have a positive effect on the wider adoption of vision for industrial applications. Already many continental European vision companies are overloaded with serious enquiries, though the conversion process is still slow and the economic case for using vision is often difficult to justify on an initial installation, if arguments of flexibility cannot be employed.

Thirdly, and this is perhaps the most important point, the flexibility which sensory-based control offers will take years to become wholly apparent, but as it is found that modifications to products can be introduced much more readily without capital cost in changing sensor-controlled systems, the advantage of sensor based control systems will become more and more apparent.

REFERENCES

[1] 'The automated semiconductor wafer fabrication market in Europe' E864, Frost and Sullivan, New York and London, 1986
[2] 'The industrial vision market in Europe' E937, Frost and Sullivan, 1987
[3] Bartlam, P. and Neilson, G. 'Vision system to identify car body types for spray painting robot'. Proc. Intelligent Robots: Third Int. Conf. on Robot Vision and Sensory Controls Nov. 1983 Ed. Casasent D. and Hall L., SPIE, Bellingham WA, pp.280-285
[4] Karlsten, P. 'ASEA Robot vision offers increased production flexibility'. Proc. 7th Brit. Robot Assn. Conf. 1984 Ed. Brock T., BRA Kempston and North Holland, Amsterdam. pp 165-169.
[5] Kelley, R. 'Heuristic vision algorithm for bin-picking'. Proc. 14th Int. Symp. Industrial Robots & 7th ICIRT 1984 Ed. Martensson N. pp.599-610.
[6] Banks, D. 'Machine Vision - the link between fixed and flexible automation'. Proc. 4th Int. Conf. on Robotic Vision and Sensory Controls Oct 1984 Ed. Pugh A. IFS (Publications) Ltd. Kempston and North Holland, Amsterdam pp.21-25.
[7] Guichard M. and Renault A. 'Industrial use of ultrasonic ranging sensors in robotics'. Proc 6th Int. Conf. Robotic Vision and Sensory Controls June 1986 Ed. Briot M. IFS (Publications) Ltd. Kempston and Springer Verlag, Berlin pp157-164.

Proc. 2nd Int. Conf. Machine Control Systems, 265-276
May 1987, © IFS (Conferences) Ltd and authors, ISBN 0-948507-52-7

Expert system workstation for machine/process maintenance, service and training

J Hadley
Texas Instruments Inc, USA

ABSTRACT

Many companies are installing computer integrated manufacturing and automated control systems into manufacturing and process plants to increase productivity. Unfortunately, actual productivity often significantly lags anticipated productivity levels. One of the factors that causes this discrepency is the inability of service and maintenance personnel to quickly and efficiently repair/maintain the automated machine or application.

Most controls and the applications under their control typically have service costs that range from 10% to 30% of the initial price of that machine or process application. This cost often translates into a cost of hundreds of thousands of dollars in direct service/maintenance costs and lost productivity due to machine or process downtime. The development of an Expert System Workstation can significantly reduce these costs by providing Expert Skills and information when and where maintenance and service personnel need it.

INTRODUCTION

The demands of todays rapidly changing process or manufacturing technology has seriously challenged the ability of traditional training/documentation methods and solutions to effectively process, present, and promote understanding of that technology to maintenance and service personnel. It is imperative that management plan ahead and seek new alternatives to effectively and efficiently deal with this problem......competitive ability will depend on finding and implementing these alternatives. Several elements of change will influence the selection of these alternatives. They include:

1. The cost of hardware and technology is decreasing while labor costs costs are increasing (figure 1).

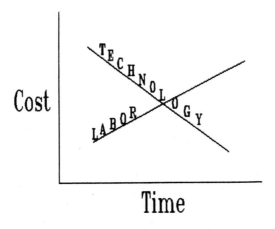

figure 1

2. Diagnostic expert systems are now available allowing for the distribution of needed expertise and information crucial to maintenance.

3. Knowledge and skill are increasingly being considered an asset.

4. Complexity of technology is increasing exponentially while the current knowledge and skill levels for maintenance and service technicians is not increasing at the same rate(figure 2).

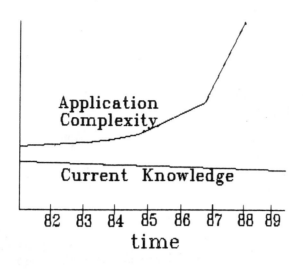

figure 2

Productivity Issues

Maintenance and service is still a labor intensive operation. In terms of productivity the primary concern is still utilization and effectiveness of resources. A closer look at the issue of productivity reveals several issues that impact maintenance utilization. They are:

1. Repair time working with the equipment making the repair
2. Availability and transit time of the maintenance expert
3. Training

time required to keep the technician knowledgeable about the applications under their charge 4. Dead time - wasted time trying to find diagrams, part locations, and absence from the plant. The measure of productivity is of course profits. Each of the above productivity issues can directly increase or decrease the product costs....reducing profitability.

In addition to resource utilization, the effectiveness component of productivity must be considered. Effectiveness is how well the repair /diagnosis was performed....the first time attempted. To repeat the diagnosis/repair of any equipment or application repeatedly can significantly increase the production cost.

Another production related issue is machine or application downtime. Maintenance and service productivity directly impact machine /equipment downtime. Downtime in a typical application can cost $5000 per minute or $300,000 per hour of lost production time. If the production line is down for days or weeks the resulting cost will significantly increase production cost and reduce long term competitive ability.

The challenge is to use technology to provide the performance, training, documentation needed in the process or manufacturing environment. Emphasis should be placed on the role of 'smart tools' like Expert System Workstations to provide the necessary expertise and information required to increase the productivity...and profitability of the technician. These 'tools provide an efficient and effective methodology for dealing with the disparity between the current technician knowledge level and what they need to know to maintain and service increasingly complex applications (figure 3). The key to the success of these Expert System Workstations is the integration of several capabilities into its' operation. The combination of maintenance /service expertise, custom documentation, repair procedures, and an understanding of the application itself all contribute to a short and long term solution of the problem...using technology as apart of that solution.

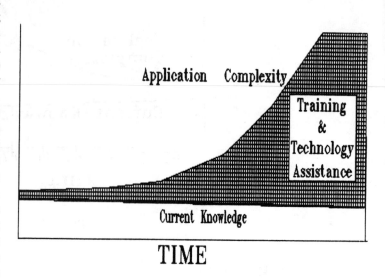

figure 3

The direct benefits would be immediate in terms of reduced machine/process downtime and a consequent reduction in process or manufacturing costs where....

Product Revenue - Product Cost = Profit

...cost reduction translates into increased profitability. In some cases, i.e. the OEM the revenue part of the equation would be increased if the Expert System Workstation was sold as a product to their end user customers....increasing profitability even more.

A potential indirect benefit is the changing of the end user or customers 'perception' of the service technician. This 'perception' could evolve from the presence of the maintenance technician on location to the presence of an on-line Expert System Diagnostic Workstation that would be accessible via phone lines for remote diagnostic capability and analysis. The maintenance or service staff would call the workstation located at some remote site and analyze the failure, determine the components required for repair, obtain the needed documentation, and the best repair procedure.... before going into the field to make the repair.

Another potential major benefit is the use of Expert System Workstation technology to assist the inexperienced technician find and fix the problem quickly. Here the workstation interacts with the technician to determine the problem and provide the necessary information and/or procedure required for quick repair. The major thrust here is to have the inexperienced technician perform like the 'expert'....to reduce equipment and production downtime costs.

The Expert System Workstation is a computerized tool that supports and imposes uniform discipline and information on the maintenance/service technicians troubleshooting strategy and procedures. Here the computer is a 'tool' that provides the 'knowledge' and 'expertise' required to find and fix machine and application problems quickly and efficiently. Typical benefits are a reduction of downtime by 10% to 15%, a reduction in the amount of paper documentation, and reduced training costs.

As the complexity of equipment and applications increases exponentially and the knowledge and skill levels of technicians decreases, the pressure on training and documentation to provide solutions increases exponentially. Here we can use the computer coupled with expert systems, interactive video, on-line documentation, and on-line diagnostic/repair capability to alleviate this pressure. Integrating all of these components into a single computer workstation provides the technician with a 'super efficient' tool. this tool will help them find and fix a problem, show them if necessary, and provide the documentation, i.e. part crib locations, repair procedures, wiring diagrams to finish the troubleshooting and/or repair job . In addition, many workstations are including 'Just In Time' (JIT) training modules to overcome the rising travel and training costs.

These costs often come in the form of lengthy training classes that are typically conducted out of the plant. Often the information covered in this type of training is forgotten and unavailable when needed requiring additional 'refresher training' be provided at additional cost. This JIT training approach provides training when and where it is needed....on-line.

THE COMPLETE PACKAGE

The system described here illustrates an approach that is currently being used to address problems associated with machinery and equipment maintenance in the process or manufacturing environment. The Expert System Workstation contains captured troubleshooting expertise for any application or process. There are several issues addressed by the Workstation that directly impact production cost and/or revenue.

These features are:

1. Diagnose/find problem quickly. The Expert System Workstation typically reduces diagnosis and repair time by 1/2 and often as much as 2/3 translating into thousands of dollars saved because of a reduction in the amount of time required to find the problem. The system is able to reduce this time through the use of a diagnostic procedure and approach used by the expert maintenance person. Once the problem is found the repair procedure used by the 'expert' is provided for quick repair. It is this 'expertise' that increases the speed and effectiveness of the application fault/problem diagnosis and repair. It optimizes the utilization and effectiveness of the maintenance/service resources.....increasing productivity.

2. The availability of expertise. Often in a large factory or plant is difficult if not impossible to locate the expert when needed. In addition, vacations, employee transfer and movement, and remote troubleshooting locations contribute to the inaccessibility of the expert when needed to diagnose and repair an application fault or failure. To the process or manufacturing maintenance technician charged with the troubleshooting and repair of failed production line equipment the Expert System Workstation will assist like The Expert...anytime, anywhere.

3. Reduction in training costs for maintenance personnel. Most maintenance departments cannot afford to train all the people working for them. The cost per individual per school can approach $4000-5000 including travel, tuition, and pay. Multiplying this figure by 5 or 10 employees it is easy to see the maintenance training budget quickly dwindle. To complicate this scenario further, each employee may be responsible for maintaining anywhere from 5 to 15 machines increasing the pressure on the training budget even more. A second training problem is the inadequate retention of the training received. Typically, if the maintenance person is lucky enough to receive training, unless used regularly, they will forget most of the material within a couple of months. Due to the high degree of reliability with certain types of controls and equipment its not uncommon to see very low failure rates, i.e. once every six months or even a year. Consequently, periodic refresher training is often needed to help maintain maintenance/service personnel knowledge of the equipment and applications under their charge. Designing and providing training on-line can alleviate these pressures and reduce overall training costs since the training is always available when and where it is needed.

4. Usable documentation. Most maintenance shops have more than enough documentation to help diagnose and troubleshoot the equipment and machinery on the plant floor. The problem is finding the information in a timely manner...if it can be found at all. There are often 2-5 manuals for each piece of equipment containing from 200 to 500 pages...all packed with information. Typically, the technician doesn't have the time to search through these manuals to find the information needed and if they do find the information they often don't understand or cannot take the time to interpret it. In addition, the overwhelming volumes of information are eliminated as only the information that is needed is provided. This feature minimizes the search time involved with finding a specific piece of information.

Providing a well organized documentation package in a format that is understandable alleviates many of these types of problems.

5. Short and long term maintenance solutions. The Expert System Workstation in addition to solving short term problems, i.e. find the failure and repair the machine quickly, also addresses a long term concern...developing the expertise within the technician. The most efficient technician is one that efficiently troubleshoots based on an understanding of the operation or process. The expert system is a

superior tool that increases the technician's efficiency and effectiveness in finding and repairing the fault/failure. However, the technician using the expert system is dependent on the system to find the problems and solve them. When using the system he/she learns how to repair a single problem. In the long term they will forget the rationale used by the system to find and fix the problem and will fail to develop the internal troubleshooting expertise required to maximize their performance. Providing training with the expert system allows the technician once the problem is repaired, to select the appropriate training module(s) to learn and understand the diagnosis and repair operations, i.e. get the 'big picture' to increase their understanding of the equipment and increase their future troubleshooting capability.

The Expert System Workstation consists of the following elements:

Modes of Operation

The Expert System Workstation approach can be used in one of two modes, i.e. off-line, on-line. The off-line mode requires the manual input of symptomatic information required by the inference mechanism to diagnose the problem(s). This manual entry is done by the electrician/technician using the system. The on-line mode requires a hardware connection between the Expert System Workstation and the machine or connections between the Expert System Workstation and the machine or process on the factory floor. The symptomatic information is automatically up-loaded through this hardware link to the expert system's inference mechanism where the problem is diagnosed. The difference being the way in which symptomatic information is provided to the inference mechanism. Once the problem is determined the repair information is provided for the technician to act on.

Hardware

The hardware is standard off-the-shelf variety and consistent with other systems found in the process or manufacturing environment. The hardware components include:

1. Texas Instruments Business Pro computer operating as an IBM-PCAT clone. The computer has a 40 Mbyte hard disk drive, 640 Kbytes of memory, a single floppy disk drive, and color graphic display capability. In addition, the computer contains video interface/control boards.

2. A Zenith touchscreen monitor that is used to input information into the computer. The touchscreen monitor is used as an alternative to the keyboard. In some applications another mode could be used, e.g. light pen, barcode, speech etc.

3. A Sony LDP 2000 laserdisk to provide audio and video information. Some applications require CD ROM instead of the laserdisk. Software The inference mechanism and the knowledge base management system was generated by the Personal Consultant (TM) tool kit manufactured by Texas Instruments. Personal Consultant (TM) allows the knowledge

engineer to rapidly generate the rule-based expert system and create a text oriented knowledge base. In addition, all future modifications and changes to the knowledge base would be through the editing capability of Personal Consultant (TM). All laserdisk I/O routines are handled by software in compiled 'C'.

Knowledge Base

The knowledge base contains the sum total of all information required by the inference mechanism to diagnose, repair, and train the maintenance technician. The knowledge base is sub-divided into procedures and operations, documentation, and training. The information presented from each of these areas is delivered or presented to the technician in one or more media formats, e.g. text, audio, video, static graphic overlays, or hardcopy printouts.

The media selected for delivery of the knowledge base's information is determined by two criterion. First, where the complexity of information is high a visual media is used. In some cases, a static graphic picture is adequate. However, where extremely complex and lengthy procedures are required, video would be used. Second, the majority of maintenance electricians/technicians tend to be 'visually' oriented. As a group, they would prefer to be shown how to rebuild a motor rather than have the same procedure described in 10-20 pages of text. Video provides a mechanism to deliver in concentrated form complex information and procedures efficiently and effectively. Since, as a group they prefer the visual format, the probability of their using the system increases...it makes interpretation and repair easier, more efficient and less error prone.

The procedures and operations section of the knowledge base contains detailed information required by the maintenance technician during the diagnosis or repair of the problem. This information can range from a simple request for the status of an indicator light to the detailed explanation of how to rebuild a motor.

The documentation section contains all the diagrams, switch settings, reference information etc. that is required to diagnose and repair the machine fault. This information is controlled by the expert system and made available when needed by the technician. For example, if the technician needed a wiring diagram the expert system would upon request printout the diagram. The need to page through volumes of documentation is eliminated as the expert system points and accesses any information that is required during the diagnosis and repair operations. In addition, documentation can be customized to provide machine specific information, i.e. switch settings for the control processor module on the stamping press and not just a general description of the switches and their function.

The training section typically contains training modules on preventative maintenance, equipment/process startup procedures, general systems operation and repair procedures. The training modules are designed to be used as stand alone tutorials or for use in the diagnosis and repair of the machine/operation fault. As tutorials, the training modules are used when the process/equipment is operating normally. Segments of the training modules can be used to provide the precise detail required to either diagnose or repair the system. For example, to identify the proper operation of the controller, the technician must use a program panel and check the status of error codes/bits contained in the controller memory. To determine the status of these error codes, the technician must know how to use the program panel and interpret the information found in memory. If these procedures are unknown or forgotten, a portion of the training module on 'Program Panel Operation' would be provided by pressing a Workstation 'HELP' key. The 'HELP' key would display information telling/showing the technician step by step what to do to gather and interpret the information required by the diagnostic portion of the expert system. Portions of training modules could be used the same way to show the proper repair procedure when 'HELP' is needed making the repair. Training modules are typically formatted in video/audio or static graphics accompanied by text explanation. These modules use a visual medium to present a concentrated or detailed form of information.

PACKAGE DEVELOPMENT CYCLE

The development of this Expert System Workstation follows the six steps explained on the following page (figure 4):

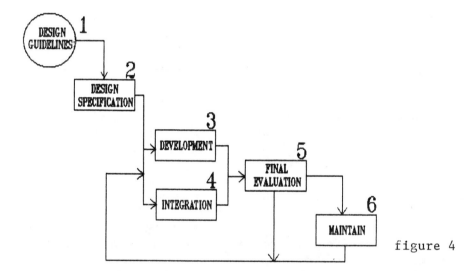

figure 4

1. Preliminary Design Guidelines - Once the project is identified a meeting of the knowledge Engineer(s) and the Domain Expert(s) is conducted to determine project guidelines, constraints, and the expert for the project. The product of these meetings is called a Requirements Summary. This Requirements Summary details in report form this information.

2. Detailed Design Specification - Once the Requirements Summary is approved the Knowledge Engineer(s) and the project Domain Expert meet to determine the specific goals, objectives, tasks, documentation and training to be covered. In addition the best media form for the information in the Knowledge Base is determined. All hardware and software required for delivery and connection to the application is also identified.

3. Development – For most problems the development of the inference mechanism is conducted in an iterative fashion as information is exchanged and modified by the Knowledge Engineer and Expert. The information is modular for easier debugging. The rules and text procedures are entered using the Personal Consultant TM Toolkit. This toolkit allows the Knowledge Engineer to quickly generate the inference mechanism for review by the Expert. The training modules, video, graphic overlays, and documentation are usually developed in parallel with the inference mechanism and reviewed by the Expert. Storyboards are used for preliminary review and approval before going into final video production. Internal evaluation and validation of all materials is conducted iteratively with the expert.

4. Integration – Once the inference mechanism and knowledge base are complete the individual training, video, graphic overlays etc. must be 'connected' or linked in software to produce the desired functionality of the workstation. All linking software is finalized here.

5. Final Evaluation – The working Expert System Workstation is moved to the plant floor environment for final testing by inexperienced technicians. If bugs or problems are detected the necessary corrections are made and the system is evaluated again.

6. Maintenance of System – The process or manufacturing environment is in a constant state of change. As changes in machinery and processes occur, corrections in the knowledge base need to be made. The corrections to the non-video portions of the knowledge base are easily made with the Personal Consultant Toolkits editing operations. This effort can be supported in-house or by an outside contractor or vendor. The amount of time required to develop a complete Workstation will vary depending on the complexity of the application. Typically development time can range from 6 man months for a small project up to 16 man months for a complex system.

SUMMARY

Unfortunately, many process or manufacturing plants ignore the complexity versus the maintenance/service knowledge level issue when planning the design and implementation of plant automation. Several automotive manufacturers have already learned that automating production and process lines does not guarantee anticipated increases in productivity. The increased production output is often offset by downtime resulting from the inability of service and maintenance personnel to keep the machinery, equipment and processes operational. It is often the failure to use technology to assist the maintenance and service organization in order to compensate for automations complexity that exacerbates the maintenance issue and increases downtime costs. Specifically, issues like downtime, availability of expertise, training, and documentation costs will increasingly become part of any automation plan. These issues need to be addresses in the initial design and planning stages to avoid costly maintenance and service problems later. The question of maintenance and service effectiveness will continue to be an issue as application complexity increases; it will be an integral part of any profitable automated assembly installation. It makes good sense to use technology to solve the new problems caused by technology....the Expert System Workstation is one successful approach that addresses this problem.

The promise for an integrated functional approach to the delivery and interaction of Expert System Workstations is impressive. Their ability to reduce process or manufacturing down- time cost is dramatic. The benefits more than justify the development of the package.

TRENDS

The promise for the industrial application of the Expert System Workstation approach is immense. However, AI in general is not a mature technology. It is in a constant state of change as well as the Expert System Workstation hardware and software used to implement this technology. There are several key trends that will have drastic effects on the direction of these vehicles:

1. The tendency is for the delivery hardware to become physically smaller....and cost less. In the not too distant future we might see the Expert System Workstation in a package the size of a notebook and costing 1/3 of the present system hardware.

2. On-line Systems are increasingly in demand. Many process or manufacturing environments have local area networks connecting manufacturing or process hardware together for more efficient, effective control and monitoring. These networks are typically connected to a mini or micro computer that performs data logging and collection. The tendency is to want the Expert System Workstation connected to the network or Host computer in an On-Line mode. Once connected the workstation could automatically up-load diagnostic information over the network, analyze the information, and show the technician what to do to fix the problem.

3. There is considerable interest in the area of predictive maintenance using the Workstation to perform an analysis based on predictive information from the field, i.e. vibration analysis, and recommend a course of action.

4. Another area of interest is dial-up diagnostic systems. Here, an expert system is located in a remote site. It is accessed through a modem and phone lines by a host computer. The remote expert system diagnoses the failure and sends the diagnosis and repair solution to the host when complete. In this example, the Workstation could be used to provide information to a host computer and/or provide repair information and documentation to the technician that is already at the remote site.

5.   In addition to reducing service related cost the workstation has the
      potential to be marketed as a stand alone product. The independent OEM
      or machine builder in addition to reduced service costs can realize
      additonal revenue from the sale of this value added capability.

REFERENCES

1.   Herrod, Richard A. and Smith, Michael O., The Campbell Soup Story: An
      Application of AI Technology in the Food Industry, Texas Instruments
      Engineering Journal, Jan.-Feb.   1986, Vol. 3, No. 1, pp. 16-19.

2.   Choat, James N., Expert System Based Machinery Diagnostics, Texas
      Instruments Industrial Systems Division Technical Newsletter, Oct.
      1986, Vol. 3, No. 2, pp. 10-13.

Proc. 2nd Int. Conf. Machine Control Systems, 277-288
May 1987, © IFS (Conferences) Ltd and authors, ISBN 0-948507-52-7

Design concepts in the 'Design to product' Alvey demonstrator

J R Harris
GEC Electrical Projects Ltd, UK

ABSTRACT

'Design to Product' is a collaborative project involving the Universities of Edinburgh, Leeds and Loughborough, HUSAT, the National Engineering Laboratory, Lucas CAV, GEC Research, GEC Avionics and GEC Electrical Projects. The project is applying advanced techniques in IKBS, MMI, and SE to produce an 'Engineering Design Support System' (EDSS) that could be used to help Designers at any stage of product development from initial design through manufacture to in-service support.

The basic objective of Design to Product is to provide the specification of such a system. The key features will be its ability to integrate diverse sources of engineering information and to provide powerful techniques for using that information. A public interface to the system will allow third party knowledge bases and specialised processes to be included as parts of a Design to Product system. In 1990 a partial implementation of the DtoP specification will be demonstrated. Subsequent developments will lead to commercial products in the early to mid 1990's.

At the heart of Design to Product are two knowledge bases, one containing general domain knowledge and the other the evolving description of the product design. The domain knowledge is all the information contained within the system that might be useful to the designer. The Product Description is a body of information that describes the product design in formal terms. The system supports 'intelligent' tools that can access these knowledge bases. The designer uses these tools to create a description of the product containing all the information required to develop, manufacture, and maintain the product. Information from this product description drives an automated flexible manufacturing system (also being developed for the project) to manufacture the designed components.

The integrated nature of the system and the power of the tools will he[lp] ensure the consistency and accuracy of a design, promote coordination [between] individuals working on a common product and reduce the time taken [to take a] product from its conception to full manufacture. The philosophy of the [Design to] Product system is to allow modular components to be added or remove[d ...]. There is a clear emphasis on distributed computing, communication[...] construction, with clear techniques for integrating third part[y software and] hardware.

1.   INTRODUCTION

The Alvey Directorate was set up by the government in 1985 and has established a national programme of collaborative research and development in four key areas of information technology, namely, Man-Machine Interfaces (MMI), Intelligent Knowledge Based Systems (IKBS), Software Engineering (SE) and Very Large Scale Integration (VLSI). As part of the Alvey programme four 'Large-Scale Demonstrators' are being funded, each devised to illustrate potential commercial applications of these key technologies. GEC Electrical Projects has been awarded the contract for one of these Large Scale Demonstrators called the 'Design to Product'.

2.   PROJECT BUDGET AND TIMESCALES

'Design to Product' has a budget of £9M (£5M from the Alvey Directorate and £3M from the industrial partners) and will last five years. There are two phases, a pilot phase followed by a full demonstrator phase each of 2.5 years duration.

During the current (pilot) phase the structure of the system and the fundamental features of its key components have been developed. The pilot phase will conclude with demonstrations of these prototype system components in September 1987.

During the full demonstrator phase of the project, the pilot phase software will be further developed and integrated into the full 'Design to Product' system. This phase will end with a demonstration of 'Design to Product' at the Lucas CAV factory in Gillingham in March 1990.

3.   THE CONCEPT OF 'DESIGN TO PRODUCT'

3.1   Design today

'Design to Product' is directed at that sector of industry manufacturing electro-mechanical products and which has a requirement for the small batch production of a wide variety of different parts.

In general terms the use of computers and computing techniques in manufacturing industry has brought some benefits but not as much as has been anticipated.
_____ ____ reasons for this, amongst the more important being

within their own skills and specialisms.

w integrated systems addressing a range of functions.

ng an important decision is frequently not available at

t encourage learning, either of system capabilities, es seldom exists.

as of CIM technology is the development of the ice and manufacturing facility. What is required is a strong information flow both in the forward and feedback directions between the design and manufacturing stages. Such a link would allow each to contribute to and learn from the other. Many believe that success in this area will provide the biggest pay back of all. Design to Product (DtoP) is addressing this concern, although in the time and with the finance available, it's achievements will point the way rather than provide complete solutions.

3.2   Engineering Design and Manufacture - The Conventional Way

Typically the procedures and operations carried out in the design and manufacture of engineered products are organised in a sequential way. Having identified the specification for a product the process starts with schematic design followed by further detailed design. There then follows separate stages for manufacturing planning, manufacture, and quality assurance before despatch to the customer who may then require maintenance and servicing facilities.

When the design, manufacture and quality assurance operations are completed a considerable volume of knowledge about the particular product will have been generated; about its
function, shape, manufacture and test performance. The problem is that some of this knowledge is lost between the different stages, and what survives is distributed throughout the organisation. Consequently some knowledge has to be recreated at different places and in different forms. This sequential structure leads to inconsistencies and difficulties when attempting to transfer knowledge in ways other than that envisaged initially. This product knowledge generation,transfer, loss and regeneration is illustrated in figure 1. Product knowledge generated is represented by the vertical axis and the sequential design and manufacturing stages are represented by the horizontal axis. The generation of product knowledge is then described by a rising "saw-tooth" form as knowledge is generated during each stage and some of it is lost between stages.

3.3   CAD/CAM and its Current Developments

The introduction of computer aided drafting/design and computer aided manufacturing systems into the traditional engineering design and manufacturing procedures has not changed the fundamentally sequential process described. What they have done is to improve the efficiency and speed with which certain stages in the sequence are performed. By their support of standard parts and part program libraries, they have improved the knowledge distribution problem in certain areas. However as they still support the sequential knowledge transfer concept they do little to correct the knowledge loss and regeneration problem.

The present developments in the CAD/CAM and CIM areas can be seen as attempts to link existing islands of computer based aids or automation: e.g. computer aided drafting to NC cutter path generation to NC part program preparation, or process planning, and part programming to production control. However, these islands are still part of the traditional sequence of the design and manufacture stages. Simply to join them up with common data bases and supply computer data links does not remove the inefficiencies inherent within this type of organisation. Although perhaps smoothed in places, the rising "saw-tooth" form generation of product knowledge still remains. The difficulties of communicating knowledge between engineering design and manufacture are also not removed, nor are the data consistency and management problems. This failure to achieve real integration using current CAD/CAM and CIM systems means that the integrated inter-disciplinary functioning and continuity of operations which is required to improve the efficiency and flexiblity of a manufacturing company is not realised.

3.4 The Concept of DtoP

An aim of the DtoP project is to remove the losses in the product knowledge generation cycle, leaving a smoothly rising line, and to solve the knowledge consistency and management problems inherent in existing design and manufacturing methodologies. The concept with which these aims are being met is that of an integrated and unified product description, whose consistency is maintained and managed by the DtoP system, and contains all the knowledge generated about a particular product at any time. Thus, it is the commonality of the knowledge required and generated during a product's design, manufacture and serviceable life which is seen as the new underlying unifying and integrating factor. Design has therefore to be seen, not necessarily as a sequence of design, planning and manufacturing stages, but as whole product generation activity comprising a number of processes that can be organised freely and flexibly as the situation demands. The introduction of flexibility and the central management of product data into the design process facilitates the feedforward and feedback of knowledge between the design stages.

In other words, the product design activity is placed at the centre of the product generation process where each stage can more easily and directly influence the others in an integrated and consistent manner.

3.5 Design using 'Design to Product'

The intention of 'Design to Product' is to provide powerful tools able to support designers at (in principle) any stage of product development. Such tools must be capable of working in conjunction with existing systems and techniques, however the much greater benefits are realised by building these tools into an integrated design support system. The design support tools of the system assist the designer to make effective decisions, and their integration enables the design data to be shared efficiently by all tools. Most importantly the system will manage the records describing the product design as they develop so releasing the designer from a very time consuming aspect of his work. This combination of powerful decision support and extensive record management will allow major improvements in design productivity.

'Design to Product' systems could be developed to support many diverse fields of design. For the project itself the target domain is the design of small electromechanical and mechanical components appropriate to diesel fuel pumps being developed by Lucas CAV. Particular tools are being developed to support the high level design of a part starting with a functional specification and to support the planning and detailing of the manufacturing operations required to machine and assemble the product.

Tools to support the analysis of parts (e.g for strength, vibration and thermal characteristics) or to simulate their operation are not being developed as part of the project. However such tools are likely to be components of a future fully developed system.

To ensure that 'Design to Product' provides facilities that match the tasks of design and manufacture requires a firm understanding of the fundamental processes used to develop a design. Within the project HUSAT is studying the procedures Lucas designers currently use to design typical diesel fuel pump parts. The insight gained from this work has strongly influenced the development of the 'Design to Product' by indicating what domain knowledge should be contained in the system, what tools would be useful and what characteristics the user interfaces for these tools should have.

4.   THE 'DESIGN TO PRODUCT' SYSTEM DESIGN

The software for 'Design to Product' has two major components, the 'Engineering Design Support System' and the 'Factory Control System'.

4.1   The Engineering Design Support System - its Structure and Operation

The Engineering Design Support System comprises a set of processes organised around an Intelligent Knowledge Base called the 'Product Description' (PD).(fig. 3) Each process supports some aspect of design activity and provides specialised tools for the user to select and operate. The EDSS is based on the premise that the user retains full control of the design process. He determines how the design problem is tackled and is free to select what tools to use and when to apply them, to accept or reject information the system provides, and to introduce his own information. The requirement for such flexibility places onerous conditions on the design of both the user interfaces to the system and the central Information Management System.

Currently the design support processes are selected and controlled directly by the user using simple interfaces. Similarly the Product Description exists only in a simplified experimental form. During the full demonstrator phase better user interfaces tailored to the user contexts will be developed to mediate between the user and the operation of the individual tools. The Product Description and Information Management System will also be fully implemented.

The user builds formal descriptions of the parts being designed in the PD by interactive sessions with the system tools. The Information Management System maintains the status of and relationships between the data records describing the design as they evolve. Any information stored in the Product Description is potentially available to any tool in the system so allowing the easy exchange of data between the tools of the Design to Product. In the eventual fully developed multi-user and multi-processor Design to Product system the Information Management System will also ensure integrity of shared data.

4.2 Design Support Processes in 'Design to Product'

Within 'Design to Product' particular effort is being directed to developing processes in the Engineering Design Support System for

- Outline specification and design ('The Edinburgh Designer System'); this work is being carried out by the team at Edinburgh University.

- Geometric modelling and the automated generation of machining data (based on NONAME, a CSG 3-D modeller developed by Leeds University); this work is based at Leeds.

- Process planning and NC part programming for machining operations; this work is being led by Loughborough University.

- Planning and control of assembly; this work is being carried out jointly by GEC-Research and Lucas-CAV.

The Factory Control System uses data from the Product Description and is part of the integrated system although it is not a design tool in the sense implied above.

5.   THE DESIGN SUPPORT PROCESSES IN 'DESIGN TO PRODUCT'

5.1   The Edinburgh Designer System

Edinburgh University are using techniques drawn from AI research to build a suite of tools to aid the user develop the design of a part, starting with its initial functional specification. Engineering knowledge in the EDS is held in a Declarative Knowledge Base (DKB) as fragments of information ('Unit modules') organised in a network structure. Each Unit Module contains declarative knowledge using formal representations developed by the project. (Fig. 2)

The aquisition of knowledge and determining its representation is a major part of the definition of any IKBS and 'Design to Product' is no exception. The structure and contents of the DKB depend totally on the design applications that the Designer System is intended to support. An extensive process of knowledge elicitation is required to formalise the design process used in a given context before appropriate information modules and knowledge representations can be defined. For 'Design to Product' this work is expected to continue throughout the course of the project.

Designs for new parts often result by refining the designs of existing parts. This requires powerful techniques for finding parts of previous designs that would provide useful starting elements. Methods must then be available for modifying the element in a controlled manner, combining elements in novel ways, and creating new elements.

The DKB provides the structures that index the elements of information contained in the knowledge base. During the development of a product description the designer examines the knowledge bases for useful information. From this examination and his knowledge of the state of the current design the designer develops the Product Description. To do this he will decide, for example, to use instances of particular unit modules, to specify values or relationships between parameters, to define the shape of or spatial relationships between modules. From these statements the system uses built in inference engines to infer any resulting consequences.

To assist the designer the powerful information management functions of the system identify conflicting design statements and the base assumptions from which these statements derive. It also allows him to temporarily constrain the development of a design to those areas of direct interest to him. By this iterative process of assertion, evaluation and modification of design statements the user progressively evolves the design description, the records of which are held in the Product Description.

Designers frequently consult colleagues, specialist books or use standard procedures to develop the detail of some aspect of the design. Subsystems called 'Specialists' within the Designer System will play a similar support role. Specialists could be developed that will assist the user to take account of manufacturing constraints, estimate costs, and assess the reliability and maintainability of his design.

Of considerable interest will be the inevitable development of large computer knowledge bases by suppliers, research bodies and other commercial organisations. Such knowledge bases are likely to support particular specialised aspects of design and will ultimately allow the designer to directly reference a supplier for product information, special design criteria and of course costs. The developments in Design to Product are being directed towards understanding what characteristics such support specialists should have and to investigate techniques for implementing them. Ultimately Design to Product will incorporate many such 'specialists' drawn from many diverse sources and covering all aspects of the product life cycle.

Other general purpose tools being developed for the Designer System support the algebraic manipulation of symbolic equations, the calculation of tolerance information, the deduction of spatial relationships and the manipulation of tabular information. In each case the intention is both to show the application of the facility and to provide a useful cost saving tool for design and manufacture.

5.2   The Generation of Manufacturing Data

Once a design has been developed to a point that it can be described geometrically then it becomes possible to generate process plans to describe the manufacturing operations required to make the part. Conventionally a production engineer will use a 'group technology' approach to process planning. In this, parts related to the manufacturers product range are categorised into families that are manufactured in a similar manner. A target part is classified into one of the predefined families and its corresponding generic process plans selected. This provides the starting point for the design of a bespoke process plan for the target part.

In Design to Product the approach is basically similar but by integrating process planning with feature visualisation, automatic generation of cutter paths and AI based process planning substantial benefits in accuracy and productivity can be achieved.

One aspect of the work in the 'Generation of Manufacturing Data' section of Design to Product is directed to developing knowledge bases for process planning. Another aspect is devoted to the design and construction of software tools to assist particular process planning activities, such as the selection of cutting tools and fixtures, machine tools and cutting processes and the ordering of process operations. The key characteristic of this work is that all the process planning tools can access both the product descriptions and the declarative knowledge bases of the system. The output of the process planning activity extends the formal description of the design held in the Product Description. This integration of functions by using a common set of knowledge bases ensures that knowledge generated early in the design process is always available for use later in the process. This contrasts strongly with the current situation where the information may well not be explicitly carried forward and has to be expensively and generally inaccurately recreated at a later stage.

Once an ordered set of operations to manufacture the part has been decided , NC part programs can be compiled. For this a proprietry part programming system is being used.

Many of the techniques being applied in this section of the project are known and being used today although not gnerally in an integrated manner. The real benefit in using formal data and methodologies in the manufacturing areas is to ensure that the design rules from which it has been derived are correct. Feedback which provides the ability to modify and improve the original data is the key difference that makes systems using an integrated approach so powerful. The emphasis is not on having the most efficient process plan or NC program, but in having an effective solution (with hopefully an alternative) quickly. Many will have experienced situations where part programmers skill is used to edit part programs to bring about small time savings while machines stand idle and operators look on. The optimisation of the whole product lifecycle is a goal of DtoP.

5.3   The Generation of Assembly Data

This area of work in Design to Product parallels the Generation of Manufacturing Data process for automated assembly. The state of the art in automated assembly is not as advanced as for automated machining and much fundamental work is required to identify the techniques for the control of robotic assembly systems before the 'Generation of Assembly Data' processes can be clearly defined. However there are many parallels between assembly and machining which suggest that in the future the two areas (at least in part) may be supported by common tools.

5.4   The Geometric Modelling Process

The geometry engine in 'Design to Product' is based on the Leeds Constructive Solid Geometry modeller 'NONAME' and will provide a vital general purpose tool supporting all the other processes in the system. Typically it will be used to calculate geometry and mass property information, evaluate dimensions, recalculate tolerance frames and generate tool paths for the NC program generation.

The physical appearance of many products is a vital aspect of their design and to support this the geometric modelling process will provide visualisation capabilities typical of conventional CAD systems. An IGES interface is included in the modeller to allow the transfer of geometry information to draughting packages or to other modelling systems.

5.5   The Man - Computer Interfaces to 'Design to Product'

The complexity of the design task combined with the flexibility and range of resources the 'Design to Product' system could provide poses many challenging problems of user interface design. Exactly what characteristics the user interfaces for the 'Design to Product' should have, have not yet been fully specified. They will depend upon the outcome of the current studies of the design process being carried out by HUSAT. The functional capabilities of the design support processes under development in the project and upon the capabilities of the Sun workstations on which the project development work is being carried out are other important factors. Currently each design support process will have its own interface for experimental purposes. The main interface implementation work will be carried out in the full demonstrator phase of the project. Although these studies have yet to be completed it is apparent that the designer must be able to call up extensive and very well developed help, support and explanation systems that tell him quickly and efficiently the why, what and how of the system state at any time. There are many techniques under development in this area, witness for example the facilities provided by the Macintosh and other personal computers. Design to Product must look and feel at least as good to be successful and to this end the project is devoting substantial resources.

5.6   The Factory Control System

The implementation of the factory systems for the project is in two phases, pilot and demonstrator. For the pilot phase a small FMS machining cell is currently under construction by GEC - Electrical Projects 'FAST' division at Rugby. The cell includes a CNC lathe, CNC machining centre with robot loading, a CNC inspection machine and the GEC free ranging AGV. The whole will be controlled by an advanced modular cell controller currently under development at Rugby. Process plans and part programs generated by the Engineering Support System can be accessed by the cell controller. Part program development can be carried out on the shop floor and then returned to form part of the evolving Product Description. By this means a consistent record of the design evolution can be maintained.

A prototype flexible assembly cells is being developed by GEC - Research at Gt. Baddow. This is based around the TETRABOT (a parallel robot being developed by GEC Research). The cell is being used to investigate assembly techniques using real-time sensor feedback and reconfigurable grippers.

Running in parallel with the GEC Research work Lucas are building an assembly cell directed towards analysing and developing techniques of assembly appropriate for flexible manufacture.

For the demonstrator phase of the project the GEC - Research work will be integrated into the cell at Lucas-CAV to produce a demonstration of flexible assembly in a production environment.

6.   FUTURE PROSPECTS

The Alvey Demonstrator projects are intended both to show possible applications of research in the four key areas and to accelerate the introduction of advanced products to the market place. 'Design to Product' will demonstrate in 1990 certain aspects of its concept in detail. Thereafter development of commercial products will continue. To be commercially valuable a 'Design to Product' system must be a tool that designers both wish to use and find helps them (in a cost effective manner) to produce better solutions to their design problems. To achieve the first the system must have effective user interfaces, provide useful design tools and have a good performance. To achieve the second requires an extensive period of knowledge engineering to create the general knowledgebases contained in the system that describe the application design environment to be supported. Throughout the life of the system these knowledge bases will have to be updated and extended. Tools to support this maintenance will be part of the system. Finally to be acceptable commercially the system must be able to work with the design tools customers currently use. Consequently the Design to Product system must provide interfaces using data exchange standards where they exist and may well have to develop standards where they do not.

7.   HARDWARE AND SOFTWARE

Design to Product is being developed on SUN single user workstations with the UNIX operating system. A variety of languages are being used, notably POPLOG (a mixed language system for PROLOG,LISP and POP11), C, FORTRAN, and PASCAL.

8.   CONCLUSIONS

Design to Product offers the possibility of a rational approach to design. It will provide specialised tools to support important parts of the design process, provide the mechanisms for integrating the tools and manage the records of the design description as they evolve. Finally by providing an integrated and direct path to the factory systems it should prove possible to move rapidly and accurately from the design phase of a product to its manufacture.

9.   ACKNOWLEDGEMENTS

This paper draws extensively on the work of all the collaborators in the 'Design to Product' project.

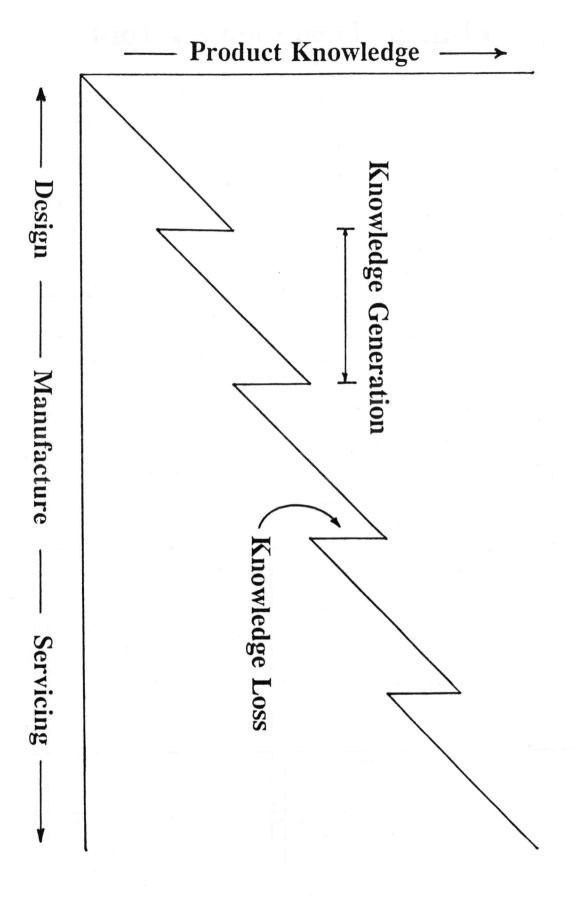

Fig. 1

287

Edinburgh Designer System

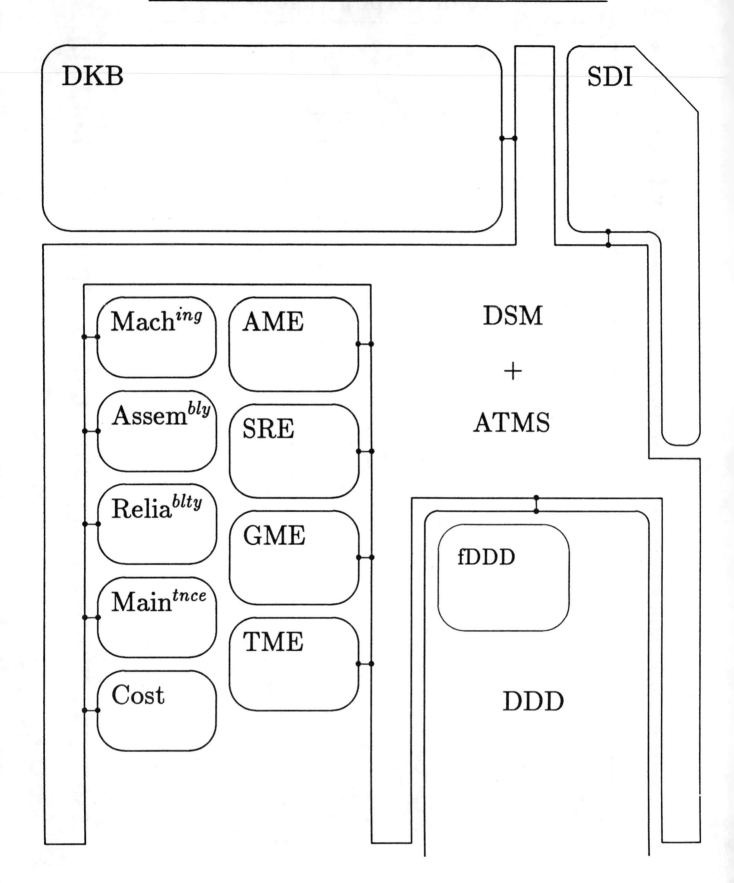

Fig. 2

Proc. 2nd Int. Conf. Machine Control Systems, 289-294
May 1987, © IFS (Conferences) Ltd and authors, ISBN 0-948507-52-7

System identification: a new modelling technique
C Boulton
Cambridge Consultants Ltd, UK

ABSTRACT

There are many benefits to be gained by modelling of systems under study, particularly for the design and development of control systems. Such modelling studies can however face severe problems in the case of complex or ill understood systems. System identification which compares inputs and outputs to give a black box model offers a cost effective modelling technique for a wide range of problems.

SYSTEM IDENTIFICATION: A NEW MODELLING TECHNIQUE

INTRODUCTION

To date a common and generally reliable technique for implementing control systems has been to put the controller in place; then run the system, and adjust the controller parameters until everything is more or less satisfactory. This approach does have drawbacks. It demands considerable skill and experience, it is very dependent upon an understanding of the controlled system, and system performance can be degraded during tuning, sometimes in a dangerous way.

Both the demand for better performance through higher efficiencies and the development of more-complex processes, have called for a more rigorous method of deriving controllers. A control design which is no better than satisfactory can represent significant financial loss in terms of a less-than-optimum performance. Market pressures demand high performance from current installations, and preclude the building of new plant. The obvious approach is to look at ways of improving the performance of existing equipment.

MODEL DEVELOPMENT

An efficient, comprehensive, and very informative way to develop a control system is via a mathematical model of the system to be controlled. This offers several advantages. Once the model has been set up it is possible to derive the necessary control algorithm and its parameters without further interfering with the plant. It is possible to experiment with the model in a way usually not permissible with a real system. Often the model itself gives an insight into the characteristics of the system, greatly aiding understanding.

Developing a model, however, is not without its concerns. The normal technique is to derive mathematical equations which describe the underlying physics or chemistry of the system. The parameters of the equations are compiled according to the system being modelled. The equations can be solved, and the solutions will describe the behaviour of the system. The control system can then be designed to modify the behaviour to that required.

Hardly surprisingly, the above procedure, encounters a few problem areas. If the physics and chemistry of a process or system are extremely complex, or ill-understood, it may be impossible to assemble the equations. A major problem of simulation is the availability of data for the equations, for example, heat transfer coefficients, fluid drag coefficients, friction levels and so on, because the fidelity of the final model hinges on the accuracy of these figures.

The evolution of a computer model is particularly valuable when an installation is at the design stage. It can aid the achievement of a deeper understanding of the system behaviour, sensitivity to particular parameters can be established, failure modes can be investigated and operating procedures developed. The very process of evolving the computer model raises questions which enhance the understanding and design of the new process.

SYSTEM IDENTIFICATION

For processes, plant, machinery and systems already in existence, deriving a fully detailed computer model can represent something of an overkill. In particular, for a single and potentially simple control system enhancement or tuning, much effort could be expended merely to get to the model stage. System identification offers a way forward.

System Identification is an approach which, instead of trying to model every aspect of the system, views it as a black box with inputs and outputs and represents the behaviour of the system as a single mathematical equation relating the outputs to the inputs.

For example, a car engine may be modelled in exhaustive detail with the chemistry and physics of the combustion process, the inlet and exhaust flow dynamics and the rotational and reciprocating dynamics with friction loads and inertia effects. If such a model is evolved it is an extremely powerful tool for answering 'what if?' questions, for predicting dynamic and non-linear effects and for achieving an understanding of operation.

However, for the design of, say, cruise control, the main variables of interest are engine speed and torque versus throttle opening. So a black box model relating these terms is entirely appropriate and would be the most cost-effective route for the development of a cruise control system. A model can be derived and the control system designed using the techniques described below.

The starting point is the particular system under study (Figure 1). The boundary around the system may be defined as required by the problem. It may, for example, be a subsystem such as a single component, or it may be an entire collection of quite large systems which are to be viewed as one. Such a system will have inputs and outputs, but will also probably be subject to disturbances over which there is no control, or noise sources which contaminate the measurements.

The principle behind system identification is to inject a known signal into the input and to measure the resulting output. Figure 2 shows a possible set of results. The input signal used here is a single step which is input at time t_1 and removed at time t_2. The output signal can be seen to follow the input. There is some delay before the output occurs, there is some oscillation before it settles down, and the figure to which it settles is slightly different from the input. Hence we can extract figures for delay, for gain and for damping. There is also noise contaminating the output, and this can be characterised separately if required. The result of such experiments may be an equation of the form:

$$\frac{\text{output}}{\text{input}} = \frac{e^{-k_1 s}}{k_2 s^2 + k_3 s + k_4}$$

(in the Laplace domain)

where $k_1 \ldots k_4$ are parameters which describe the response. This equation can be used as a general model of the system. It is linear, of minimum complexity and unconfused by detail.

If the system is unknown but unvarying, we can collect data, then generate the model. This technique is known as batch processing. For systems which may vary with time it is necessary to continue acquiring data and updating the estimate of the parameters ($k_1 \ldots k_4$ above). Recursive system identification allows us to create models which evolve with time and track the variation in the system, and can be used for fault diagnosis or as a basis for adaptive control.

Obviously there are applications where the injection of a signal on the inputs is unacceptable. Often there are sufficient disturbances at the inputs which serve to perturb the system. Our experience todate has been that this is common. It is such perturbations which excite the dynamic response of the system and allow the model to be identified.

APPLICATIONS AND RESTRICTIONS

The ideal application examples are those where there may be complex physical effects acting. Friction effects, flow effects in pipelines or orifices, valve characteristics and dead zones are typical examples. Systems with clearly defined inputs and outputs can be modelled with minimum complexity with a view to establishing a control system in a quick and cost effective manner. Examples exist where system identification techniques have been used to extract a few select parameters of sub-components in a system. These parameters were then used as part of a larger simulation for predictive purposes.

It can be seen that by using system identification techniques to track the underlying changes in a process there are a range of possibilities. For example by cascading a system identifier with a control design algorithm the result is an adaptive controller which will adjust its performance to track the evolution of the process.

By matching particular characteristics of a process with particular parameters extracted by system identification one can detect incipient changes to the characteristics. If such characteristics are related to faults the result is a fault detection technique of particular sensitivity. CCL is currently working on the use of system identification techniques for diesel engine health monitoring.

As expected there are limitations to the technique. The most fundamental restriction is that the system under study must exist, hence the technique is not appropriate for entirely predictive model studies.

The models produced are generally linear. Although non-linear extensions are possible they represent a significant increase in complexity. Because the real world is non-linear, the restriction of linearity must be appreciated, and hence the models should not be used to make inferences about significantly different operating points.

IMPLEMENTATION

While simple in concept, system identification needs to be undertaken with some care in terms of the choice of software, algorithms and test procedures. Our approach has been to develop two parallel routes, one suite of programs on an in-house mini computer which allows close interfacing with control design software; the second route is a compatible portable facility running an a Compaq PC (IBM look-alike).

The Compaq is complemented by a co-processor for faster processing and by data acquisition modules which perform analogue-to-digital conversion and sample and hold. Data acquisition can be performed continuously at up to about 200Hz across eight channels. To observe very high speed phenomena sampling can be carried out at up to about 65kHz but the results are then processed in batch mode.

The software is built on that developed at Oxford University, and allows batch identification using techniques of Generalised Least Square, Maximum Likelihood and Instrumental Variables. We have developed recursive identification facilities and added some utilities to make the system easier to use.

In developing the facility we have sought to produce a portable unit which will easily interface with a potentially wide range of system sensors. The ability to use the facility on site allows the evolution of experiments, early confirmation of results, and a very much greater confidence in the progress of work. Aspects such as sampling rates, injected sequence characteristics, noise models, and parameter variability can be quickly assessed on site.

CONCLUSION

System identification has emerged from the academic environment and has a place as a useful tool in understanding and developing processes and machinery across a range of industries. It is a powerful, particularly efficient and cost effective means of rapidly deriving the characteristics of complex or ill-understood systems. The information extracted can be used for the whole range of development activities, machine development, control system design, through to large scale system improvement.

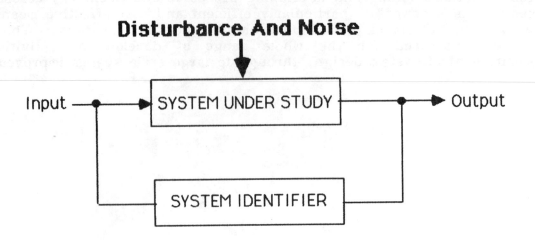

Disturbance And Noise

Input → SYSTEM UNDER STUDY → Output

SYSTEM IDENTIFIER

Figure 1

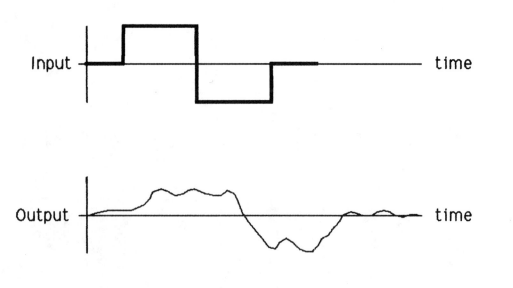

Input — time

Output — time

Figure 2

LATE PAPERS

Proc. 2nd Int. Conf. Machine Control Systems, 295-302
May 1987, © IFS (Conferences) Ltd and authors, ISBN 0-948507-52-7

Procurement of a highly automated facility for the manufacture of diesel engine connecting rods

D Roberts
Cummins Engine Co Ltd

ABSTRACT: This paper describes the procurement and development of the control systems used by Cummins in the purchase of a Flexible Conn Rod Line for its Shotts Factory. Particular emphasis is placed upon the role of Honeywell as Consultants in the Specification of the main Control system.

Capital for the facility was justified upon normal JIT premises (ie lower work in progress, reduced inventory, faster response to customer demand, improved quality, less scrap). The ability to produce more than one type of Conn rod was a factor in being able to maintain high machine utilisation in a low volume market. The facility, eventually intended to produce at volumes of 800 rods per day, is designed for relativly low volume demands, such as model startup and service parts. A reduction in headcount (against the line to be replaced) was made possible by the use of CNC and PLC controlled machine tools coupled with an advanced control system strategy. In the project justification stage Honeywell were employed as consultants to advise on the control system strategy.

After capital investment had been approved, Honeywell were used as consultants in the control system area in helping us generate Invitations To Tender (ITT's) for machine suppliers. The facility was divided into nine discrete manufacturing cells by operational groups and ITT's issued for each 'cell' formed. Machine suppliers were asked to quote to supply complete cells, including a cell control system with common features in each cell.

Responses to the ITT's from machine suppliers revealed that they were stretched to provide the main control systems, 'systems houses' being used as sub-contractors in quotations to provide the cell controller functions. Eventually contracts were placed with machine tool suppliers to provide basic machines only due to financial and project time constraints. At this stage Honeywell was asked to write Functional Design Specifications for control of two of the major manufacturing cells, and also for a 'limited line control' system.

Honeywell worked with Cummins to produce the required FDS's. During this period Cummins personnel worked to establish a commercially available local area network for communication between machine controllers and Honeywell (using a limited number of point to point serial lines), and communications facilities required in the machine controllers (both CNC and PLC).

Honeywell subsequently quoted for the provision of the cell and line controllers. Cummins decided not to commit to the purchase of cell and line control systems at this time, and to review the status at the end of the year.

There are several reasons that Cummins has not committed to purchase the cell and line controller facility at this time. This is explained below:-

1

The projected installed capacity of the line at the time the decision on cell and line control systems was made was 450 rods/day. As can be seen from Fig. 1, projected demand remains below 450 well up to the end of 1988. Installed capacity could be increased to 600 rods per day (the planned capacity of the line) by capital expenditure. In these times of capital restraint, this capital will not be committed until such time as increased capacity is required.

Installed capacity can be increased by either of two methods from 450 to 600 Conn Rods per day (see Fig. 2).

a)   Install cell controllers for Cells 1 and 2 and a 'limited' line control system.

b)   Purchase a new CNC machine for both Cells 1 and 2.

The decision as to which option is chosen to increase capacity will be governed by:-

.   The capital and support costs of each option.

.   The ability to use the manufacturing capability of additional resources (e.g. machine tools) should predicted market volumes fall.

3

The Technical Project Team (both Honeywell and Cummins) had resolved a control system design which pushed control downwards, and thus allowed a step-by-step implementation of cell controllers and, later, a line control system whilst maintaining a capable production facility. A Honeywell project review resulted in much of of the control and database functionality being moved upwards from cell to line control for a number of technical reasons. The result of this was that cell installation only would have been difficult to achieve and, for practical purposes, line control must be installed with cell control, involving higher initial capital than the earlier design which allowed a progressive installation.

4

It will be easier to install cell and line control systems once machine tools are installed and producing, rather than installing all systems at the same time. This separates the installation, testing and de-bugging of:-

i)   The manufacturing system, and

ii)   Special communications and control functions required by the cell and line control systems.

There are a number of lessons to be learnt from our experience.

1

The main lesson being that if the end user becomes responsible for the integration of several suppliers within a control system a good technical knowledge is required of the control functions and communications media used. This will occur if the end user requires to maintain capital costs at realistic levels whilst maintaining the full benefits available from a high level control system, unless a complete 'turnkey' system is purchased.

Within this project this has resulted in Cummins generating an expert knowledge in the programming and use of PLC's and the communications network, so that we are able to generate any communication telegrams necessary. The control functions of the PLC's required have all been supplied by the machine builder for reasons of health and safety. In addition Cummins has developed a diagnostics system such that all faults occurring on PLC's are recognised and handled in the same way within the PLC, the communications network and the proposed Honeywell system. With CNC controllers we found it necessary for the machine builder to be responsible for any communications links due to the complexity and specialisation of CNC controllers. Again the end user must be sure of the functions required of the CNC machines, so that the correct facilities are purchased.

2

As the overall design of the facility (from process, operational and control aspects) becomes complete and is fine tuned, small changes in requirement can have colossal implications into the details of the control system.

Example: Within Cell 1 of the Conn Rod Line, a change from an automatically loaded gauge to a manual gauge system , the following items required review and, in some cases, drastic change:-

Robot	Sequence
First Off Gauging	
Action on Gauge	Failure
Action on Gauge	Warning
Railcar Routing	Procedures
New Pallet Coding Editing Facilities	

3

Changes to traditional purchasing policy. Aside from the justification required for purchasing new technology, there are some further aspects in procurement that should be considered.

The 'total' design should be finalised as soon as possible. Only when this is completed should machine tool orders be placed. Machine tool ordering will require a small 'F.D.S.' for each main item of equipment, outlining the following:-

i) Controller

ii) Process Capabilities of the Machine.

iii) Process Control Functions of the Machine.

iv) Communications Standards Required.

v) Information required from the machine control via the communications link.

vi) Control functions required to be initiated via the communications link.

vii) List of all main fault conditions and an understanding of how these can be made available via the communications link.

4

    The study required to produce the FDS's for cell and line controllers involved a deep, detailed look at the manufacturing philosophy, in particular in the areas of:-

i) The rules controlling material movement (push vs. pull philosophies).

ii) The exploitation of pallet coding systems (when they are required) to the full potential benefits they make available.

This study resulted in small, but very significant changes, to control of the Conn Rod Line, allowing a far more robust solution, both with and without cell and line control.

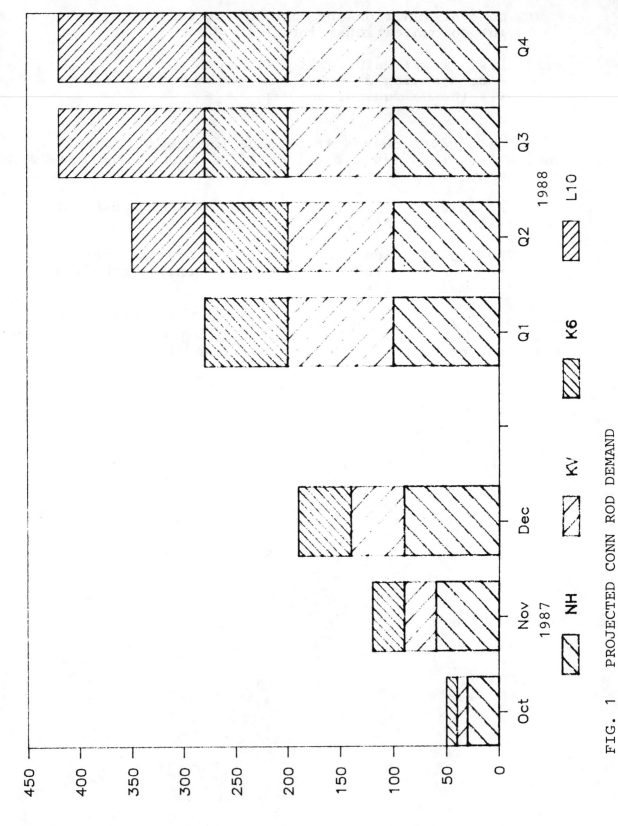

CONN ROD CAPACITY vs DEMAND

RODS PER DAY

FIG. 1   PROJECTED CONN ROD DEMAND

| | Cell 1 | | Cell 2 | | Cells 1-9 |
	3 Mc	4 Mc	5 Mc	6 Mc	
Hourly Output	30	40	35.2	41	40
21.5 Hrs. @ 70%	450	600	530	617	602
24 Hrs. @ 80%	576	768	675	787	763
24 Hrs. @ 100%	720	960	845	984	960

1A (between 3 Mc and 4 Mc), 1B (between 5 Mc and 6 Mc), 2 (below, between columns)

Capacity Improvement

1A New machine installation for Cell 1
1B New machine installation for Cell 2
2   Install Honeywell Cell & Line Control System

Utilisation Losses   (With Cell & Line Control)

10(5)%   Losses due to Changeover

10(5)%   Losses due to Tooling Management

10%   Planned Maintenance, Quality Checks and Breakdowns.

FIG. 2   CAPACITY PLANNING

Proc. 2nd Int. Conf. Machine Control Systems, 303-312
May 1987, © IFS (Conferences) Ltd and authors, ISBN 0-948507-52-7

A generic approach to integrated manufacture through area control systems

M Nichol and A Fitzgerald

Scicon Ltd, UK

The pressures of technology and market on U.K. manufacturing industry are examined and the need to provide a link from administration systems to shop floor control systems is identified. A generic approach to the implementation of this link is described and the approach is backed up by a case study. Finally, the paper concludes by examining the consequences of ignoring this vital link.

INTRODUCTION

The recent political, academic, media and practitioner outpourings on the state of the manufacturing industry are legion. A distillation of these outpourings is useful in setting the scene of this paper, and indeed in justifying the "Generic Approach to Integrated Manufacturing through Area Control Systems".

Manufacturing industry is reacting to two potentially conflicting pressures. The market place has become much more sophisticated and is demanding a wide product range with many variants and shorter product lead times. Product life cycles are shortening, reducing the window of opportunity. High quality and low price are essential weapons in gaining business.

These market pressures are being applied in an era of tough economic constraint, against a background of recession in the manufacturing industry. Two million jobs in manufacturing have disappeared, since 1979, and the erosion continues at the rate of two or three thousand per month today. Certainly, productivity has shown a significant (3.6%) increase, but overall output is still 3.9% below the 1979 level.

Manufacturing industry is reacting to these problems, but, in general is reacting by doing what it knows, better, rather than analysing the overall problem and developing a business solution.

Certainly, technology has developed significantly over the last ten years. Large amounts of capital have been invested in automating the manufacturing production process, and, especially since 1983 in the use of computer systems in the manufacturing business. Unfortunately, it is generally true to say that these investments have suffered from being piecemeal, blinkered and relatively ineffectual in terms of the overall business needs of the manufacturing enterprise.

In an environment where organisations have similar manufacturing resources, the competitive edge will develop through flexibility and responsiveness. Competition will focus on price. The competitive edge will be gained only through better planning and management of the manufacturing resource. The 'intellectual assets' of the enterprise now become the single differentiating factor. These assets are the management information and control systems, and the people who manage the business through use of these systems. Managements' task becomes different. It develops into the creation and nurturing of the intellectual assets and the recognition of the overall business needs of the enterprise.

The implementations are fragmented and the applications are too frequently isolated. Computer Integrated Manufacturing requires that Process Mechanisation and Automation be integrated with Information Systems that facilitate control of the manufacturing enterprise.

The majority of Information Systems (CAD, CAPM, CAPPE, CAM) are dedicated to specific departments in the enterprise. Access to relevant information is technically difficult and politically hindered; data becomes trapped in systems inside departments. Pressures build on the 'owners' of information to share that information within the enterprise.

The path to improvement is to Simplify, Automate then Integrate. A
simple view of the information systems functionality of the Manufacturing
Enterprise is illustrated in Figure 1. It is through this view that the
Area Control System has such an important part to play.

FUNCTIONALITY OF THE CAM BRIDGE

Having discussed the development of the higher or 'Enterprise' level of business control; being the application of computer aids to design, analysis, process and resource planning; and the use of advanced manufacturing technology on the shop floor, we can now address the functionality required for the mid-ground or 'bridge' between them. It has long been the "no-mans land" between management and the shop floor, where relatively little progress has been made when compared to the other areas. Traditionally the role of the 'bridge' has been vested in the shop foreman or supervisor, who matches the requirements of the 'enterprise' level with the capacity and capabilities of the manufacturing units. As long as the delivery dates are met or the output of the plant matches the flow of orders, nobody minded or cared to examine the hour by hour or minute by minute progress. Today this approach needs radical change. The just-in-time philosophy has heightened our awareness of the problems that excess stockholding, work in progress and high scrap levels brings; together with utilisations that are not appropriate to the needs of todays companies.

Information must flow up and down throughout the organisation for better control of resources and materials and to provide management with data that is timely and relevant. This should enable management to take a far more pro-active role.

Area control systems directly address this underdeveloped middle ground by providing systems that 'bridge' the gaps. The functionality of these systems will depend on the respective levels of technology above and below them; but generically they should fulfil many of the following functions.

- o   Short term scheduling
- o   Distribution of CNC/NC programs
- o   Tool management
- o   Transport control e.g. conveyor/AGV
- o   Collection of Management Information for analysis/display
- o   Simulation for 'what if' scenarios
- o   Error control/Tracking
- o   Manufacturing database management

In most cases these would be implemented as part of a factory-wide communications system that is fast becoming essential to Automation generally.

Two major inputs are usually required to an area control system. Firstly there are the 'works orders' which tell what to make by when (due dates). Secondly in order for decisions to be made, the 'process plans' or the "how to make" details must be supplied. Both of these may be input to the area controller manually or integrated with computer aided systems such as MRP II or CAPP (Computer Aided Process Planning). Scheduling together with other tasks should then performed by the area controller system which then matches manufacturing data (NC Part Programs) with the tooling required before launching the job schedule onto the network, for distribution to the appropriate node in the system. Additionally transport (conveyor or AGV) control is initiated for blank or part movements as necessary.

Naturally the traffic flow should not just be one-way to the shop floor. Management information (shop and part status) and error conditions (if appropriate) must be collected from the shop floor by the area control system. This enables management to 'snap-shot' the production situation with virtually real-time data. Thus timely decisions may be made using current rather than historical data. Let us now consider in more detail some of the major functions of such a system.

The Scheduler

Scheduling is often concerned with a unique set of conflicting requirements that each company prioritises in different ways. As such there is rarely any point in developing a 'standard' scheduler, as tailoring is nearly always required. However by adopting a core software approach we may then optimise the schedule by a variety of due dates or other criteria. The inputs to this short term or shift scheduler may arise as outputs from an MRPII system, which usually works on 1 or 2 weekly time buckets.

This scheduler function defines the order of execution of work orders based on the availability of system resources, i.e., tooling, materials, and machine tools. Optimisation constraints may be defined by the system buyer based on the unique requirements of the particular system.

Once this schedule has been determined, the processing is modelled to determine tooling and material resource requirements. This step creates all necessary resource data files for control of cutting tools, fixture build, and raw material staging. These data files are presented to the storage/retrieval system, tool room, and load station, as appropriate, to ensure that all requirements for parts production are met. When a job in the scheduled work queue reaches the top of that queue, these resource requirements and machine tool availability are re-checked to ensure that no resource is unavailable prior to job start. If these conditions are met, the appropriate messages are sent to the material loading station to enter the required raw material into the system.

When a resource exception status occurs during production, such as a machine tool or tool breakage, the resource requirements for the work-in-process are recalculated and any job that cannot complete due to this change is suspended and appropriate messages and status conditions are set. Similarly, when maintenance or tool service update status is entered, the contents of the work-in-process queue are re-examined and where appropriate, jobs that have been suspended due to resource availability are re-activated in the priority order established by the Shop Load file.

Distribution of Manufacturing Data

An area control system uses a variety of manufacturing data files in order to plan and control optimally the execution of the assigned work. These files contain detailed manufacturing routing information, numerical control data for machine tools; robots, inspection machines, tool data catalogs, fixture catalogs, and the like. The system provides a complete data base management system for coordinating these files, including the ability to add, delete, and modify their contents.

These data files are usually contained within the area control system in the host computer's database. When released to the shop floor machines, via the network, the local copy resides in the controllers' memory.

To cater for the large variety of machine tool controllers, and to convert from the network protocols, there is usually the need for some sort of interface unit or gateway.

Local tape prove out will usually still be necessary, and the modified program data must be sent back to the area control system for updating purposes. This same network is used for the overall shop floor control function.

The Shop Floor Control function performs overall line control and individual machining station cell control. The line control level principally affects material handling activities. The cell control level scans and evaluates the data contained in the shop status image file and issues control commands to the shop floor devices. These functions operate as status-driven programs that react to changes in system status per a fixed algorithm based on a system model.

For instance, when a CNC reports an end-of-program condition, the line control function will issue material handling commands to move the finished workpiece to its next operation and deliver a new workpiece to that cell. The cell control function issues a command to delete the current part program from the CNC storage.

Tool Management

Control of cutting tools and fixtures is extremely important for successful operation of any area control system. These features, in effect, replace the senses, i.e. eyes and ears, of the machine tool operator, as well as perform the tedious clerical details associated with tool servicing support.

The system should provide the complete tool management function, including complete tool load planning, tool back-up, tool life prediction and monitoring, and tool data set-up.

In any efficient manufacturing system it is imperative that tooling arrives at the work station ready for use before, albeit just-in-time, actually needed. As we strive more and more for highly flexible manufacturing systems, having tools available for rapid changeovers becomes essential.

Benefits of a Generic Area Controller

In the main the benefits of utilising a generic area controller approach lie in the savings (tangible) to be made in the following areas:

-       Cost decrease in the inventory carrying charges associated with the expected reduction in work in progress.

-       Cost reduction in the operator personnel due to the 'unmanned' nature of certain aspects of the manufacturing system.

- Cost reduction in the shop scheduling support services timekeepers, progress chasers and expeditors.

In addition to these measurable benefits a number of intangible benefits accrue that one more difficult to quantify.

- Improved delivery time response.

- Better control of costly resources.

- Reduction in scrap levels.

- Balanced work-flows.

Implementation of An Area Control System for Flexible Manufacturing at New York Air Brake Corporation

New York Air Brake Company is in the process of implementing a flexible area control manufacturing system. The base for this system uses six Cincinnatti T-10 horizontal machining centre cells together with a 130 station Cincinnatti Tool storage carousel and materials handling equipment.

The system produces machined piece parts from castings and barstock blanks utilising Cincinnatti Milacron T-10 Machining Centres for the metal cutting operation. Raw materials are clamped in fixtures, which are mounted on tombstones, that are positioned on pallets, which are interchanged into the, machining centres' operational envelope. The system contains ancilliary equipment and work stations that allow complete finishing operations to be accomplished by the system operators. Quality is controlled with a unique implementation of statistical techniques that is truly optimising total process control. The total system configuration allows input of raw materials in lot sizes of one and output of "A" items of inventory as completely machined parts in a queueless flow that is in compliance with all piece part specification.

Very early in the implementation NYAB was able to realise many of the benefits of this mode of manufacture. Lead times were reduced to the point where the master brake control valve for a subway car could be manufactured, assembled and tested in a 48-hour period, down from previous methods which required 16 weeks. In achieving this rapid throughput, raw materials inventory was reduced to a maximum of one week supply through some creative efforts of the Purchasing Department. Loss due to obsoleted or noncompliance of components was minimised because of the small amount of work in process. The effect of engineering change on final configuration and test results is so rapid that production facilities can be used for product enhancement activities at cost profiles which are many times lower than prototype costs.

Cutting tool management was also systemised during phase one planning. The initial planned workload was carefully examined for redundant geometry, commonality of geometry and compatibility of tolerancing. Even though the machine configuration allowed for 360 active tools in the system, every effort was made to minimise tool requirements initially in order to accommodate added workload. Process Engineers examined machining methods and increased multiple use cutting tools. Time cycles were allowed to extend in some areas with the allowable criteria that production requirements on a daily basis must be met. Engineering changes were requested to accommodate minimised tool requirements. Final analysis of this effort showed that, with a 3% increase in production time and some engineering change on every piece part drawing, the initial tooling requirements for 48 machined parts were reduced by 25% to 218 tool assemblies.

Phase one implementation and operation lasted for a period of 30 months. It truly was a period in which a great deal of knowledge was obtained by everyone at NYAB. The Manufacturing personnel involved completely understood the interactions of all variables within the area control system. The Design Engineering Department found a source for rapid prove out of anticipated design changes. The Marketing Department found a responsive Manufacturing Department capable of producing an amount of variation in its products that was unheard of in previous NYAB operations. The Financial Department found a product cost profile that was very favourable as compared to selling price in a shorter period than was anticipated for cost to fall in line.

NYAB is now implementing the full automated capability to schedule the system operations, supervise system material handling, monitor and record system conditions. The system is able to simulate system operation, conduct actual operations, monitor system operation and report variance in system operation. Based on inputs of workload, cycle time and tooling requirement, the system simulates system operation in an accelerated time frame. The results of the simulation can be reviewed by Production Control personnel. Adjustments can then be made in workload and cell configuration to optimise production. Planned downtimes for preventive maintenance and prototype production can be accommodated as well as unscheduled machine outages. The optimised system workload can be exported to the shop floor for processing over an Ethernet Local Area Network. The same network allows monitoring of shop floor parameters from the Product Control Department.

The company is now able to achieve finite scheduling every 4 hours.

The next area of integration being planned is into the two main business data bases. A highly successful MRP system is in place at NYAB and Manufacturing can extract production requirements from that data base. Cell operation must be observed and fully understood because this capability will require more cell intelligence. Cell parameters will have to be altered by artificial intelligence in order to achieve meaningful system operation. This capability is not existent at this time but careful observation of system operation should provide avenues for this capability. Additionally, the development of MRP integration will provide the tools necessary to integrate the CAD data base. The integration of that database will assure that the latest Engineering information is utilised in production.

In conclusion, NYAB has travelled a long road towards development of the Flexible Area Control system. Great knowledge was gained; careful planning limited mistakes and the stage was set for future capabilities. The system has become a self-preserving entity, because as a result of its capability, NYAB has gained 75% of the market share of Mass Transit Braking Systems.

THE FUTURE

Over the next twenty-five years, the automated factory concept will certainly be realised. The analysis above identified the key component in the realisation of that concept. It is this "CAM Bridge" that provides the means of moving on from the current generation of factory systems which maintain an historic view (ie keeping score) of the enterprise to the pro-active situation of control of the enterprise in real time (ie getting the score right).

The characteristics of currently implemented systems are based on a Departmental focus, Labour orientations and an environment of direct labour reporting and overhead allocation. Systems of the future will have a Product/Market focus, will be machine directed and will control an environment of new performance measures, fixed costs and overhead labour reporting. The systems of the future will be implemented in one of four scenarios, Green Field, Retrofit, Band Aid (patching up existing short comings) or Ostrich (generally ignored!). Few Green Field sites will emerge, the majority of installations being retrofitted into existing system infrastructures.

Successful implementation of systems of the future depends on the Management of Change. The Enterprise must establish a CIM task force under the control of a Director of Manufacturing Technology. The role of the Director for Manufacturing Technology is crucial in the development of business strategy for the enterprise, and the translation of that business strategy into Manufacturing Strategy. The implementation of the Manufacturing Strategy will require the establishment of a systems infrastructure and the operation and nurturing of the enterprises Intellectual Assets. New computer and manufacturing technology skills will be required.

The generic supervisory control system which provides the "CAM Bridge" exists now. SCIMACS (Scicon's Manufacturing Area Control System) is a core product which can be tailored to meet the needs of the manufacturing enterprise.

The major step necessary to implement such systems is not technological, it is managerial. The future depends on the successful management of change. The price of failure is that the problem no longer exists .....
and neither do YOU!